John George Hall

A History of South Cave and of Other Parishes in the East Riding of

the County of York

John George Hall

A History of South Cave and of Other Parishes in the East Riding of the County of York

ISBN/EAN: 9783337429324

Printed in Europe, USA, Canada, Australia, Japan

Cover: Foto ©ninafisch / pixelio.de

More available books at **www.hansebooks.com**

A

HISTORY

OF

SOUTH CAVE

AND OF OTHER PARISHES

IN THE EAST RIDING OF THE COUNTY OF YORK,

BY

JOHN GEORGE HALL

Author of "Notices of Lincolnshire," &c.

'EVERY MAN'S CONCERN WITH THE PLACE WHERE HE
LIVES HAS SOMETHING MORE IN IT THAN THE MERE
AMOUNT OF RATES AND TAXES HE HAS TO PAY."
TOULMIN SMITH.

HULL :

EDWIN OMBLER,

7, GEORGE STREET & 27, DOCK STREET,

1892.

TO

CHARLES EDWARD GEE BARNARD, Esq., J.P.,

LORD OF THE MANORS

IN

SOUTH CAVE,

THE FOLLOWING PAGES ARE RESPECTFULLY

DEDICATED.

LIST OF ILLUSTRATIONS.

INTRODUCTION.

THE present age is undoubtedly to a great extent one of sensational productions, and the details of local topography may probably appear uninviting even to those who feel some degree of interest in the sayings and doings of their predecessors, and are desirous of realizing the ancient condition of the district in which they reside.

The increasing intelligence of the age seems to demand the adoption of some new and striking method of presenting antiquarian truths, so that they may be interesting as well as instructive.

This has been our aim, but how far we have succeeded in doing so we must leave the reader to judge.

The present work is far from professing to give an exhaustive account of the various matters connected with the parishes in the district; but as this particular portion of the county seems to us to have been greatly neglected in the past, we venture to send it forth as a kind of pioneer, until some abler pen shall delineate more fully a district so rich in historical associations.

INTRODUCTION.

The following pages have been compiled in the hope that they may not only prove of interest to both residents and visitors in the district, but may also be the means of preserving for the use of some future historian many interesting particulars which might otherwise be lost. Shortly after the commencement of the present work, the materials so rapidly accumulated on our hands, that it became absolutely necessary either to omit altogether several of the parishes enumerated in the Prospectus, or to greatly curtail the particulars respecting them; and eventually the latter course was adopted, as being likely to cause the least amount of disappointment to our subscribers.

To Mr. William Richardson, of South Cave, the work to a great extent owes its existence. He suggested its collection and publication, and, by the sacrifice of much time and labour, has materially assisted in its compilation.

To the Clergy of the district for their uniform kindness in readily permitting access to Parish Registers, &c., we tender our sincere thanks. To T. Sturmy Cave, Esq., of Strawberry Hill, London, for much valuable help; to Mr. and Mrs. Barnard of Cave Castle, for free access to documents, and for important assistance; to the Dean and Chapter of York, with their valued Clerk, Mr. Whitehead, for permission to copy from the Torre MSS.; to Sir A. K. Rollit, M.P.; T. T. Wildridge, Esq.; W. G. B. Page, Esq. (Assistant Librarian, Hull Subscription Library); Jas. Reckitt, Esq.; F. R. Pease, Esq.; T. W. Palmer, Esq.; Mr. M. Foster, Sancton; Captain Judge; G. E. Weddall, Esq.; and others, who have rendered us valuable assistance, our best thanks are due.

Hull, March, 1892.

SOUTH CAVE.

ESTLING in a valley at the south-western foot of the Wold Hills few places are more pleasantly situated than South Cave. It is a small town and parish about three miles north of the River Humber, thirteen miles from Hull, and seven miles south of Market Weighton; in the South Hunsley Beacon division of Harthill Wapentake, Beverley Union and County Court District, Rural Deanery of Howden, East Riding Archdeaconry, and Diocese of York.

The Parish, which has a rateable value of £9,881, with 949 inhabitants and an area of 4,337 acres, formerly comprised the townships of South Cave, Bromfleet, and Faxfleet, containing together 1,100 persons and 7,480 acres, but in 1861 Bromfleet and Faxfleet were severed from the parish. The principal land-owners are Mr. C. E. G. Barnard, J.P., Cave Castle; Mr. W. H.

Harrison-Broadley, J.P.; and Mr. G. G. Macturk, in addition to a large number of freeholders and copyholders.

Under the Bailiwick or Manor Paramount of South Cave there are three copyhold manors, namely, East Hall; Faxfleet, in South Cave; and West Hall; formerly held by the families of Malet, Deyvill, Vavasour, Danby, Harrison, Girlington, Idell, Washington, and Lloyd, but all three manors are now vested in Mr. Barnard. The township is remarkably healthy, the greater part of it resting upon a bed of gravel, and sheltered from the east by the Wold Hills.

The old Roman street, from Brough to Market-Weighton, would pass the site of the present village, and being in a pleasant valley and in near proximity to the Roman Station of *Petuaria* it is not unlikely that the spot would be selected by officers of the Roman Legions as a suitable one for residential purposes. In the month of January, 1890, a discovery was made in the neighbourhood, of an interesting relic of the Roman lead trade. When ploughing in a field near the "Cliffs," a farmer came upon a block of lead measuring 22 inches in length, 5½ inches in breadth, 4½ inches in depth, and weighing 9st. 9lbs. An inscription appears upon the block in well-executed raised letters, as will be seen from the engraving. The title may be expanded thus : *Caii Iulii Proti Britanicum Lutudense ex argento*—that is (the lead of), C. Julius Protus, British (lead) from Lutudæ, prepared from silver. C. Julius Protus was the capitalist who worked the mines, and the mine itself was at Lutudæ, a place which was probably in South Derbyshire. The lead is said to have been prepared from silver, because the silver was always extracted. * This highly inter-

* For a full and most interesting account of inscribed pigs of lead see "*A propos d'un Saumon de plomb antique trouvé a Saint Valery-Sur-Somme, Notes Epigraphiques et Historiques*, par. V. J. Vaillant," published at Boulogne-sur-Mer, 1888.

esting relic is now in the possession of Mr. Barnard, the owner of the field in which it was found. It is curious that long ago—probably before the year 1700—a portion of another block of lead was found at Brough. It was a fragment only, with the letters, B R E X A R G.

DOMESDAY.

In Domesday Book there are numerous references to South Cave, amongst which we find the following :— *

'Cave. Land of the Archbishop of York. In Cave is one carucate and six oxgangs to be taxed, where there may be one plough. Eldred, Archbishop,

BLOCK OF LEAD FOUND AT SOUTH CAVE.

held this for one Manor. Now the Canons of St. Peter's [York Minster] have it under Thomas, Archbishop, and it is waste, except that one Farmer (censorius) pays ten shillings and eightpence.'

'Land of Earl Hugh. In Cave, Basin and Ulf, and Torchil, had two Manors of six carucates and two oxgangs to be taxed, and there may be four ploughs. Nigel now has of the Earl in the demesne one plough ; and five villanes with two ploughs. Value in King Edward's time, forty shillings, it is the same at present.'

'Land of Robert Malet. Manor. In Cave, Gamel had twenty-four carucates of land to be taxed where there may be twelve ploughs. Robert Malet has now four ploughs in the demesne there, and thirty villanes having eight ploughs. There is a Church and a Priest there, and the site of two Mills. Wood pasture and coppice wood one mile long and one broad. The whole Manor seven miles

From Bawdwen's translation.

long and one broad. Value in King Edward's time twelve pounds, now one hundred shillings.' *

CHARTER.

During a period of a century after the date of Domesday we have very little information respecting this parish, but in 1291 a Charter was granted "to the Master and Brethren of the Knights Templars in England, and their successors, for a market on Monday in every week at their Manor of Suth Kave; and one fair there every year for four days, namely, on the eve, day, and morrow of the Holy Trinity, and on one day following. Witnesses: R. Bishop of Bath and Wells, and others. Dated at Berewyk-upon-Tweed, 10th August." †

The Order of Knights Templars was suppressed in 1312, and in the following year a Charter was granted to Peter Deyvill for a fair and market, which was confirmed in the 22nd of Richard II., and again in the first of Henry IV., as appears by an "Inspeximus" dated 31st May, 1400, with the Great Seal attached, now in the possession of Mr. Barnard, and in a good state of preservation.

The following is a translation of the Charter granted to Peter Deyvill. ‡

' **Edward**, by the Grace of God, King of England, Lord of Ireland, and Duke of Aquitain, To all Archbishops, Bishops, Abbots, Priors, Earls, Barons, Justices, Sheriffs, Provosts, Officers, and all Bailiffs and others his faithful subjects, greeting. Know ye that we have granted, and by this our Charter have confirmed, to our beloved and faithful Peter Deyvill, that he and his heirs for ever may have one Market every week, on Monday, at his Manor of South Cave, in the County of York, and one fair there every year for three days to con-

---

* The great depreciation which had evidently taken place in the value of land since the time of King Edward (the Confessor) would be accounted for by the fact that the country between the Humber and the Tyne had been devastated by command of the Conqueror.

† Charter Roll, 19 Edward I., No. 17.

‡ Variously spelled Deyvill, De Eyvill, Dayrill, and Davill.

tinue, to wit, on the eve, on the day, and on the morrow of the Holy Trinity, unless that market and that fair be to the hurt of the neighbouring markets and fairs. Wherefore we will, and firmly command for us and our heirs, that the aforesaid Peter and his heirs for ever may have the aforesaid Market and Fair at his manor aforesaid with all liberties and free customs to the said Market and Fair belonging, except that Market and Fair be to the hurt of the neighbouring Markets and Fairs aforesaid. These being witnesses : The Venerable Father William Archbishop of York, Primate of England : Gilbert de Clare, Earl of Gloucester and Hertford, Humphrey de Bohun, Earl of Hereford, and Essex, Henry de Percy, Hugh le Despenser, Marmaduke de Thwenge, Edmund Mauley Steward of our Household, and others. Given by our hand at York, the seventh day of May in the seventh of our Reign.' *

Peter Deyvill paid a fine to the King, of forty shillings, "for having one market and one fair at his Manor of South Cave." †

From the record of proceedings connected with the confirmation of the Charter in the reign of Richard II., it appears that an Inquisition had been taken at Hull,

"on Friday next, before the ffeast of St. Dunstan, in the twentieth year of the reign of King Richard II., after the conquest of England, before Peter de Buckton, Escheator of the Lord the King, in the County of York, by virtue of his office, by the oath of Richard Lelorn, John Withernwick the elder, Lawrence Drenge, Roger Franklain, Thomas Rose, of Goodmanham ; and John Clark, of North Cave ; Thomas of Ellerton, John Grigg, of Ellerker ; Elyat Well, of Hessle ; Robert Dirkin, John Ellison, of Hessle : and Thomas Ellerton, jurors, who say upon their oath that Thomas Dayvill, of South Cave had, and exercised, one market every Monday in the week, and one fair every year, in the Feast of the Holy Trinity, at South Cave, upon the grounds of the Templars there for twenty years last past, without the Kings license or special warrant, and which said market and fair the said Thomas aliened in fee to Thomas of Metham, Chivaler, without the King's license, which said market and fair were held of the Lord, the King. in capite, and of the value in all issues, according to the true value thereof, by the year, six marks : and the said Thomas, the issues and profits of the said market and fair for twenty years last past, did receive and take, from whence he is responsively to the Lord the King. In testimony whereof, to this Inquisition, the jurors aforesaid have set to their seal."

Enrolled on Charter Roll. 7 Edward II., No. 5.
† Originalia Roll, 7 Edward II., m 19.

Deyvill pleaded that he "ought not to account to the King, and
that the market and fair in the hands of the King ought not to remain, because that he saith that one, Peter Davyll, his cosen, whose
heir he is—to wit—son of William, son of Roger, son of the aforesaid Peter, was seiz'd of the aforesaid Manor of South Cave, with
the appurtenances, to him and his heirs in the time of King
Edward."

The matter was still pending at the death of the King, and in
the first year of Henry IV. (1400), it was agreed " that the justices
of our Lord and King, assigned to take the Assizes in the said
County of York, should be appointed, by commission of this Exchequer, to enquire of the premises." The justices made a return
to the writ as follows :—

"To wit, on Monday, in the first week in Lent, in the within menconed first
year of ye reign of King Henry ye Fourth, after the Conquest, at York, in
the County of York, before John Markham and John Cockhayne, Justices of our
Lord, the King, assigned to take the Assizes aforesaid in the County, came
Thomas Dayvyll, of South Cave, within named, by his attorney, within named,
and the jurors being likewise called, came, and upon publick proclamation,
made as the custom, is, ' If any knew, or would prosecute, or inform the said
jurors for our Lord, the King upon the matters aforesaid within contained, that
then he should come there more fully to inform the said jurors for our Lord,
the King ;' and hereupon came William Gasteign* and Robert Tirwhite, the
King's Serjeants at Law ; William Lodington, the King's Attorney at Law :
Richard of Norton, Alexander of Lounde, Thomas of Sancton, John of Pocklington, and Robert of Sancton, and offered themselves to inform our Lord, the
King, concerning the premises ; whereupon it is proceeding to the taking of
the Inquisition aforesaid by the jurors first impannell'd, and now appearing, which
said jurors, being elected, tryed, and sworn to speak the truth concerning the
premisses, in the presence of the aforesaid William Gasteign, Robert Tirwhite,
William Lodington, Richard of Norton, Alexander of Lounde, Thomas of Sanne-
ton, John of Pocklington, and Robert of Sancton, say upon their oath that Peter
Dayvyll, within mentioned, was seized of the Mannor of South Cave with the
appurtenances within menconed to him and his heirs in the time of King

* This would doubtless be the famous Judge Gascoign.

Edward, son of King Henry, to which said Peter the said Lord Edward, * late King of England, progenitor of the now King, did grant and confirm by his Charter —shown in evidence to the above jurors, and within enrolled—that the said Peter and his heirs for ever should have one market every week on Monday at the mannor aforesaid, and one fair there every year, to continue three days, to wit, on the vigil, on the day, and on the morrow of the Holy Trinity, as in the aforesaid Charter, is more fully contained, and say that the said Peter, by vertue of the grant and confirmation aforesaid, was seized of the market and fair aforesaid, and that all the heirs of the aforesaid Peter were in like manner seiz'd of the market and fair aforesaid, until the taking of the Inquisition aforesaid, whereof mention is within made at the mannor aforesaid, as was lawful for them without that; that the aforesaid Thomas Dayvyll, or any of his ancestors, the market and fair aforesaid, did hold upon the ground of the Templars ; or that the said Thomas Dayvyll the said market and fair to the aforesaid Thomas of Metham, within named, did alien in ffee as by the Inquisition aforesaid, for the Lord, the King, is within supposed ; and they say further that the aforesaid Thomas Dayvyll is heir of the aforesaid Peter Dayvyll in manner as the said Thomas Dayvyll hath within alleged, and the aforesaid Thomas Dayvyll demands judgment upon the premisses ; and the premises being seen by the Barons, and having been deliberated thereupon among themselves, it is considered that ye aforesaid Thomas Dayvyll should be acquitted of the account required of him to be made to the King concerning the premises, and that the hand of the Lord the King, of and from the market and fair aforesaid, with the appurtenances, should be amoved, and that the market and fair aforesaid, together with the issues and profits thereof received from the time of taking the same into the King's hands should be to the said Thomas Dayvyll, free to hold and exercise according to the form of ye grant of the King abovesaid, always saving the King's *accou* if he should otherwise complain thereof ; and we have brought the Tenor of the Record and Press aforesaid at the prosecution of the aforesaid Thomas Dayvyll to be exemplified under the Seal of our said Exchequer. Witness : L. Allerthorpe, at Westminster, the one-and-thirtieth day of May, in the first year of our reign."

The yearly fair was formerly much resorted to, but is now very little used except as a pleasure fair, when it is the custom to make extra provision for the accommodation of visitors, including an ample supply of the now famous "Cave Cheesecakes."

* The Justices appear to have been under the impression that the Charter was granted to Deyvill by Edward I. and not Edward II.

To give an idea of the former importance of the fair and weekly market, it may be mentioned that Mr Barnard has a document dated in 1782, signed by eighty-eight persons "being corn-factors, merchants, farmers, and tradesmen, agreeing, with the consent and approbation of Leuyns Boldero Barnard, Esq., Lord of the manor and soil, and proprietor of the tolls thereof, that the market should commence at 10 a.m. instead of 4-30 p.m. (the hour mentioned in the Charter), for the convenience of those who resort here from a distance ; " and the late Mr. George Petfield, joiner who acted as an enumerator at the census in June, 1841, has left a memorandum in his books as follows : " Total residents in the town, 972. Visitors, cattle dealers, and drovers that came to Cave Fair on Sunday night, 293."

The following fines, &c., refer to the time of the Knights Templars :—

" Fine between Alan, Master of the Knights Templars in England, plaintiff, and Gundretha, who was the wife of William de Saunton, impedient, concerning four bovates of land at Cave. The right of the Master is acknowledged."—*Feet of Fines*, 10 *Henry III.*, 22 *(old No.).   From Catalogue.*

" Fine between Gundretha de Bayville, demandant, and Alexander de Santun, tenant, concerning one carucate of land in Sutheave. The right of Alexander is acknowledged : to hold of Brother Robert, Master of the Knights Templars in England."—*Feet of Fines, 15 Henry III., 72.   From Catalogue.*

" Fine between Robert de Samford, Master of the Knights Templars in England, plaintiff, and John Gundi. Roger de Mulbray had destrained the Master for scutage to the amount of 6s. 8d. (when the fee was taxed at 40s.) for his free tenement in Sudeave, viz., one carucate of land ; and also to do suit every three weeks at Roger's Court of Tre k. The Master alleged that the said John ought to acquit him from these services, as being mesne between the Master and Roger. John acknowledges the right of the Master to hold in frank almoign, and will acquit and defend him from all secular service, &c."—*Feet of Fines, 29 Henry III.   From Catalogue.*

" Fine between Roger de Eyvill, demandant, and Brother Robert de Turevill, Master of the Knights Templars in England, concerning one toft and two bovates of land in Suth Cave. The right of the Master is acknowledged." *8 Edward I.*

"John de Mercato, [of the Market] who brought a writ against the Master of the Knights Templars in England, that he should permit him to have common of the pasture in Suthcave, does not prosecute ; therefore let him and his pledges be amerced, viz., Ralph de Ripplingham and William le Vavasur of the same."—*Assize Roll, York, 8 and 9 Edward I., York X, 1-9, m, 12d.*

We have also found further references to South Cave in the Feet of Fines, Assize Trials, and Post-Mortem Inquisitions of the period, some of which are given below :

"Fine between Hugh de Branton, demandant, and Elias de Flamavill, Thomas de Brabancun, and Thomas de Houne, tenants, of one carucate of land, with appurtenances, in Cava, on an assize of *mort d' ancestre.* The tenants acknowledged the right of demandant, and gave him two bovates of land— part of the premises. The demandant then granted all the residue of the said carucate to the said Elias and Thomas, and the heirs of Elias to hold of him by Knight service, as much as appertains to the said land, whereof ten carucates make one Knight's fee, for all service."—*Feet of Fines, 4 John. From Catalogue.*

"An assize comes to acknowledge whether Geoffrey de Behlun, brother of Nigel de Behlun, was seised in his demesne [as of fee] of four bovates of land in *Kave* ; and whether William de Aivill holds two bovates, and Alexander de Santon, two bovates thereof. Aivill vouches to warranty Nicholas de Behlun, whom he is to produce for aid of the Court. Santon says he claims nothing in that land, except the service only. Nigel says that Santon, since the Writ was sued out, has given that land to Roger, his brother. The jury say that the gift was made previously ; therefore Nigel is amerced, 'he is poor.' Afterwards Nicholas de Bellhum came and warranted. An agreement [or Fine] was made between the parties."—*Assize Roll, 15 Henry III., York, X, 1-1—2m, 1d.*

"An Assize comes to acknowledge whether John Mauleverer, John de Hadenay, and Ralph Foliot unjustly dis-seised William Russel of his free tenement in Cave. John de Hadenay says that William Russel had of his gift, in the time of the war, 12s. of rent, which he used to receive from William Foliot, father of the said Ralph ; and Russel received that rent for three or four years ; and because that gift was made in the time of the war, he (John), believed that he could not [be said to] disseise Russel thereof. As he acknowledged that Russel was enfeoffed, and that he disseised him without judgment, it is considered that Russel shall recover his seisin, and John be amerced. Russel is amerced for a false claim against Mauleverer; and Ralph Foliot is ordered henceforth to pay the said rent to Russel, &c."—*Assize Roll, 15 Henry III., York, N, 1-1--2, m, 6d.*

"Fine between John, son of Richard de Cave, demandant, and Alexander de Sancton, whom Peter Fitz Alexander vouches to warranty, and who warrants to him by Ernald de Cave, clerk, concerning two bovates of land, with appurts, except one toft and one-and-a-half acres of meadow in Sutheave; and between the same John, demandant, and the said Alexander, whom William, Master of St. Leonard's, York, vouches to warranty, concerning one acre of meadow in the same vill. John remitted to Alexander all right in the said land and meadow; and Alexander gave to John one bovate of land and two-and-a-half acres of meadow in the same vill, at a yearly rent."—*Feet of Fines, 33 Henry III.*

"Fine between John de Kava, demandant, and Roger de Eyvill, whom William, son of John de Walkinton, vouched to warranty, concerning ten acres of meadow in Sukave; and between the said John, demandant, and the the said Roger, whom John Lockes vouched to warranty concerning two-and-a-half acres of land in the same vill. The right of John is acknowledged; he rendering a yearly rent."—*36 Henry III.*

"Richard Dunper (or Dimper), of South Cave, and Richard at the Cross, present themselves against Henry, son of Elias de Braydwayt, of a plea that Richard Dunper should render to Braydwayt one bovate of land (except two acres) in Suth Cave, and that Ric. at the Cross should render to him one toft and one bovate of land (except two acres) in the same vill. Braydwayt was plaintiff, but did not appear, &c."—*De Banco Roll, 2-3 Edward I., m 8.*

"An Assize comes to recognize whether John, son of John Lokis brother of Emma, wife of Simon le Teler, and of Isolda, wife of John de Adelingflet, and of Juliana, sister of the same Emma and Isolda, was seised in fee of one toft and four acres of land in Market Cave, on the day when he died; whereof Roger Doel and Elizabeth, his wife, hold one toft and two acres, and Roger De Eyvill holds two acres. Doel and wife appear and vouch Roger de Deyvill to warranty. The parties came to an agreement; Roger giving 20s. to "Simon and the others."—*Assize Rolls, 8 and 9 Edward I., York, N 1-7, 2, m 60.*

"Alex. de Hothum, parson of the church of Batelesford, who brought an assize of novel disseisin against Agnes de Vaux, of Suth Cave, and others, in a writ concerning tenements in Suth Cave, does not prosecute; therefore let him and his pledges be in mercy, viz., Geoffrey Hayne, of Hotham, and William Swayn of the same."—*M 30 d.*

" Roger de Eyvill presents himself against Robert de Eyvill concerning a plea of two bovates of land, with appurtenances, in Suth Cave. Defendant does not appear, and failed to do so on a previous occasion, when the Sheriff was ordered to seize the land. Judgment is now given that Roger shall recover it, and that Robert be amerced."—*Assize Roll, York, N 1-9, 1, m 37.*

" Grant to Peter de Eyvill and his heirs, of free warren in all their demesne lands of Suth Cave, Byrland, and Spaldington, in the County of York, provided those lands are not within the bounds of the King's Forest. Witnesses: R. Archbishop of Canterbury and others. Dated at Byflet, 21st November." *Charter Roll, 2 Edward, II. 47.*

" Fine between John de Ellerker, senior, plaintiff, and John de Marche [or De Mercato], Suthcave, and Dionisia, his wife, deforciants, concerning one messuage, four bovates of land, and eleven acres of meadow in Suthcave. The right of John de Ellerker is acknowleged."—*Feet of Fines, 13 Edward II., 106.*

" Fine between John de Ellerker, senior, plaintiff, and Roger de A. Keny, Joan, his wife, and Simon de Stocking and Agnes, his wife, deforciants, concerning three messuages, six tofts, six bovates of land, eleven acres of meadow, and 72s. of rent, in Suthcave, Drewton, and Waldeby. The right of the plaintiff is acknowledged."—*12 Edward III., 10.*

" Fine between Nicholas Donnyby, of Hotham, plaintiff, and William Darryans, of Drewton, deforciant, concerning messuages, lands, &c., in Drewton, Southcave, Braythwayt, and Etton. Nicholas has part of the premises of the gift of William, and for this, Nicholas grants to William " the same tenements," with the homages and all other services of Master Thomas de Cave, clerk, and others (named), and their heirs. Sundry remainders are set out."— *Feet of Fines, 13 Edward III., No. 75.*

" Fine between Sir Thomas Brounflete, Knight, plaintiff, and John Yeversley and Agnes, his wife, deforciants, concerning sixty acres of land and sixty acres of meadow in Southcave, called Bagflete. To hold to John and Agnes for their lives, rendering one rose yearly; the reversion to Sir Thomas and his heirs."—*Feet of Fines, 4 Henry V.*

" Fine between John Ellerker, of Risby, plaintiff, and Thomas Taillour, of Ellerker, and Cecily, his wife, deforciants, concerning three tofts, forty acres of land, twenty acres of meadow, forty acres of pasture, and 18d. of rent, with appurtenances in Bagflete and Southcave. Deforciants release to plaintiff."

" Isabella, wife of John Ellerker is mentioned in another fine."—*8 Henry V.*

" Fine between John Ellerker of Risceby, and Isabel, his wife, plaintiff, and Edmund Lund and Elizabeth, his wife, deforciants, concerning six mes-

suages, two tofts, ten bovates, and seventy-two acres of land, six acres of
meadow, and 3s. of rent, in Southcave, Swanland, Elneley and Bagfleet. Defendants release to deforciants."—*Fines, York, 6 Henry VI.*

A dispute between the burgesses of Beverley and the inhabitants of South Cave engaged public attention during the reign of
Henry VI. It arose from a claim made by the burgesses of ex-
emption from toll in South Cave.

"Legal proceedings had been resorted to during the reign of Richard II.
by one of the burgesses, against the collector of tolls in South Cave, for having
unjustly enforced payment ; and the cause had been decided in favour of plaintiff. A similar claim having been renewed at this time, the Governors of
Beverley procured an exemplification of the former plea of trespass, and verdict
thereupon, between Thomas Chandler, a burgess of Beverley, and Thomas
Davill, Lord of the Manor and owner of the tolls of South Cave ; in which it is
recorded that the jury found for Thomas Chandler, the plaintiff. This exemplification was exhibited as a decisive proof that the burgesses of Beverley were
legally exonerated from toll within the parish of South Cave, and their right was
reluctantly admitted." *

THE MANORS OF SOUTH CAVE.

As before stated, there are three manors in South Cave, namely,
the Bailiwick or Manor Paramount of 'South Cave, with East
Hall ;' the Manor of 'South Cave West Hall, otherwise West Hall,
in South Cave ;' and the Manor of 'South Cave, otherwise Faxfleet, in South Cave.'

It will be seen from Domesday Book that the manor was at
that time held by Robert Malet, and most probably it was then
undivided, and included the townships of Bromfleet and Faxfleet.

Subsequently we find four manors within the parish, namely,
East Hall, West Hall, Faxfleet, and Bromfleet. Though Fax-
fleet and Bromfleet, are now severed from the parish, Faxfleet in
South Cave is still a manor therein, but no part of Bromfleet
Manor is now within South Cave.

* Corp Rec., 23 Henry IV., 14c.

The original parish was not only of considerable extent (as mentioned in Domesday) but, having three or four resident lords of the manors, it must have been one of importance

These manors have been held by numerous families, and, until the year 1785, they never appear to have been all held by the same lord.

We will first give a concise list of the lords of each of the three manors, and then we purpose giving a short history of each manor separately.

OWNERS OF THE BAILIWICK, OR MANOR PARAMOUNT WITH EAST HALL.—Robert Malet, Deyvills, Vavasours, Danbys, Harrisons, Henry Washington, Idell, Boldero Barnards.

OWNERS OF WEST HALL.—Sir Alexander Cave, Sir Alexander Lound, Lord Sheffield, Girlingtons, Harrisons, Lloyds, Dunns, Boldero Barnards.

OWNERS OF FAXFLEET IN SOUTH CAVE.—The Knights Templars, John Strivelyn, Stephen le Scrope, John Earl of Bridgewater, Thomas Tyte, Esq., Sir William Holcroft Knt, Sir John Cuttler, Bart., Edmund Lloyd, Edward Marshall, Elizabeth Marshall, Boldero Barnards.

THE BAILIWICK OR MANOR PARAMOUNT OF SOUTH CAVE, WITH EAST HALL.

As before mentioned, the original grant by William the Conqueror was to Robert Malet : and the Charter to Peter Deyvill, the Lord of the Manor, for a Market and Fair, was dated in 1314. From the "Inspeximus" in 1400, it was clear that the Deyvills were at that date still in possession. They were an important family, and some interesting particulars respecting them will be found in our reference to Faxfleet.

In the reign of Edward III., Thomas Deyvill was one of the two Knights elected as Members of Parliament for Yorkshire, namely, in 1328, 1331, and 1333. *   The arms of the Deyvills were among those depicted in the windows of York Minster. †

The manor passed from the Deyvills to the Vavasours, and in the 38th of Elizabeth (1596) there is a grant of a Royal License to Edward Vavasour, to sell the Manor Paramount to Sir Thomas Danby. This Sir Thomas Danby appears to have been the head of the very important Leeds family of Danby, of Farnley Hall. ‡ Their arms are still incorporated with those of the town of Leeds, and a well preserved shield of Sir Thomas Danby's Arms, dated 1586, and bearing his initials, was found some years ago in a wall of the stable yard at Cave Castle. He certainly resided here, and the record of his burial appears in the Parish Register for the year 1590, in the following terms : –

"*Venerabilis Vir Thomas Danby, Miles, Sepultus fuit decimo quinto die mens Septembris.*"

He left the manors to his son Richard, who was succeeded by his son, Sir Thomas Danby, who died in 1660, and he was followed by his son, Francis Danby, who also resided here, and entries appear in the Registers of Births and Deaths of his children from 1636 to 1646. Francis Danby, the last Lord of the Manor of this family died in 1663 but is not buried here.

The Danbys were Loyalists and mortgaged their property in South Cave to a Mr. Jermins, Sergeant-at-Law, to enable them to pay, amongst other debts, the fine of £320 inflicted on Francis Danby by the Commissioners for Compounding, during the Com-

* Park's Parliamentary Representation of Yorkshire, p 8.

† Drake's History of York.

‡ "Sir Christopher Danby, of Farnley Hall," was High Sheriff of Yorkshire in 1545.

monwealth. His release, dated 1650, and signed by the Commissioners, is amongst Mr. Barnard's papers. The mortgage on the Danby property in South Cave passed into the hands of a Mr. Francis Harrison, who, as well as his son, Thomas Harrison, of Dancers Hill, South Mimms, Hertfordshire, had previously lent various sums of money to Sir Thomas and his son, Mr. Francis Danby, and in 1649 the Danbys agreed to sell their Manor of South Cave to Harrison for £3,200. Harrison paid certain sums amounting in the aggregate to £1,725, and then refused to pay anything further. In the year 1653, Francis Danby commenced a Suit in Chancery, "to enforce the said Mr. Harrison either to pay the purchase money or relinquish his bargain upon being reimbursed the money by him expended and disbursed about the same." Nothing, however, came of the suit, and after Harrison's death, his son Richard remained in possession. Richard married Eleanor, daughter of Sir William Lowther, of Swillington, Yorkshire, by whom he had five daughters, viz. :—

Anne who married Henry Fairfax, Esqre., of Towleston.

Diana, who married Captain Richard Moore. —She was buried here 22nd January, 1691.

Eleanor, who married (October 7th, 1689) Henry Washington.

Elizabeth, who married Richard Lloyd, Esq. —She was buried here 13th January, 1724. and

Mary who married Charles Nodon.

Both Richard Harrison and his wife are buried here.

At Richard's death (March 16th, 1682) the estate went to his five daughters and co-heiresses.

So far as we can ascertain from old documents in connection with the Chancery Suits affecting the estate, and which, fortunately, have been carefully preserved, the marriage of Eleanor Harrison and Henry Washington was the first connection of the Washingtons with South Cave, consequently the old tradition that John Washington, grandfather of the General, emigrated from South Cave to America in 1657 cannot be sustained. The South Cave Washingtons may have been, and probably were, members of the family from which the President sprung, but they were not his immediate ancestors.

In the year 1689, Miss Jane Danby, the only surviving child of the former owner, thinking probably, that in those more settled times she might have a better chance of success, filed a Bill in Chancery against Richard Harrison's five co heiresses. Mr. Henry Washington, being a solicitor (and at that time Under-Sheriff of Yorkshire), acted for his wife as well as for the other defendants, and the Chancery Suit dragged on for many years, not being settled till the year 1703.

Miss Danby bitterly complained of the repeated delays caused by the defendants' Attorney, Henry Washington, as will be seen from the following extract from a petition filed by her :—

"But the defendant, Washington, having the carriage of the Commission, refuses to let them proceed, declaring that he cared not how long he delayed the cause, for that he, being the solicitor therein for himself and other defendants, doubted not but to get as much thereby as his wife's share came to, and turned one of the plaintiff's witnesses out of the house, and threatened to send him to goale when he was attending to be examined for the plaintiff on the last commission." For this he was condemned to pay the plaintiff £15 for her costs for attending on the defendant.

During the progress of the Chancery Suit, Henry Washington wrote a letter to a Mr. Hoy (who was probably his agent), which is of such an interesting nature that we give it entire :

5 April, (16)93.

"Mr. Hoy,

Not knowing how to direct to you I sent this to Mr. Consett. I have given Sir Ab. Danby notice of ye execution of our Com., on ye 24th instant. Mr. Consett will this weeke receive a box full of old bills, answers.

and deposicons, and also a copy of a decree which wee have under seale, which pray look over.   I find ye draught of a conveyance from all ye Danbys to Tho. Harrison, but whether itt was ever executed I know not.   Wee have ye bond menconed in ye cop. of ye account being or charge which wee found with Tho. Harrison's writings, and Mr. Justice Jermin's mortgage, the order for ye discharge of ye sequestracon, but to save a long recital I send you a copy of itt. Now, these being proved previously, I hope wee need not prove them again, but only what money has since been laid out in repaires and what losse has been by ye insolvency of tennants, for if we must prove them then or interr. you will find are short.   Part of ye estate is a wood of about twenty-six acres.   And I find that by their last Com. they endeavoured to prove that wee had felled or cut downe abundance of the wood.   Now if itt be necessary for us wee can prove that old Danby cutt downe ye wood before wee entred, and that wee never cutt downe any but for ye repaires and fencing of ye cottages and closes, but then wee must have an interrogatory to lead to itt.   The workmen who were formerly imploy-ed in building or repaireing ye houses and cottages are most of them either dead or gone, soe that what wee prove must be by hearsay and beleife.   I would faine have our answers seriously perused, for I hope that we have not lett them in. And in case wee have not, then pray advise me what wee must doe, for wee vallue not expense if we could att any rate gett ye Bill dismissed.   Not but that our money due, could we prove ye same effecually, is full ye vallue of ye land according to ye rents itt now gives.   I shall bee shortly in towne, and then, or in the meantime, if you want itt, will supply you with more money, soe pray take what advice you think convenient.   Mr. Jones draw our answers.   I desire you to send mee two lines to Yorke where I now am, and you will oblige.

Your ffriend and servant,

HEN. WASHINGTON."

Evidently our local Washington had not that utterly unselfish disposition which characterised the great American patriot, and a little extra money seemed to be no object if he " could att any rate gett ye Bill dismissed." We part very reluctantly with the old tradition that General Washington's ancestors were born here, but fail to find any evidence in support of the statement, though dili-gent search has been made among old papers relating to the Cave Castle Estate.

In 1694 Jane Danby died, leaving her lawsuit still undecided, and

C

it was carried on by Sir Abstrupus Danby,* her cousin, (described as heir of Jane Danby, as well as grandson and heir of Sir Thomas Danby, of Farnley Hall), against Henry Washington and Nodon.

The lawsuit proceeded for some years, but on July 2nd, 1702, Sir Abstrupus Danby came to an arrangement with the defendants Washington and others, by which he resigned all claim against the the co-heiresses on payment to him of £320 10s., and so ended this long-pending lawsuit.

In August, 1702, a deed was executed by the co-heiresses and their husbands empowering Ralph Nodon gent, of the Middle Temple, London, to sell the Manor of South Cave East Hall.

In 1706 Henry Washington advanced £2,830 to pay off the "remaining" claims of his wife's sisters ; he himself claiming besides this sum, £1,655 for his wife's share and his own expenses in the suit though he appears to have previously received £902 7s. 6d. on her account, and in 1707 the manor was conveyed to Washington "and his heirs for ever."

By his will, dated 6th October, 1717, Mr. Washington devises his property to Eleanor, his wife, for life, with reversion to his son Richard, and £50 apiece to three younger children.

On January 14th, 1719, Eleanor Washington, and her son Richard, agree to sell the manor to Mr. John Idell, to whom Henry Washington had mortgaged it before his death.

Mr. Idell had married Anne, Eldest daughter of Henry Washington.

In connection with this sale from Washington to Idell the following letter from Richard Washington is interesting :—

* Sir Abstrupus was one of the Members of Parliament for Yorkshire in 1698.

" Brother Idell,

Above are all the deeds I have in my power or custody or know anything of relating to South Cave, which I sent down by the Hull carrier yesterday, directed to you at Mr. Short's, cooper, in High Street, Hull, Yorkshire, carriage paid, and I hope you will receive them safe. My mother hopes very shortly to hear from you, with a Bill for the remr. due to her, and I assure you she wants it. We are ready to receive the money and assign as you shall think proper, and pray let me know when you shall be prepared, that I may order mrcs. accordingly. I am, with humble respects to all friends, and love to yourself and family.

January 7th, 1723.   Your affectionate brother,

R. WASHINGTON."

Mr. Idell appears to have paid £3,000 on account of the purchase money, and to have given Mrs. Washington and her son, a mortgage on the estate to secure the balance of £2,000. In response to the appeal so forcibly made in Mr. Richard Washington's letter, Mr. Idell seems to have taken steps to procure this £2,000 elsewhere, and the mortgage was assigned October 25th, 1725, to a Mr. Walker, from whom it passed to Mr. Christopher Kirby, of Kingston-upon-Hull.

In 1744 Mr. Idell gave an additional mortgage of his manor for £500 to Mark Kirby, Esq., brother and heir to Christopher Kirby, deceased, and in 1748 Mr. Idell and his son, John Idell, sold the manor to Leuyns Boldero Barnard, Esqre.

MANOR OF WEST HALL.

This Manor was at one time held by the Cave Family, whose history dates back to the time of William II. In 1316, Sir Alexander de Cave is returned as joint Lord of South Cave, North Cliff and South Cliffe. For a fuller account of this family, the reader is referred to the separate chapter on the subject ; and here we need only trace the family so far as it is connected with the Manor of West Hall.

Maud, the daughter and heiress of Sir Alexander Cave, married Sir Alexander Lound, of Lound Hall and of South Cave, and the latter would doubtless have then become owner of the Manor. Mr. Barnard has in his possession a deed dated in 1433, which refers to Alexander Lound, as will be seen from the following translation :—

" Know all men present and to come that we, John Persay. John Daunay, Esquire(s), and John Coldon, Rector of the Church of Little Coldon, have given, granted, and by this, our present Charter, confirmed to Alexander de Lound, of Suth Cave, Esquire, all our manors, lands, tenements, rents, reversions and services, with all their appurtenances, in the County of York, which we had of the gift and feoffment of Thomas Lound, Knight : To have and to hold all the aforesaid, manors, lands, tenements, rents reversions, and services, with all their appurtenances, as it is aforesaid, to the aforesaid Alexander, his heirs and assigns for ever, of the chief lords of those fees, by the services therefore due and of right accustomed. And also we, the aforesaid John Persay, John Daunay, and John Coldon, will warrant and defend all the aforesaid manors, lands, tenements, rents, reversions, and services, with all their appurtenances, as it is aforesaid, to the aforesaid Alexander, his heirs and assigns for ever against all men by these presents. In witness whereof we have affixed our seals to this present Charter. These being witnesses : Henry Brounflet, Edmund Darrell, Richard ———— --, Ralph Graystok, William Tempest, Knights. Dated on the first day of November, in the twelfth year of the reign of King Henry VI., after the Conquest of England." [1433].

The Lounds are also frequently referred to in connection with Wallingfen Common. The old Manor House for West Hall is marked on a map of the parish made in 1759, as " Mr. Lloyd's House," he being then Lord of the Manor. Doubtless both Sir Alexander Cave and Sir Alexander Lound had resided there. The house in 1767 was occupied by Thomas Mead, who was probably the last tenant, and it then went out of occupation. Some portions of the walls remained for many years afterwards, and the fish ponds were filled up less than half-a-century ago.

Janet, the daughter of Sir Alexander Lound married Robert Sheffield, ancestor of the Lord Sheffield and Earls of Mulgrave.

The following is a copy of a portion of a Suit-Roll, or list of tenants of the manor during the reign of Queen Elizabeth, which is interesting, as giving the names of some of the copyholders at that time connected with the manor :—

"A suyte role for the Lord Sheffield Manor of Southcave, for the lands and tenants belonginge to the same vt. sequitr. :—

Henrie Earle of Darbie.

Sr. Thomas Danby, Knight.

Wyllm Ellerker, Esquire, for a tofte in Ellerker.

Rychard Langdayll, Esquire, for land in Sancto.

Thomas Elwod, gentleman, for lands in Myddleton.

Robert Constable, gent, for lands in Drewton and Euthorpe.

Necolas Babthorp, gentle., for lands in North Cave.

Thomas Rychardson for a tofte in Hothom.

Wyddow Elwarde for lands in Cotta.

Wyllm Johnson, gent.

Wyllm Waudbie for land in Everthorp.

Robert Waell.

Georg Iddle."

The first Lord of the Manor to whom we have any reference among the records belonging to this manor is Edmund, third Lord Sheffield, who, in the fourteenth year of James I. was constituted President of the Council for the North. In the reign of Charles I. he was created Earl of Mulgrave. By his first wife, Ursula, the daughter of Sir Robert Tirwhit, he had six sons, first, Charles who died young and unmarried ; second, Sir John Sheffield ; third, Edmund ; fourth, William (drowned in France) ; fifth, Philip, and sixth, George. Sir John, Edmund, and Philip were unfortunately drowned in the passage of Whitgift Ferry (over the River Humber), and George broke his neck in a new riding house which his father had made out of an old consecrated chapel, as says Sir William Dugdale.*

* See The works of John Sheffield Earl of Mulgrave, Marquis of Normanby, and Duke of Buckingham, Vol 2

Lord Sheffield was succeeded by the Girlington family, who appear to have purchased property here about the same time as the Danbys. The earliest mention of the Girlingtons in the Parish Registers is in 1592, when the following entry occurs : "*Anthoniis Girlington filius Nicholaus, bapt 23rd April 1592.*" Nicholas Girlington seems to have been the head of the family here, and the entry of his death is made in large letters as follows : "*Mr. Nicholaus Girlington, armiger, sepult, April 4th, 1637.*" His son William had pre-deceased him on 21st July, 1617, leaving only surviving issue an infant daughter, Katherine Girlington (baptised January, 1617). We have found no Court Rolls between the years 1588 and 1591, when Nicholas Girlington, armiger, was Lord of the Manor, and they continue to bear his name until the year 1607. From that date they are missing until 1658, when we find that the court was held for the " Worshipful John Girlington," for whom Samuel Jobson was steward. Nicholas Girlington would no doubt keep the manor until his death in 1637, when his grand-daughter—who in all the papers is described as " Domina," or " Dame " Katherine Girlington—succeeded him. This lady was a devoted Loyalist and must have held very considerable property, as, by the following extract taken from a list of those Loyalists who compounded for their estates during the Commonwealth, it will be seen that she paid a much larger amount than Danby, the Lord of the Bailiwick.*

	£	s.	d.
Jobson, Samuel, of Brantingham, Yorkshire ...	40	0	0
Danby, Francis, of South Cave, Yorkshire, gent. ...	320	0	0
Girlington, Dame Catherine, of Southam Cave, Yorkshire	800	0	0
Marshall, John, of South Cave, gent.	13	10	0

The Samuel Jobson referred to was the benefactor to the poor

* Scaum's History of Beverlac.

of South Cave, who, though he lived at Brantingham, was buried in the Church at the former place.

We have not found any of the Court Rolls of this lady; but in a list of the tenants in Faxfleet Manor, made in Lord Bridgwater's time, "the Domina Katherina Girlington" appears "*pro manorio sua.*" She died about the year 1658. In 1660 John Girlington sold the manor to Francis Harrison, the then owner of the Bailiwick and East Hall, who is followed by Thomas Harrison in 1666, and by Richard Harrison in 1669. At the death of the latter in 1682, his five daughters and co-heiresses appear as the Ladies of the Manor. In 1669 the manor was allotted by "The Great Partition Deed" to Richard Lloyd, Esq., in right of his wife Elizabeth, which he held until his death. By his will, dated 7th July, 1703, we find he had land in Southwell, Nottinghamshire, and other places. He was succeeded by his son Richard, married in 1717 to Isabella Leybourne. He died 22 June, 1724, and is buried here. Mrs. Isabella Lloyd acted as guardian for her son Richard—the third of the name, from 1725 until 1737. He is variously described as of the Parishes of Edwinstow, in Nottinghamshire; of Newton in the Thistles, in Warwickshire; and of the Rectory of Foremark, in Derbyshire.

In 1762 Mr. Lloyd let the West Hall Manor House, with the orchard, garden, park close, brewery-house, stable (for two horses), &c., to John Dunn, gentleman, of Howden, for a term of seven years, at a rental of £33 per annum, and in 1764 he sold the manor and all his property in South Cave, amounting to 163 acres, to Mr. Dunn for £5,000, reserving the Manor House, the closes adjoining it, and some fields on the Wolds, which had been settled on his wife Eleanor for her jointure. In 1772 Mr. John Dunn dates his letters from Howden. His brother, Thomas Dunn, previously described as yeoman, of Newbald, lived then at Mount Airy, and acted as his agent. The West Hall Courts were held for John Dunn, gentleman, of Howden, from 1764 until 1776, when he was succeeded by Elizabeth Dunn, spinster, whose name appears as Lady of the Manor from 1777, to 1781, and she by Mary Dunn, spinster, whose name is on the Court Rolls of 1782, 1783, and 1784.

In 1785 Miss Dunn sold the manor and all her property to Henry Boldero Barnard, Esq., when, for the first time on record, all the three manors in South Cave came into the same hands.

MANOR OF FAXFLEET.

The Lord of the Manor in 1643 was John, first Earl of Bridgwater, son and successor of Sir Thomas Egerton, Baron of Ellesmere, who was Lord Keeper of the Great Seal in the reign of Elizabeth, from 1596 until her death in 1603, and Lord High Chancellor of England in the Reign of James I., from 1609 until 1616. Lord Bridgwater married the Lady Frances Stanley, one of the daughters and co-heiresses of Ferdinando, Earl of Derby, by whom he had four sons and eleven daughters. He died in 1649, and is buried at Little Gaddesden, County Hertford.*

The next name on the Court Rolls of Faxfleet, dated 4th October, 1667, is that of Thomas Tyte, armiger, Lord of the Manor, for whom Samuel Jobson acted as steward. Mr. Tyte was succeeded in 1668 by Sir William Holcroft, Knight, who retained Samuel Jobson as his steward.

In 1672 Sir John Cuttler, Baronet, was Lord of the Manor. He was the notorious miser immortalised by Pope in his III Epistle

See Collin's Peerage.

to Allen, Lord Bathurst, on the use of " Riches." Immediately following the well-known description of the death-bed of Villiers,
Duke of Buckingham, beginning, " In the worst inn's worst room,"
&c., occur the following verses relating to Sir John Cuttler:—

> " His Grace's fate sage Cutler could foresee,
> And well (he thought) advis'd him, ' Live like me.'
> As well His Grace replied, ' Like you, Sir John !'
> ' That I can do when all I have is gone.'
> Resolve me, reason, which of these is worse,
> Want—with a full or with an empty purse ?
> Thy life more wretched, Cutler, was confess'd.
> Arise, and tell me, was thy death more bless'd ?
> Cutler saw tenants break and houses fall ;
> For very want he could not build a wall.
> His only daughter in a stranger's power ;
> For very want he could not pay a dower.
> A few grey hairs his reveren'd temples crown'd ;
> 'Twas very want that sold them for two pound.
> What ! e'en denied a cordial at his end,
> Banish'd the doctor, and expell'd the friend ?
> What but a want, which you perhaps think mad,
> Yet numbers feel, the want of what he had !
> Cutler and Brutus, dying, both exclaim,
> ' Virtue ! and Wealth ! what are ye but a name !'
> Say, for such worth are other worlds prepared ?
> Or are they both, in this, their own reward ?"

Sir John Cutler (or Cuttler) left no sons, and was the only
baronet of his name.*

On the Court Roll of 12th October, 1693, Edmund Lloyd,
Esq., is Lord of the Manor, and continued until 1715. He is
described in a Deed of Sale, as of the Parish of St. Paul's, Covent
Garden, County Middlesex, and he sold the Manor to Edward
Marshall, senior, of Tadcaster, gentleman. The latter died in

* See Kimberley's Baronetage.

1742 leaving the manor to his wife, Elizabeth, to be sold, and the proceeds to be applied in paying his debts and legacies to his three daughters, Elizabeth Harrison, widow: Margaret, and Jane; to his son Leonard, and to his grandsons, Edward, son of James Plaxton Marshall; and Edward, son of Edward Marshall. In 1750 a sale was carried out according to his wishes, and Leuyns Boldero Esq., bought Faxfleet in South Cave.

ALL SAINTS, SOUTH CAVE.

Pedigree
of Barnard of Cave.

William Barnard = Elizabeth
living, 1579.

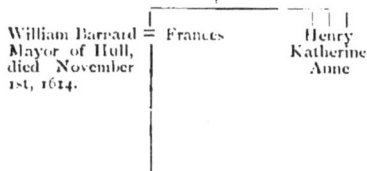

William Barnard = Frances   Henry
Mayor of Hull,   Katherine
died November   Anne
1st, 1614.

William Barnard, of West Heslerton, m. Elizabeth, daughter of Leonard Bushell, of Whitby.	Margaret m John Ramsden, twice Mayor of Hull. ob. 1637; buried at Holy Trinity, Hull.	Peter and James	John, twice Mayor of Hull; ob. Sept. 20th, 1656; buried N. Chancel Holy Trinity, Hull. m. Mary, daughter of Richard Sykes, Alderman of Leeds.	George, Rector of West Heslerton and Cowlam, ob. 1631. S.P.	Henry twice Mayor of Hull; ob. Aug. 4th, 1661; buried N. Aisle, Holy Trinity, Hull. m. Frances, daughter of Peter Spurrier.	Leonard m. Elizabeth, daughter of Sir John Lister, Knt., M.P. for Hull. leaving issue, John, William, and Elizabeth.	Frances m. Robert Legard, of Anlaby, leaving issue ten children.	Anne.

(1)   (2)   (3)

Continued on next page.

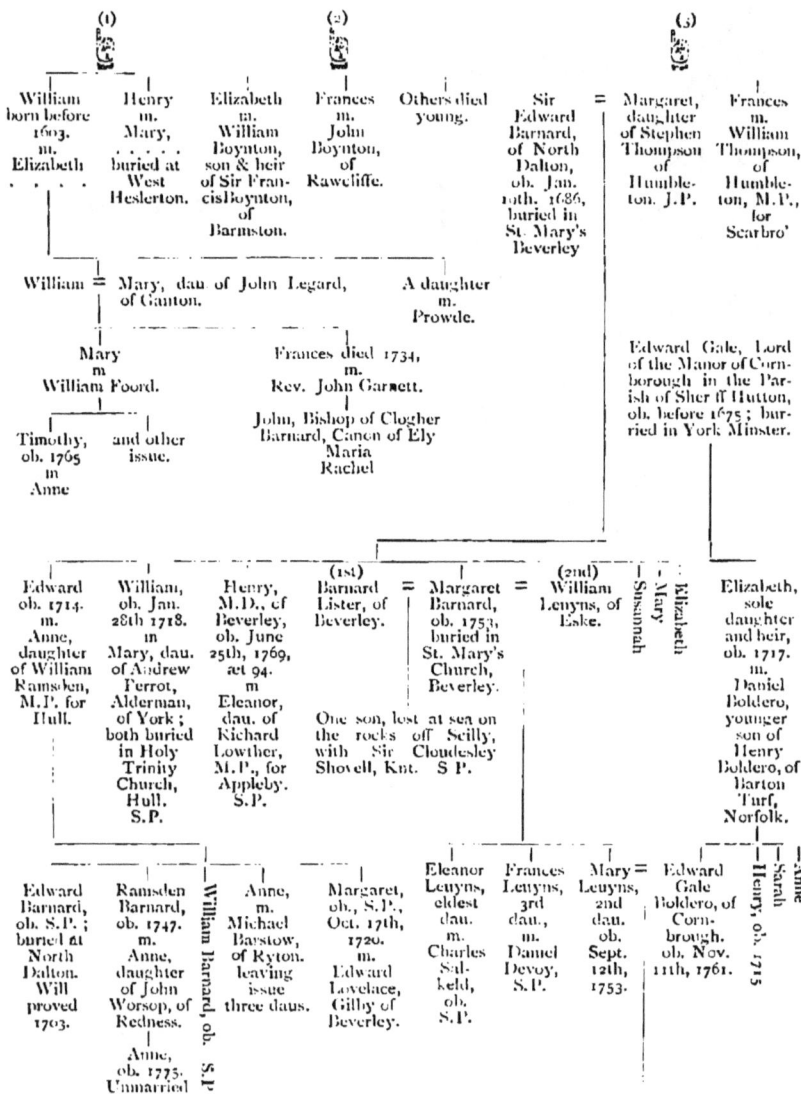

(1)   (2)   (3)

William
born before
1603.
m.
Elizabeth
. . . .

Henry
m.
Mary,
. . . . .
buried at
West
Heslerton.

Elizabeth
m.
William
Boynton,
son & heir
of Sir Fran-
cis Boynton,
of
Barmston.

Frances
m.
John
Boynton,
of
Rawcliffe.

Others died
young.

Sir   =   Margaret,
Edward   daughter
Barnard,   of Stephen
of North   Thompson
Dalton,   of
ob. Jan.   Humble-
10th. 1686,   ton. J.P.
buried in
St. Mary's
Beverley

Frances
m.
William
Thompson,
of
Humble-
ton, M.P.,
for
Scarbro'

William = Mary, dau of John Legard,   A daughter
            of Ganton.   m.
                                         Prowde.

Mary
m
William Foord.

Frances died 1734,
m.
Rev. John Garnett.

John, Bishop of Clogher
Barnard, Canon of Ely
Maria
Rachel

Edward Gale, Lord
of the Manor of Corn-
borough in the Par-
ish of Sher ff Hutton,
ob. before 1675 ; bur-
ried in York Minster.

Timothy,
ob. 1765
m
Anne

and other
issue.

Edward
ob. 1714.
m.
Anne,
daughter
of William
Ramsden,
M.P. for
Hull.

William,
ob. Jan.
28th 1718.
m
Mary, dau.
of Andrew
Perrot,
Alderman,
of York ;
both buried
in Holy
Trinity
Church,
Hull.
S.P.

Henry,
M.D., of
Beverley,
ob. June
25th, 1769,
æt 94.
m
Eleanor,
dau. of
Richard
Lowther,
M.P., for
Appleby.
S.P.

(1st)
Barnard   =   Margaret   =   (2nd)
Lister, of   Barnard,   William
Beverley.   ob. 1753,   Lenyns, of
                 buried in   Eske.
                 St. Mary's
                 Church,
                 Beverley.

            One son, lost at sea on
            the rocks off Scilly,
            with Sir Cloudesley
            Shovell, Knt. S P.

Mary
Susannah

Elizabeth

Elizabeth,
sole
daughter
and heir,
ob. 1717.
m.
Daniel
Boldero,
younger
son of
Henry
Boldero, of
Barton
Turf,
Norfolk.

Edward
Barnard,
ob. S.P. ;
buried at
North
Dalton.
Will
proved
1703.

Ramsden
Barnard,
ob. 1747.
m.
Anne,
daughter
of John
Worsop, of
Redness.

Anne,
ob. 1775.
Unmarried

William Barnard, ob. S.P

Anne,
m.
Michael
Barstow,
of Ryton.
leaving
issue
three daus.

Margaret,
ob., S.P.,
Oct. 17th,
1720.
m.
Edward
Lovelace,
Gilby of
Beverley.

Eleanor
Lenyns,
eldest
dau.
m.
Charles
Sal-
keld,
ob.
S.P.

Frances
Lenyns,
3rd
dau.,
m.
Daniel
Devoy,
S.P.

Mary = Edward
Lenyns,   Gale
2nd   Boldero, of
dau.   Corn-
ob.   brough.
Sept.   ob. Nov.
12th,   11th, 1761.
1753.

Anne

Henry, ob. 1715

Sarah

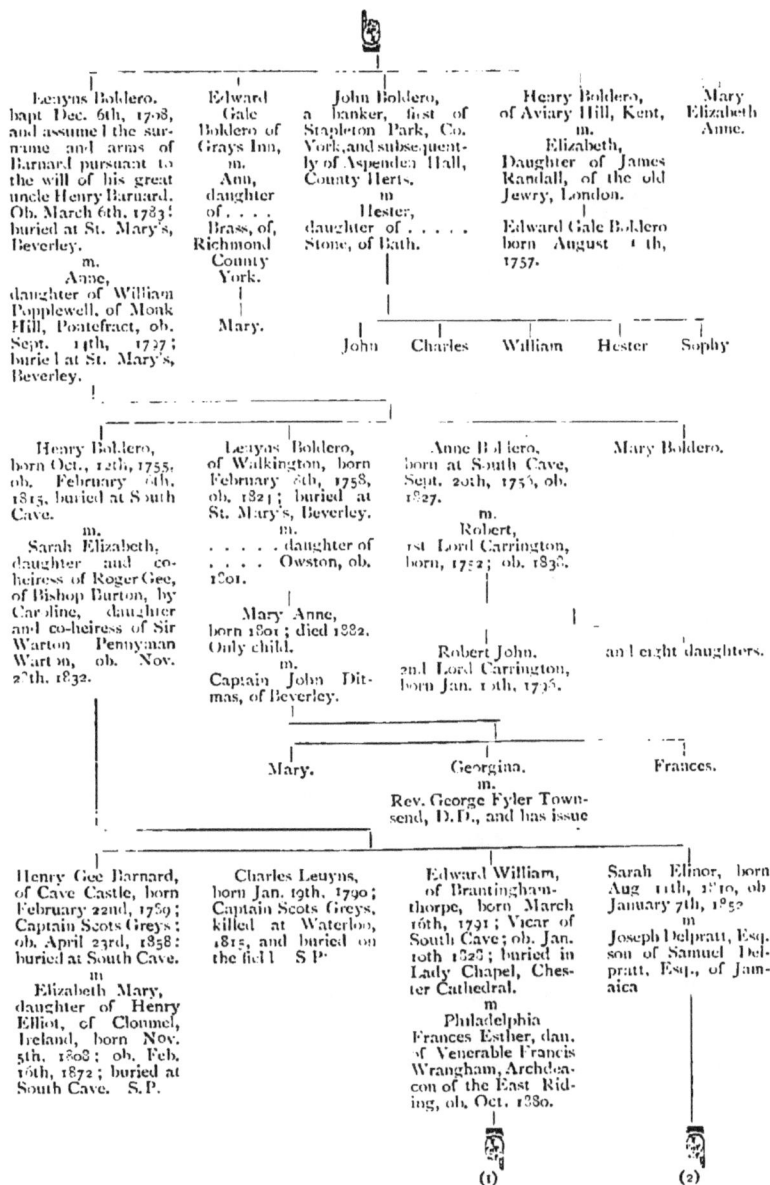

Leuyns Boldero. bapt Dec. 6th, 1708, and assumed the surname and arms of Barnard pursuant to the will of his great uncle Henry Barnard. Ob. March 6th, 1783; buried at St. Mary's, Beverley.
m.
Anne, daughter of William Popplewell, of Monk Hill, Pontefract, ob. Sept. 14th, 1797; buried at St. Mary's, Beverley.

Edward Gale Boldero of Grays Inn, m. Ann, daughter of . . . . Brass, of, Richmond County York.
Mary.

John Boldero, a banker, first of Stapleton Park, Co. York, and subsequently of Aspenden Hall, County Herts. m Hester, daughter of . . . . . Stone, of Bath.

Henry Boldero, of Aviary Hill, Kent. m. Elizabeth, Daughter of James Randall, of the old Jewry, London.
Edward Gale Boldero born August 4th, 1757.

Mary Elizabeth Anne.

John Charles William Hester Sophy

Henry Boldero, born Oct., 12th, 1755, ob. February 6th, 1815, buried at South Cave. m. Sarah Elizabeth, daughter and co-heiress of Roger Gee, of Bishop Burton, by Caroline, daughter and co-heiress of Sir Warton Pennyman Warton, ob. Nov. 20th, 1832.

Leuyns Boldero, of Walkington, born February 6th, 1758, ob. 1824; buried at St. Mary's, Beverley. m. . . . . . daughter of . . . . Owston, ob. 1801.
Mary Anne, born 1801; died 1882. Only child. m. Captain John Ditmas, of Beverley.

Anne Boldero, born at South Cave, Sept. 20th, 1755, ob. 1827. m. Robert, 1st Lord Carrington, born, 1752; ob. 1838.
Robert John, 2nd Lord Carrington, born Jan. 16th, 1796.
and eight daughters.

Mary Boldero.

Mary. Georgina. m. Rev. George Fyler Townsend, D.D., and has issue Frances.

Henry Gee Barnard, of Cave Castle, born February 22nd, 1789; Captain Scots Greys; ob. April 23rd, 1858; buried at South Cave. m Elizabeth Mary, daughter of Henry Elliot, of Clonmel, Ireland, born Nov. 5th, 1808; ob. Feb. 16th, 1872; buried at South Cave. S.P.

Charles Leuyns, born Jan. 19th, 1790; Captain Scots Greys, killed at Waterloo, 1815, and buried on the field S P

Edward William, of Brantingham-thorpe, born March 16th, 1791; Vicar of South Cave; ob. Jan. 10th, 1828; buried in Lady Chapel, Chester Cathedral. m Philadelphia Frances Esther, dau. of Venerable Francis Wrangham, Archdeacon of the East Riding, ob. Oct. 1880.

Sarah Elinor, born Aug 11th, 1810, ob January 7th, 1852 m Joseph Delpratt, Esq. son of Samuel Delpratt, Esq., of Jamaica

(1) (2)

(1)   (2)

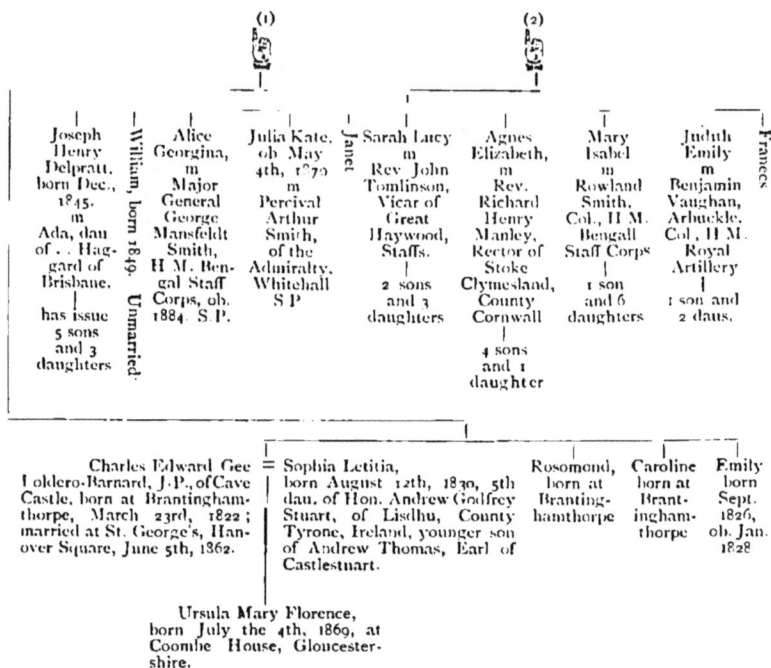

| Joseph Henry Delpratt, born Dec., 1845. m Ada, dau of . . Haggard of Brisbane. has issue 5 sons and 3 daughters | William, born 1849. Unmarried. | Alice Georgina, m Major General George Mansfeldt Smith, H. M. Bengal Staff Corps, ob. 1884. S.P. | Julia Kate, ob May 4th, 1870 m Percival Arthur Smith, of the Admiralty. Whitehall S P | Janet | Sarah Lucy m Rev John Tomlinson, Vicar of Great Haywood, Staffs. 2 sons and 3 daughters | Agnes Elizabeth, m Rev. Richard Henry Manley, Rector of Stoke Clymesland, County Cornwall 4 sons and 1 daughter | Mary Isabel m Rowland Smith, Col., H M. Bengall Staff Corps 1 son and 6 daughters | Judith Emily m Benjamin Vaughan, Arbuckle. Col., H M. Royal Artillery 1 son and 2 daus. | Frances |

| Charles Edward Gee Loldero-Barnard, J.P., of Cave Castle, born at Brantinghamthorpe, March 23rd, 1822 ; married at St. George's, Hanover Square, June 5th, 1862. | = | Sophia Letitia, born August 12th, 1830, 5th dau. of Hon. Andrew Godfrey Stuart, of Lisdhu, County Tyrone, Ireland, younger son of Andrew Thomas, Earl of Castlestuart. | Rosomond, born at Brantinghamthorpe | Caroline born at Brantinghamthorpe | Emily born Sept. 1826, ob. Jan. 1828 |

Ursula Mary Florence, born July the 4th, 1869, at Coombe House, Gloucestershire.

THE BARNARD FAMILY.

The Barnard family settled in Holderness at a very early date, and were in possession of lands in Hedon, Preston, and Burstwick in the thirteenth century. We find in 1296 that King Edward I. escheated a writ to Thomas de Weston, his bailiff of Holderness, desiring him to pay for lands belonging to Lucie, daughter and heir of John Barnard, which the King's late escheator, Thomas de Normanvill, had enclosed within the Royal Park of Burstwick. Frequent mention is made of the Barnards in the old writings relating to Hedon*. In 1413 Henry V. confirms a Charter to this town, granting great liberties to the mayors and

* Poulson's History of Holderness.

burgesses, and Hugh Barnard is one of the first jury. In 1472
Thomas Barnard is Mayor of Hedon, and is re-elected ten times
between that and 1493. In 1505 William Barnard is Mayor ; soon
after which the family seems to have migrated to Hull, though they
still retained their property in Holderness. There is at the present time a close near Hedon which goes by the name of "Barnard's Croft," by which name it was known in the reign of Henry
III. being mentioned in a Deed of that period.

At a Court Leet held 9th November, 1597, William Barnard
and Elizabeth, his wife, surrendered land at Patrington for a term
of twenty-one years Their son, William Barnard, was the first of
the family who seems to have settled in Hull.

On May 2nd, 1711, Dr. Henry Barnard, youngest son of Sir
Edward Barnard, Knight, made a surrender of lands, inherited
from his father, in Lelly and Preston, near Hedon. The rest of
the property belonging to the family in Holderness, in Storke,
Sandholme, Hollym, Rye-hill (otherwise Ryhill), Camerton, Lelly,
and elsewhere, under the will (bearing date 16th January, 1747) of
Ramsden Barnard, Esq., of North Dalton, grandson and representative of Sir Edward Barnard, passed on the death of his only daughter
and heiress. Anne Barnard, on 3rd May, 1775. to his friend, William
Bethell, Esq., second son of Hugh Bethell of Rise, he having
been the sixth mentioned in the entail created by this will.

There are numerous tombstones to members of the Barnard
family both in St. Mary's Beverley, and in Holy Trinity Church, Hull.
The oldest, in the latter, now entirely defaced, is that of William
Barnard, son of the William and Elizabeth Barnard, alive in 1597.

De la Pryme, gives the following as having been the inscription of this stone in the north aisle of the chancel :—

"Here lieth in peace, William Barnard, Merchant Adventurer, of Kingston-upon-Hull, who departed this life the 1st November. 1614."

De la Pryme's manuscript says :

" Both their portraits are upon the stone *i.e.*, both his and his wife's, with nine sons at man's estate, and three daughters."

These portraits and the inscription have since disappeared, and two of the nine sons must have died before their father, as only seven are mentioned in his will.

This William Barnard was Lord of the Manor of Melton, and owner of the Parish of Cowlam, besides possessing considerable property in Holderness and other parts of Yorkshire. In 1589 he was Chamberlain of Kingston-upon-Hull, and Mayor in 1602. In his will, dated 1603, he bequeathes various sums to the charities and ministers of the town, and leaves to each of his sons landed property of considerable extent. It reads strangely to us in the nineteenth century to find included in his fifth son Henry's portion : " My sheepwalks, with six score sheep gates in Myton, now in the occupation of John Mawson ; and also my sheepwalks and closes, with all the sheep gates thereunto belonging in the same lordship, now in the occupation of John Thirkell, glover, being freehold land." Of the seven sons mentioned in the will, three took an active part in public affairs in Hull during the Civil War. John and Henry were each twice Mayor, whilst Leonard—many of whose letters are extant among the Corporation Records—acted as special envoy to Parliament on several occasions. He married a daughter of Sir John Lister, Knight, and was executor of his will under which large charities were left to Hull.

Sir Edward Barnard, of North Dalton, Knight (born 1632), eldest son of Henry, was the most noted man of his family and was knighted by Charles II. He was Recorder of Hull from 1669 to 1684, when he was discharged by James II. He was also Recorder of Beverley from 1663 to his death. Sir Edward is described by Gent as having been "the honor of Kingston, the delight of Beverley, and an ornament of the law." He must have been a man of great energy, as besides attending to his public duties and the management of his large estate, he found time to fill several volumes with reports of law cases (among others, of the trial of Sir Harry Vane) in a beautifully clear handwriting. These volumes are now in the library at Cave Castle. He died in 1686, aged 54, and is buried at St. Mary's, Beverley. He was succeeded by his son Edward, as Recorder of Beverley, and in 1697, "at the request of the town," Mr. Edward Barnard also became Recorder of Hull.

Sir Edward's male issue failing on the death of his youngest son, Dr. Henry Barnard (he having no children by his wife Eleanor, daughter of Richard Lowther, of Malmesmeburn, M.P. for Appleby), his branch of the family is now represented by the descendants of his eldest daughter, Margaret, who, by her second husband, William Leuyns, Esq., of Esk, left three daughters and co-heiresses. One of these three ladies, Mary Leuyns, married Edward Gale Boldero, Esq., of Cornbrough, in the North Riding, and their eldest son, Mr. Leuyns Boldero, on the death of his great-uncle, Dr. Henry Barnard, at the advanced age of ninety-four, assumed, in compliance with his will, by Royal License dated 30th November, 1769, the name and arms of Barnard, in addition to the name and arms of Boldero.

Mr. Leuyns Boldero. had, previously to this, bought the Manor of South Cave, and settled here.

Mr. Leuyns Boldero Barnard's great-grandson, Mr. C. E. G. Barnard, therefore, now represents this old and once numerous family ; the eldest branch, the Barnards of West Heslerton, having become extinct, in the male line, in the beginning of last

D

century, as will be seen from the pedigree ; and though the late Lord Willoughby de Brook, as well as the Barnards of Bigby in Lincoln-shire, and elsewhere, claimed to be descended from the same family, they have not been able to trace their exact connection with it.

It may be mentioned, that the Bolderos are a very old family, and, there is a tradition, that they are descended from the Danish "Balder," who settled in Suffolk in the ninth century. Their pedigree in the present Mr. Barnard's possession commences about 1420.

The Daniel Boldero, whose son married Miss Leuyns, was born in 1620. He was M.A. of Jesus College, Cambridge, and was the son of Henry Boldero, of Barton Turfe, Norfolk, and Hepworth, Suffolk. Daniel Boldero married Elizabeth, only daughter and co-heiress of Edward Gale, Esq., of Cornbrough Manor, in the North Riding. He died in 1711, and is buried in the South Aisle, St. Helen's, York.

Soon after 1748, when Mr. Leuyns Boldero purchased the South Cave Estate, he began to plant extensively and was the first to propose the enclosure of Wallingfen. He was a man of great energy and ability, and it is to his care in the preser-vation of important MSS. that we are indebted for valuable documents which have materially assisted in the preparation of the history of the manors.

His eldest son, Henry Boldero Barnard, who succeeded him, modernized and enlarged the house and was looked upon as a model country gentleman. He commenced the collection of pictures at Cave Castle, as well as the library. By his wife, Sarah Elizabeth, eldest daughter and co-heiress of Roger Gee, of Bishop-Burton, he had three sons and one daughter. His eldest son, the late Henry Gee Barnard, educated at Eton, entered the army in 1806 and became Captain in the Scot's Greys. Soon after the death of his father he retired on half pay, and he married (8th April, 1834) at Paddington Church, London, Elizabeth Mary, daughter of Henry Elliot, Esq., of Clonmel, Ireland, by whom he had no issue. He died in 1858 universally beloved and respected.

The second son, Charles Leuyns, born 1790, entered the army at the early age of fourteen, and served with distinction in the 14th and 38th Regiments, and with the 1st Dragoon Guards in Germany, as well as through nearly the whole of the Peninsular War, in which he was severely wounded, and where he was honorably mentioned in the despatches. He was captain at the age of sixteen, and, having obtained his brother's troop early in 1815, at the battle of Waterloo he led into action the right squadron of his regiment and fell on the field. It may be mentioned as a remarkable fact, that he was the only officer in the Scots Greys who had been in action previous to that day.

The Rev. Edward William Barnard, of Brantinghamthorpe, the third son was M.A. of Trinity College, Cambridge, and Vicar of the parish of South Cave from 1818 until his premature death of fever in 1828. He was a scholar and man of refined taste: a poet of no mean order, and his " Trifles, imitative of the style of Meleager," and his "Translations of the Poems of Flaminio " are highly prized by connoisseurs, as are also the few fugitive poems that have been published since his death. The following specimen has a local interest :—

Lines by the Rev. E. W. Barnard, written at Brantinghamthorpe on the ninth anniversary of the death of his brother, Captain Charles Leuyns Barnard (Scots Greys), killed June 18th. 1815, aged twenty-five.

Thrice three years have pass'd away
Since when I stood on Airey's brow
And thought of many a holiday
Pass'd with thee at our home below.

I scarce believed the lapse of time :
  But, when fond memory called again
The playmate of my boyhood's prime,
  I shrank to feel she call'd in vain.

He sleeps, alas ! a soldier's sleep
  On thy red bosom, Waterloo ;
And I have ceased his loss to weep,
  And girt me to the world anew.

But hours like this will reach me yet,—
  When something heard, or seen, or spoken
Stirs up within my heart regret,
  Mellow'd by time, but never broken.

Here, on this very breezy hill,
  When July's eve brought gentle weather,
How often have we communed, till
  Our hearts would leap and cling together.

How often in the arduous chase—
  Emulous, but from envy free—
We've paused abreast, and laugh'd to trace
  The laggards on yon miry lea !

How often into Fate's dark book,
  Prophetic both, but ah ! unwise—
Our eager spirits dared to look,
  But look'd alas ! with hope's young eyes !

We read not, that thy lot was seal'd,
  Admired by all, in youth to die !
My real fate was unreveal'd ;
  Still much is with futurity.

We read not that domestic joy,
  Life's dearest gift, was stored for me :
We read not, that a gallant boy,
  In name and look recalling thee,

Should rise beneath my fostering care—
  A light to gild my humble way
And keep thy memory fresh and fair
  Even to thy brother's latest day.

And now I should be loath to see
   The leaf, my latter end disclosing ;
For life has yet been good to me,
   And haply ill may vex its closing.

But chief, my little ones, for you
   I dread to read what fate may bring !
The fairest flowers, that earth e'er knew,
   Have perished in their natal spring.

And thou, dear Charles, hast taught me now
   That worth is impotent to save ;
That manhood's bravest plume must bow
   Before thy breath, insatiate grave !

Mr. Edward Barnard was also author as well as poet, though, with the exception of " The Protestant Beadsman," he had not published any prose work. He was an ardent admirer of nature and delighted in all field sports. He married in 1821, Philadelphia Frances Esther, eldest daughter of the late Venerable Francis Wrangham, Archdeacon of the East Riding, and of Dorothy, daughter of the Rev. Digby Cayley, and left three children : Charles Edward Gee, the present head of the family, born 23rd March, 1822 ; Rosamond and Caroline, all now living.

The present Mr. Charles E. G. Barnard, married 5th June, 1862, at St George's Hanover Square, Sophia Letitia, fifth daughter of the Hon. Andrew Godfrey Stuart, of Lisdhu, County Tyrone, son of Andrew, Earl of Castle Stuart, and Sophia Isabella, eldest daughter of George Lenox Conyngham, of Springhill, County Derry, by whom he has had issue Sophia Isabel, born and died January 14th, 1867 ; a son born and died 25th April, 1868 ; and Ursula Mary Florence, born 4th July, 1869.

THE RECTORY AND PREBEND.

South Cave was one of the thirty-six Prebends anciently

attached to the Cathedral Church of St. Peter's at York. This Prebend consisted of the Impropriations of South Cave and Wadsworth, and Advowson of the Vicarages, and also a moiety of Otley Impropriation. It was rated A.D. 1534 at £87 yearly for first fruits. The following is a list of the Prebendaries :--

——	John Lethbroke	1422	John Selowe
1269	Thomas de Passelewe	1438	Thomas Kempe
1312	Neapol Card.	1442	John Stopendon
1342	Robert de Kildesby	1447	Thomas Kempe
1350	Henry la Zouche	1449	Stephen Wilton
1351	Henry de Ingleby	1457	William Worsley
1375	—— -——	1499	Hugh Oldham
1380	John Fordham	1504	Geffrey Simeon
1381	Nicholas de Heth	1509	John Wethey
1383	John de Waltham	1509	Geffrey Wrenne
1383	William de Noion	1512	John Withers
1399	William Waltham	1534	William Hogill
1416	Henry Bowet	1549	John Wilson.

Mr. Wilson, the last incumbent, was, according to Mr. Torr, "placed here in order to alienate it, which he forthwith did the same year, viz., 1549, by passing it away to Sir Michael Warton, since which time it hath become entirely dissolved and extinct."*

The Rectory and Prebend were granted by a patent in 1552 to Sir Henry Nevill, Knight, "in Tayle Male" and by a deed, dated 1586, William Johnson is to pay to Sir Henry Nevill £380, a fine for his instalment to farm for twenty-one years at £30.

In 1604, the reversion of the Rectory and Prebend was granted by a patent to Sir Henry Nevill, of Pillingbeare. This Sir Henry Nevill's widow, the Lady Elizabeth, married Sir John Thorowgood, to whom the guardianship of Richard Nevill, her son, was assigned and granted by the Earl of Pembroke and Montgomery, Chamberlain to the King.

Old History of York Minster, Vol. 2 p. 198.

By Sir Henry Nevill's will his Rectory and Prebend were to be sold to pay his debts and give portions to his daughters, viz.:—

To his eldest daughter, Katherine Nevill   £800

,,   Mary, his second daughter   500

,,   Philiss, his third daughter...   300

In 1637, the Prebend, &c. of South Cave were purchased by Sir John Thorowgood, of Pillingbeare, County Berks. By his will, dated 1656, Sir John Thorowgood leaves the Rectory and Prebend to his wife, Lady Elizabeth, for her life (with an annuity of £20 to his step-son, Richard Nevill, for his life) with remainder to his brother William Thorowgood.

1676-80.—Henry More, Clerk, Sub-Chantor and the Vicar Choral, claims forty shillings per annum out of the dissolved Prebend of South Cave from William Thorowgood, and William Clarke, his farmer. Henry More states in a bill exhibited in His Majesty's Court of Exchequer, " It so happened that between the 27th year of the reign of King Henry VIII, late King of England, of famous memory, and the end of the same King's reign, divers and sundry of the said Prebends or Prebendshipps were dissolved and the numbers reduced . . and were seized into the hands of the late King, who continued some in his own hands and disposed of others at his Royal Majesty's pleasure ; yet, nevertheless, the said pensions from the time of the dissolvement of the said Prebends were from time to time continued to be paid, as well as by the said King Henry VIII. and his successors, Kings and Queens of England for those corpses of the said Prebends, ... and the orators further show that there is now due to them out of the Rectory of South Cave, in the County of York, which was the ancient corpse of the dissolved Prebend of South Cave, which was a Prebend belonging to the said Church of St.

Peter, the arrears of a pension of forty shillings, and amounting in all to the sum of thirty-two pounds."

In 1694, Samuel Wise, of the Parish of St. James', Clerkenwell, in County Middlesex, who had inherited the Rectory from his uncle, William Thorowgood, left it by his will to his son, Samuel Wise, subject to the several charges by the will of William Thorowgood, Esq., deceased.

In 1706, Samuel Wise mortgages to Jonathan Eddowes, haberdasher, in London, his Rectory, &c. of South Cave for £1,050, and, being unable to release it, sells it to Jonathan Eddowes on a further payment of £736., in the year 1710.

In 1744, Jonathan Eddowes leaves the Rectory, &c. of South Cave by will to his grand-daughter, Anne Ruggles.

In 1766, Mr. and Mrs. Walford (the Anne Ruggles of Jonathan Eddowes' will) as owners of the Great Tithe, stopped the agreement which had been come to respecting the enclosure of the township, by the Lord of the Manor Paramount and all the other proprietors, insisting on having more in lieu of their tithes.

In 1785, Mr. Henry Boldero Barnard bought the Rectory etc. of South Cave from the Rev. William Walford, son of Mrs. Walford, for £11,550.*

The Rector, or Lay impropriator, as such, has the power to grant marriage licenses. The Rev. Digby S. Wrangham, of Darrington, is the present Surrogate ; but of late years " banns " have almost superseded licenses, and none have been granted since 1872. There was also a court for proving wills.

The Church.

From the account in Domesday, it appears that the village

* The Walfords were descended, in the female line, from Jane Cromwell, sister of the Lord Protector, Oliver Cromwell.

had a Church and Priest at the time of the Norman survey. No portion of that church is now in existence, having, it is supposed, been burnt down about the year 1600—a few years after the date when Glover, the Somerset Herald made his itinerary through Yorkshire; and it is a fortunate circumstance that he has given us such an interesting list of the monuments and inscriptions in that earlier church. The old square font now in the north chapel may have occupied a position in the church in Saxon times, and is of the same shape and form as the very ancient one at St. Etheldreda's, Ely Place, London.

The church is dedicated to All Saints, and from an inscription on a pillar near the tower, it seems to have been re-erected in 1601. It is situated on a slight eminence midway between the market-place and "west-end," and consists of a nave, north aisle, south transept, (called the Faxfleet aisle), a north chapel, chancel, south porch, and a tower at the west end. The dimensions are—Nave 50 feet by 36 feet, (including the aisle) ; chancel, 32 feet by 21 feet. At the west end of the north aisle is a painted window of two lights, in memory of the Rev. Herbert Ferreman Inman, M.A., Vicar. The west window in the tower is also a memorial window in memory of Henry Gee Barnard, Esq, erected by his widow, A.D. 1859. The chancel was re-built in 1847 at the cost of Mr. H. G. Barnard, the patron and impropriator who also had the east window (of four lights) filled with old richly-stained foreign glass. The north chapel is separated from the chancel by two fine pointed arches of an early character. In 1848, Faxfleet transept or aisle was re-built by the late Mr. George Baron, proprietor, of the Faxfleet Hall Estate. It is separated from the nave by a lofty pointed arch. In the south wall is an ancient piscina, over which is a tablet recording that

"This Ile was repaired at the proper cost and charges of the Right Worshipfvl Henry Garwaie, Esqvir, Alderman of the Cittie of London, 1633." *

The tower contains three bells with the following inscriptions :

(a)   "Gloria in Excelsis Deo, 1676."

(b)   "Cum Sono Busta mori cum pulpita vivere disce. 1742.

PETER HICKINGTON, Vicar.

MAT. BURLEY,   } Churchwardens."
JOHN BUTTERFIELD, }

(c)   "Populum Voco Deum Laudare, 1744."

LIST OF VICARS.

The following particulars, with the list of vicars are taken from "Torr's Peculiars," in the library of the Cathedral Church at York.

" There are in South Cave, of the fee of Mowbray, twenty-four oxgangs of land, where eight oxgangs make a carucate, and sixteen carucates a knight's fee, which was held by the heir of the Deyvill's : the whole town containing fifteen carucates. The Prebend of South Cave hath in the town one carucate or eight oxgangs of demesne land and meadow, and manor, and several tenants held of him over which he held full jurisdiction. The Prebend is also Rector of the Church of South Cave, having there his rectory, with the vicarage appendant, and the predial tythes of the whole town, and tythe of hay in all the meadows ; also tythe of wool and lamb, excepting of all cattle belonging to the Lords or the Knights Templars of the House of St. Leonard's Hospital, in York."

A CLOSE CATALOGUE OF THE VICARS OF SOUTH CAVE.

Temp Instit.	Vicarii Eccle.	Patroni.	Vacat.
2nd Nov., 1327 ...	Domini Thomas....................	Prebend of }	Mort.
23rd Oct., 1349 ...	Hugo de Leverton..................	South Cave. }	....
23rd Nov. 1349 ...	John de Driffield	....	Mort.
Jan., 1350	Ric de Pykering....................	....	....
26th May, 1367 ...	Robt. de Horton	....	Mort.

* In the "Particulars of the Parsonage in 1633," as given on another page, it will be seen that Mr. Garway farmed the "Tithe of the Demesne of Faxfleet." Sir Henry was Lord Mayor of London, 1639-40. He was a most interesting character, and there is a good account of him in the *Dictionary of National Biography*, Vol. XXI., p. 13. The family seems to have been immensely wealthy and to have possessed estates in various parts of the kingdom.

Temp Instit.	Vicarii Eccle.	Patroni.	Vacat.
19th Aug., 1399...	Joh Winthorpe		Resig.
Sept., 1401 .	Johe Yorke		Resig.
23rd April, 1402...	John de Popilton		Resig.
27th Sept., 1403...	Wm. de Spenser		Mort.
15th Nov., 1403...	Thos. Harold		Resig.
6th July, 1425 ...	Will Berneby		Mort.
6th Nov., 1454 ...	Will Welles		Resig.
13th Mar., 1472...	John Staveley		Resig.
7th July, 1489	Ric. Staresman		Mort.
3rd Oct., 1506 ...	Joh. Sympson .		Resig.
13th May, 1515 ...	Adam Carver ...		Resig.
25th April, 1550...	Lambert Ketilwell	*	Mort.
15th Nov., 1580...	John Baldwyn		Resig.
29th Aug., 1581...	Thos. Flint		Mort.
1st Jan., 1621	Thos. Brabbs		
7th Jan., 1623	Thos. Brabbs, B.A.		Mort.
3rd July, 1638 ...	John Seaman. M.A.		Mort.
27th April, 1662...	Rich. Remington		Mort.
26th July, 1671 ...	Alex. Macingtosh		
8th July, 1675	Robt. Sharpe		

CONTINUATION LIST OF VICARS.

Temp. Instit.	Vicarii Eccle.	Patroni.	Vacat.
1684	John Lambert		Mort.
1702	Peter Hickington	Samuel Wise ...	Mort.
1754	John Robinson	Miss Ruggles ...	Mort.
1783	Daniel Garnons	Mr. & Mrs Walford	
1817	Edward William Barnard	H. G. Barnard	
1828	———— Creyke	,,	Resig.
1834	E. Hotham	,,	Resig.
1844	Edwd. W. Stillingfleet	,,	Resig.
1857	Herbt. F. Inman	Mrs. Barnard ...	Mort.
1859	Digby S. Wrangham	,,	Resig.
1875	Wm. C. Stuart	C. E.G. Barnard	Resig.
1880	Wm. T. Mackintosh	,,	Resig.
1888	Thos. H. McDougall	,,	

* Torr gives the Patrons after the Reformation, but there being some doubt as to their accuracy, we have omitted them.

TESTAMENTARY BURIALS.

On Saturday after the Feast of St. Matthew, A.D. 1346.

DOMINI THOMAS, Pptual Vicar of South Cave, made his will, proved; whereby he gave his soul to God Almighty and his body to be buried in the church porch thereof; and bequeathed to Sir Alex. de Cave two silver pitchers.

6th Decr. A.D. 1479.

JOHN WRIGHT, of temple-garth in Faxfleet, made his will—proved 27th Aug., 1481—giving his soul to God Alm., St. Mary, and all saints, and his body to be buried in the Ch. of All Saints, South Cave, and bequeathed 13s. 4d. to a fitt priest to celebrate for his soul for the space of one year, and 10s. to the Friars Augustines to say a trental for him.

24th Decr., A.D. 1483.

WILLIAM WELLES, Chaplain, Vicar of S. Cave, made his will—proved 25th Nov., 1483—giving his soul (*ut Supra*), and his body to be buried in the Quire of the Church of All Saints, S. Cave.

2 Sept., A.D. 1491.

ROBERT GREEN, farmer of the Rectory of S. Cave, made his will—proved 20th Oct. 1492—giving his soul (*ut Supra*), and his body to be buried in the pshe. Ch. of S. Cave.

9th July, 1506.

RICHARD STARESMAN, Vicar of South Cave, made his will—proved 22nd July, 1506—giving his soul (*ut Supra*), and his body to be buried in the Ch. of S. Cave, before his stall.

ANCIENT MONUMENTS, &c.

The following account of the monuments, inscriptions, and arms in South Cave Church, is taken from the "Visitation of Yorkshire (in 1584), by Robert Glover, Somerset Herald."* There are at present no traces of any of these monuments, and they would doubtless be destroyed when the church was burnt down about the year 1600.

I. "An old Knight and his wife kneeling with His Cote Armor on Both Theyre Backs and This written over Theyre Heads, 'Dominus Alexander de Cave, Dame Jone de Cave.' Argent fretty azure, Cave fretty of four in most

* "Glover's Visitation," Edited by Foster, p. 439.

places" (there is clearly some error here either in Glovers' MS., or in some subsequent copying, as the ar. and az. should be reversed).

"A Knight kneeling in ye windowe and his two wives with Cave on the out Garment, and theyre own in the Inner."

II.   "Argent, a lion rampant azure impaling Cave."

III.   "Azure, a bend argent impaling Cave."

IV.   "Gyronny, argent and gules, impaling Cave."

VI.   "Cave impaling argent, a bend between three roses gules.. under this Woman, Written :

'**Orate pro animabus Petri Santon,**' " the rest broken.

VII.   "Cave impaling vert a bend flory or."

VIII.   "A Knight Kneeling, with his Coat Armor, and his wife by him, with Cave on her outward garments and the other on the Inner, (the writing is gone) Azure fretty argent a crescent for difference, impaling Azure fretty or, a chief of the last."

IX.   A Knight carved all in Alabaster Lying as big as the life with these armes paynted about ye sides and under his head upon the Helmet this crest A° 1416. Armes Azure fretty or an annulet for difference Crest, out of a ducal coronet or a falcon of the last."

X.   "Upon a stone on the ground, and no arms to be seen, was written :

Hic jacet Dus, Gerardus de Loade, Miles, qui obiit XX° — An' Dni MCCCCLXXX. quorum animabus propicietur Deus, Amen."

"These Following are paynted on ye Walls, very ould."

XI.   "Quarterly 1 and 4 Cave 2 and 3 gules 3 mullets argent."

XII.   "Argent on a bend. cottisied sa. three escallops—gules, impaling three mullets in pale argent."

XIII.   "Quarterly 1 and 4 on a bend three cresents 2 and 3 on a bend cottisied sa. three escallops qu."

XIV.   "Gules a cross patonce."

XV.   "Quarterly 1 and 4 on a fesse dancettie sable 2 and 3 ar on a bend cottised sable three escallops gules.

XVI.   "Quarterly 1 and 4 are on a bend cottised sable three annulets or (argent) 2 and 3 Cave."

XVII.   "Gules three mullets argent, Hansard. A Knight kneeling of the Caves with his two wives these arms on their garments."

XVIII.   "Cave impaling argent, a bend engrailed between three martletts sable. (broken) Tho ————— Margaret."

XIX.   "Cave impaling, a blank shield ' Tho —————Cecilia.'"

XX.   "Argent three fusils in a fesse gules impaling Cave."

XXI. "Quarterly 1 and 4 argent three bars gules over all a bend engrailed sable 2 and 3 Cave."

XXII. "Quarterly 1 and 4 argent a cheveron between two taus in chief sable and a gart in bas. or (sic) 2 and 3 Cave."

MONUMENTS &c., NOW IN THE CHURCH.

Within the altar-rails there is a stone on the floor with the following inscription :

"Here Lye the Bodies of Frances Daur. of Mr. Northend, of Hunsley, and Eliz. Daur. of Mr. Hall, of Brough. The Wives ; and also of Francis Eliz. and James, the Children of Peter Hickington, who has now been Vicr. of this Church, and That of Elloughton, thirty-two years. A.D. 1734.

Here also lieth the saidd Peter Hickington, who died March the 7th, 1754, Aged 80.

William, Son of Peter Hickington, died Septr. 29th. 1772, aged 42.

> Life's giddy scene by Fate at length is clos'd
> And still in earth the body lies repos'd.
> The Soul superiour spurns the mould'ring clay,
> For, sprung from Heaven, she Homeward wings her way,
> Soaring she sings. Be this grand truth confesst
> Repentance only can give hopes of rest :
> Go then, proud scorner, seize this instant hour
> Perhaps thy Last, and make thy calling sure."

Another stone, also within the altar-rails, has the following :—

"Beneath this Stone lies the remains of The Revd. Danl. Garnons, Clark, Vicar of this Parish 34 years, who departed this life, the 30th day of April, 1817, obiet 73."

In what is now used as the vestry, on the north side of the church, there is a large vault with this inscription :—

"Here lyeth the body of Richard Harrison, Esquire, Lord of this Manor, who departed this life the 16th day of May, A.D. 1682.

Here also lyeth the body of Eleanor, his wife, who was one of the daughters of Sir William Lowther, who departed this life the 23rd day of March, A.D. 1692-3."

A few years ago, during some alterations that were being made in the vestry, an old black marble tomb stone was discovered under the floor, bearing the inscription : " Here lyeth the body of the Dame Catharine Girlington, who departed this life . . ." (the date 1562, has been cut on the stone within the last few years, but is inaccurate, as will be seen on reference to the History of West Hall Manor, ante). On the same stone there is also this inscription : " Here also lyeth the body of Susanna Washington, daughter of Mr. Henry Washington." This stone has now been placed near the Harrison vault

- ON THE NORTH WALL OF THE CHANCEL.

" Beneath the centre stone of this chancel are deposited the remains of Henry B. Barnard, Esq., who died February 6th, A.D. 1815, aged 59. His amiable qualities will ever be remembered by those who knew him, and long will the neighbouring poor regret the magistrate who protected them in all their sufferings, and the friend who for thirty years dispensed among them the wages of honest labour ; which he rightly esteemed to be the choicest gifts of charity."

Also on the north wall of the Chancel :

" This tablet is erected to the memory of Captn. Charles Leuyns Barnard, of the 2nd R. N. B. Dragoons, who fell at Waterloo, 18th June, 1815, aged 25 years, and was buried on the field of battle. He served a campaign in Germany, and nearly the whole of the Spanish War, in which he was severely wounded. At the Battle of Waterloo he led into action the right squadron of his highly-distinguished regiment, and displayed, before he fell, talents and courage, that gained him the admiration of all his brother soldiers.

Ye that respect the union of virtue, valour, and ability, pause, 'ere ye pass this tablet ; and if ye have sons, pray that their lives may be as fair, and their death as glorious as his."

Also on the north wall of the Chancel :

"In memory of Edward William Barnard, M.A., Vicar of this Parish, who died at Chester, 10th January, 1828, aged 36 years."

TABLET ON SOUTH WALL OF CHANCEL.

" Sacred to the memory of Sarah Elizabeth Barnard, widow of the late H. B. Barnard, Esq., of Cave Castle, and eldest daughter and co-heiress of the late Roger Gee, Esq., of Bishop Burton, who died 28th Nov. 1831, aged 62."

TABLET ON SOUTH WALL OF CHANCEL.

" To the memory of Sarah Elenor Delpratt, wife of Joseph Delpratt,

Esq., of Old Charlton, in Kent, and only daughter of the late H. B. Barnard, Esq., of this place, who departed this life January 7th, 1852, aged 42 years."

On South Wall of Nave.

" Elizabeth Mary Barnard, to her beloved husband, Henry Gee Barnard, Esq., born 1789; died 1858. In grateful remembrance of a happy union of twenty-four years."

In South Aisle.

"Here lieth the body of John Clapham, who died the 18th day of Sept. 1754, aged 62; and Ellen, his wife, who died 14th March, 1760, aged 64."

Floor South Aisle.

"Sacred to the memory of Isabella Leeson, who departed this life on the 3rd June, 1833, aged 28 years."

In the Tower.

"In memory of John Hill, Esq., for thirty years surgeon of South Cave, who died Feb. 23rd, 1865, aged 63 years."

On the North Wall of Nave.

A tablet to the memory of Joseph Blanchard Burland, of South Cave, who died 29th March, 1868, aged 65 years.

Tablet in Faxfleet Transept.

"To the memory of John Robinson, whose remains are deposited in the family vault, in the churchyard. He departed this life the 10th day of Feb., 1838, aged 53 years."

In the churchyard is a stone of white marble, covering the grave of the late Mr. Henry Gee Barnard, who died April 23rd, 1858, and also that of his wife Elizabeth Mary, daughter of Henry Elliot, Esq., of Clonmel, Ireland, who died in London, February 16th, 1872.

In the churchyard there are tomb stones to the following :—

Giles Bridgeman, who died Nov. 21st 1804, aged 80 years.

Teavil Leeson who died Oct. 6th, 1865, aged 90 years.

Thomas Macturk, who died January 16th, 1857, aged 64 years.

And Thomas Scatcherd's tomb with its well-known verse :—

" That Ann lov'd Tom was very true,
Perhaps you'll say ' what's that to you.'
Who 'ere you are, remember this,
Tom lov'd Ann, 'tis that made bliss."

CHURCH TERRIERS, &C.

" The particulars of the Parsonage of South Cave as now it is let per annum, 1633."

	Per Annum.
	£ s d
Imprimis eight oxgangs of arable land being glebe and sixteen acres of meadow in the Salt Ings...	16 0 0
Item - certain Forby lands belonging to the same ...	2 0 0
Item —the Tithe Corn the Wool and Lamb	80 0 0
Item—the Tithe of the Ings	16 0 0
Item—the Tithe of the Manor of Faxfleet and Oxmardike	30 0 0
Item—the Town of Faxfleet and Boothby Garth	10 0 0
Item—the Tithe Corn and Hay of Broomfleet, with the Wool and Lamb	22 0 0
Item—the Tithe of the Province	6 0 0
Item—the Tithe of Kettlethorpe	2 13 4
Item—the Tithe of Weedley	2 0 0
Item —the Tithe of the New Field	2 0 0
Item—the Tithe of Ratten Closes Pest Ings and between Closes	2 0 0
Item—the Tithe of the yards and garths about the Town ...	2 0 0
Item—the Tithe of the Cornfields...	2 13 4
Item—the Tithe of Bagfleet's closes...	3 6 8
	£198 13 4

The outrents paid to the Prebends at York and to the singing men about the Minster, per annum, £2 13s. od.

I know not the rent to the King whether there be any or not, I did never pay any.

The gift of the Vicarage goeth with the Prebend or Parsonage.

There was a lease from Sir Henry Nevill for other tithes about Ottley and other places but you may inquire more of one Mr. Hamond who was Sir Henry's Steward for I think they were all one Prebend.

THE ESTATE OF THE RECTORY OF SOUTH CAVE.

All Buildings about the Parsonage very ruinous part therof lately but meanly repaired.

The Parson as Patron presents the Vicar. The now Incumbent Mr Brabbs. The Vicarage worth per annm. £30.

* From an old paper in the possession of C. E. G. Barnard, Esq.

E

The Vicarage in all its Buildings well maintained.

To this Rectory belongs eight oxgangs of glebe land ; every Oxgang containing nine acres of arable, three of pasture and two of meadow.

William Simpson, tenant to four oxgangs payeth for the same eight pounds per annum.

Charles Wadman tenant to the other four payeth the like sum.

There are also ten acres of arable land called Forbylands belonging to this Rectory used by Mr. Danby worth per an. £40.

There are in South Cave six score Oxgangs of land, an oxgang usually let for five pounds per ann, the Tithe of South Cave and Weedley used by Danby and Tindall.

This estimate by Oxgang rate which I conceive the most certain and sure Valuation amounteth to £60 per ann.

Tithe Wool and Lamb by credible information worth per an. £50.

For the Tithe of South Cave and Weedley with the Forbadge lands possessed by Mr. Danby and Mr. Tindall worth per an. £110.

The Tithe of Broomfleet now let to Matthew Richardson and Charles Wilson for £20 per ann.

Tithe of the Township of Faxfleet let to Richd. Mandril for £10 per ann.

Tithe of the Demesne of Faxfleet let to Mr. Garroway for £30 per ann.

The Rectory of South Cave worth per ann. £170.

Note : There are belonging to this Town exceeding great and good commons much advantageous to the Parsonage, therefore many desire to be Tenant to the same."

The following is a copy of a Terrier dated September, 1716, bound up with the Parish Registers.

"A Terrier of all and singular the housing, lands, Grounds, Profitts and Ecclesiastical Dues belonging the Vicaridge of South Cave, Exhibited September, 1716.

All the buildings belonging to this Vicaridge are a dwelling house and a Dove coat, and a Cow House, whose Dimensions are as follow.

The dwelling house is one streight building eighteen yards long and six yards broad. The dove coat is six yards square.

The ground belonging it is a Small Orchard, a fore yard and a Close or Croft containing in ye whole about three acres and an halfe

To this Vicaridge belong all manor of Tythes (Except corn and hay, wool and Lamb) and are paid as follows :—Every Messuage pays four pence for a Hen, Every Cottage two pence. At Weedly ye Great House pays twelve pence

for Hens and the little house six pence. Every Oat meal Mill pays two shillings.
Cow and Calfe three-half-pence ; uncalved one peny. Plough a peny. Every
Bee skepp three pence : or Honey in Kind. A foal two pence ; Geese, Ducks,
Pigs, Turkies, fruit, potatoes, turnips and mustard seed in Kind or as we can
agree : a Dove coat is one shilling and sixpence ; a Dove Chamber one shilling ;
for Lime twelve pence per peck ; for Hemp sixpence, or in Kind when sown in
small parcels or upon ground that has been used to it ; when in large quantities
and upon fresh ground five shillings per acre as ye Act of Parliament directs.

Offerings for every person thats sixteen years old or upward two pence ; for
Rapes the full twelfth part of ye price or to allow a crown per Last for Dressing
and delivery and then to have the full tenth of the price it is sold for.

Note : that the people of Broomfleet within this Parish pretend that all the
Grounds within their township wch is called the Lords lands are exempt as from
great so also from all small Tythes. Tho. Mr. Robert Sharpe many yeare
Vicar of Cave now lately Deceased gave it under his hand to Mr. Peter Hickington the present Incumbent that in his time he always recd. the small Tythes for
those grounds as they became due even When the great Tythes were not paid
for the same.

Mortuaries are paid in this Parish according to the Act of Parliament for
every wedding with Licence ten shillings, without two shillings and eight pence,
Churching fee one shilling, for burying in the Church yard with a Coffin two
shillings and fourpence ; without a Coffin one shilling and four pence ; for
burying in the body of the Church four shillings and eightpence to the Minister
and six shillings and eightpence to the Churchwardens to be accounted for ;
in the Chancell to the Vicar ten shillings, to the Impropriator or his Tenant as
they can agree."

In a Terrier dated 14th July, 1853, we have the following
particulars :—

" A sum of money (about £59) received for land sold to the Hull and
Selby Railway Company has been vested in the public funds.

The furniture of this church consists of three bells and an old clock, a bar-
rel organ and a time piece.

The Communion plate consists of one small silver cup, one draining spoon,
one silver gilded chalice, one silver patten for bread (the gift of Nathaniel
Rogers in 1732), one silver flagon and two silver plates, the three latter articles,
and two ancient oak chairs were presented by Henry Gee Barnard, Esquire."

THE PARISH REGISTERS.

The Registers commence with the year 1558. The earlier ones

had been copied on loose sheets of parchment, which were handsomely bound in 1877 at the expense of Mr. Barnard.

Christian names generally in use during the first hundred years of the Registers were Thomas, William, Edmund, John, Margaret, Annas, Allezon, Katherin, and Jennat; and among surnames we find Dudding, Danby, Harryson, Teavill, Richardson Freeman, Cave, Girlington, Willson, Chappellow, Snarforth, Spofford, Sparrow, Gibson, Norman, Pinder, Kirlington (of Bromflect) and Marshall. The latter surname appears to have been very common, and between 1684 and 1693 there are references to five John Marshalls who are distinguished in the registers as "blew John," "two pence John," "Soldjer John," "Cambridge John, Senr." and "Cambridge, John, Junr." The following are extracted from the registers :—

1558. Allezon Nisyaile was buryed ye 7th day of January.

1565. George Sparrow and Annas Birde were marryed the viith day of October

1566. Ffrancis Chotseth was christned ye last day of August, Maister Clatun, ffrancis Vavazor, and Mrs. Elizabeth Ellerker, suerties.

1590. VENERABILIS VIR THOMAS DANBY miles sepultus fuit decimo quinto die mens Septembris.

1617. Johnes Harryson fuit sepult 28° die Aprilis.

1671. Katherina Girlington Guilimi filia bapt 10° die Iunij.

1623. Samuell Jobson Richardi fils fuit bapt decimo sexto Novemb.

1637. Willm. Danby fils Mr. ffrancisci fuit bapt.

1654. A Marriage Intended to be made betwixt Peter Palmer, of South Cave, woolen webster, and Dorothie Norman, daughter of Willia Norman, of the same Towne, spinster, was published in South Cave Market Place on three market dayes. That is, to wytt, upon the first of May, the 8th of May, and the 15th of May, 1654. In three severall weekes next following betweene the houres of eleven and tow, according to the late Acte of Parliamt. in that case prvided, and noe pson. alledged anything to the contrary. Witness hereof, Jo. Langthorne, Register for South Cave Parish.

Be it Remembred that Peter Palmer was marryed to Dorothy Norman this prsent sixteenth day of May, 1654, in the prsence of Robert Carlin, Tho. Sheppard, Tymothie Hobman.

Phil. Saltmarshe.

1682. May 18th. Richard Harrison de South Cave armiger sepult.

1684. January. Johanes Marshall (*Vulgo dict*, 2 pence John), sepult.

1684-5. Willielmus Spoffard (alias Butcher) de South Cave, sepult.

A Register of all yt are buryed in woollen within ye Parish of South Cave, in ye yeare of or. Lord, 1686, and ye 2nd of ye Reigne of King James ye II.*

Robert, ye Sonne of Wm. Cooke of South Cave, buried March 26th. } Affidavit made.

John Belton of South Cave, buryed January ye first (16 . . .). { Affidavit and Certificate according to ye Act of Parlt. for burying in woollen was brought to me January ye first.

1686-7. Samuel Jobson de Hotham in Ecclesia huig parochia sepult.

1689. October 7th. Henricus Washington and Elianora Harrison, matrimonio conjunct.

1693. Christophore Lonsdale, Generosuss, Sepult, Martij 15th.

1693. Elinora Lonsdale, Marita Dnni Xpofori Lonsdale sepult Martij 25th

1694-5. Susannah filia Henrici Washington, Generos : bapt, Martii 24.

1695. Susanah, daughter of Hen. Washington, Gent., bur Apr. 23rd.

1696. Jan. 13th. Elizabeth filia Henrici Washington, generos bapt.

1700. May 3rd. Richard Thornton, Shoomaker, sepult.

1700. October 27th. Nicholas fil Ambrosij. Fisher de Bromflit bapt.

1724. Thom filius Georgii Leak, sepult.

1721. Jany. 8th. Johanes filius Johanis Idell, Gener. bapt.

1724. June 30th. Richardus Lloyd, Armiger, sepult.

1727. Johanes Marshall (vulgo Cambridge) sepult, 11th May.

1726. Eliz. Uxor Johanis Lonsdale de Drewton, Sepult. 20th February.

EXTRACTS FROM THE CHURCHWARDEN'S ACCOUNTS.

1705.	Spent wh. ye French was beaten by the Duke of Marlborough	0	6	0
	Spent on ye Ringers, &c., att Burtons	0	16	0
	Spt. in ale at several times to ye persons yt. helpt to remove ye frame when ye steeple was rought cast	0	2	6
1727.	Sp. at ye Coronation in meat, drink, and powder ...	1	8	2
1765.	Paid Robt. Marshall for whiping ye Doogs	0	5	0
1791.	Pade Charles Holborn for Clock	7	7	0

* To encourage the home wool trade, Acts of Parliament were passed in 1666 and 1678, requiring burials to be in woollen, and the Clergyman was to make an entry in the register that an affidavit had been brought, and the law duly complied with.

1795.	Pd. for a prayer for Prince of Whales...		0	0	6
	Pd. Thos. Glasby for bringing form of Prayer ...		0	0	2
1798.	Paid Saml. Shaw, Warrener, for a Fox head	...	0	1	0
1799.	Paid singing Master for instructing Singers	...	7	7	0
1807.	Paid John Arnel for keeping silence in the Loft	...	0	2	6

CHARITIES.

JOBSON'S CHARITY.—The Jobson family had been settled in South Cave from the sixteenth century. The first entry in the Parish Register is that of "Anna Jobson, buried 1610."

Mr. Samuel Jobson, the donor of the charity bearing his name, was baptised in 1623, and his father, Richard Jobson, was buried in 1643.

Samuel Jobson's name, and that of his wife Ursula, appear on the West Hall Manor Court Roll of 1685 as surrendering a tenement in the West end of the town. He must always have been a person of some consideration, as he was steward of the Manors of Faxfleet under three successive Lords, and steward of the West Hall Manor in John Girlington's time.

Samuel Jobson was buried within the Church, March 22nd, 1687, and by his will gave a cottage and about five acres of land adjoining Brantingham Church, together with some land on the west side of the South Cave and Brough Road, to the poor of South Cave. The gift is recorded on a board in the Church as follows:—"The Gift of Mr. Samuel Jobson to the Churchwardens of South Cave and their successors for ever, commencing at Easter, 1697. Mr. Jobson, by his last will, gave to his beloved wife:

"All that his Cottage in Brantingham adjoining on the Church Garth during her natural life, and after her decease he gave the same premises to the Churchwardens of South Cave and their successors for ever upon condition that they and their successors for ever pay yearly, after his said wife's decease, the sum of twenty shillings for an anniversary sermon to be preached every Easter Tuesday, and likewise, upon condition that on the same day, yearly, immediately after the sermon, they distribute to the value of twenty-five shillings in white Bread to the Poor. Daniel Garnons, Vicar, 1809, Samuel Ayre and Thomas Clegg, Churchwardens."

The cottage and land were sold a few years ago to Mr. Christopher Sykes, M.P., and the purchase money was invested in consols. In the year 1883 the Charity Commissioners approved of a new scheme for the future management of the charity—which is vested in a body of trustees who meet quarterly. In the scheme it is stated that the endowment consists of the sum of £2,917 12s. 8d., consolidated three per cent. annuities, and the income is to be applied as follows :—£15 a year to the Vicar of South Cave ; the remainder of the income to be divided into three equal parts, two of such third parts to be applied for the benefit of deserving and necessitous persons resident in the original parish of South Cave, in any of the various ways therein described, as should be considered most advantageous to the recipients ; and the remaining third part of the income to be applied towards the repair of the Parish Church.

Mrs. Barnard's Charity.

The late Mrs. Elizabeth Mary Barnard, who died February 16th, 1872, by her will bequeathed a sum of £1000 to the poor of South Cave ; the interest to be distributed by the Vicar and Churchwardens among six of the poorest and most deserving females, (widows being preferred —other things being equal), who shall have lived in the township of South Cave, for five years prior to the yearly distribution of the gift, on the 22nd of February, being the anniversary of her husband's birthday.

Rev. James Bayock and the Congregational Chapel, West End.

A tradition has lingered in the parish that the Rev. James

Bayock, who was said to be the Vicar at the passing of the Act of Uniformity in 1662, refused to conform, and purchased a tithe barn which he converted into a meeting-house. This is not altogether accurate, as will be seen on reference to the list of vicars given on another page.

Probably Bayock (whose name singularly enough appears to have been spelled in books and documents, both in his own time and since, as "Baycock," though he always signed Bayock), may have been a young clergyman residing in the parish or neighbourhood without a charge at the time, and this view is favoured by the fact that in Calamy's "List of Ejected Ministers in the North and East Ridings," he mentions a "Mr. Baycock" as one of three ministers "who were not fix'd." *

On the passing of the Act in 1662, Bayock having purchased a tithe barn then for sale, converted it into a meeting-house, and began a ministry which continued for about half a century.

The old meeting-house survived until seventeen years ago, when it was pulled down and gave place to the present chapel.

Mr. Bayock had at one time a congregation of about 400 hearers, many of whom came from a distance, which may account for the fact that in the year 1702 he conveyed a house and a piece of ground in St. Katherine's yard, near his chapel, to a body of trustees who were to hold the same at "the rent of one Peppercorne att the ffeast of St. Michael the Arch-Angel," to the intent that the trustees might erect a stable on such piece of ground, most probably for the accommodation of vehicles belonging to members of the congregation.

By a deed dated 30th May, 1730, Mr. Bayock conveyed the

* Calamy (1713 Edition) Vol. II., p. 835.

chapel and premises to trustees "upon the special trust and confidence, and to the absolute intent and purpose that the said House, Chappel, or building shall be used and imployed as a Chappel or Meeting House for religious worship for such persons as are, or shall be knowne or distinguished most commonly by the name of Presbyterians." *

The following is a copy of his will, which is a quaint and interesting document :

"I, James Bayock, of South Cave, in the County of York, Clark, an unworthy Minister of Jesus Christ, whose doctrine I have preached, tho' with weakness, more than fifty years, being at present sound in my Intellectuals, yet indisposed by an aguish distemper and knowing the uncertainty of mortal life, tho' I believe " *Quod terminus vitæ humanæ sit fixus et immobilis*," do make this my last will and Testament. First, I bequeath my Soul to the Father of Spirits through Jesus Christ, looking for Salvation onely by the merit of Jesus Christ, not by works of Righteousness which we have done. I believe the Holy Scriptures of the Old and New Testament to be the only Rule of Faith and Manners. My body I committ to the ground till the Resurrection of the dead, but to be buried on the backside of my Chappel or in my orchard by my Executors, knowing Superstition first brought Bodies to be buried in Churches, according to Doctor Fuller's History, Century the Eight, whose words are these : 'Anno 758. About this time bodies were first brought to be buried in Churches, when before neither Prince nor Prelate was to be buried within the Walls of a Cyty, till Eadbert, King of Kent, granted it to Cuthbert, Archbishop of Canterbury ; also the Law of the twelve Tables of Rome did forbid Bodies to be buried within the Cyty, though it be now a custome, yet in Cytys it is prejudical to the health of the living.' All my real personal estate in this world I give and dispose of in the following manner : First I give unto my dear Wife, Mary Bayock, all my real estate in land, viz., my Dwelling freehold house in which I live, in South Cave, with ye Orchard, Dovehouse, and all other houses and buildings belonging thereto, also ye little close att ye Orchard end ; all which I give to my said dear, very dear wife, aforesaid, and her heirs for ever. Also I give unto my dear wife, Mary Bayock, my little park in the Newfield, and the freehold House besides our Chappel, standing upon ye same ground called St. Katherine's

* The original deeds from which the above extracts are taken are deposited at the Fish Street Congregational Church, Hull.

Yard, with common rights and all right belonging to ye same, all which abovesaid I give to my said dear Wife and her heirs for ever. As for my personal
estate, my goods, household, and books, which ar of small value I give to my said
dear, very dear, wife, which real and personal estate will hardly be a competency
for her. God knows I never sought riches by being a non-conformist, but
know I exposed myself to poverty and persecution as many others have done.
Lastly I make my dear Wife sole Executrix of this, my last Will and Testament,
written by my own hand, revoking all other. I can give nothing legacies but a
shilling to each of my Brother Bayock Daughters and a shilling to each of my
Sister Wheelright Daughters and sons, because my personal estate will not pay
what I owe, and funeral charges—which I desire may be without any pomp and
charges. Those now last lines also I make a part of my last Will and Testament. Sealed, signed, and delivered in ye presence of the Witnesses under
written. In testimony whereof I have hereunto set my hand seal this 12th day
of March, 1731-1732, James Bayock (L.S.), Will. Hall, William Weedley, John
Carlill, John Lyon."

The fourth day of October, 1737, the Will of James Bayock, late of South
Cave, in the County of York, Clerk, was proved in the Peculiar Court of South
Cave, by the oath of Mary Bayock, widow, the Relict, the sole Executrix in the
said will named, to whom administration was granted, she having been first
sworn duly to administer." *

We had considerable difficulty in ascertaining the date of Mr.
Bayock's death, but, sometime ago, we were fortunate enough
to meet with a copy of a register of deaths, compiled by the Revs.
Oliver Heywood and T. Dickenson, of North Owram, in the West
Riding, between the years 1644 and 1752, and on page 322,
occurred the following entry in the year 1737. " Mr. ———
Bayok, of South Cave, near Hull, bur. Sept. 29th, aged 90 or up-
wards. A dissenting Minr., supposed to be the oldest Minr. in
England." It was this entry which first led us to suspect that
" Bayock " was an improper spelling of the name.

Mr. Bayock was followed by the Rev. Thos Hickington, who
died in 1754, at the age of eighty-two, having been a minister above

* Extracted from the District Probate Registry at York.

fifty years. Succeeding ministers, and the years in which they respectively entered, were as follows:—Ellis, 1773; Blackburn, 1780; Grimshaw, 1781; Tapp, 1791; Nettleship, 1821; Kelsey, 1824; Stott, 1831; Allen, 1839; Roberts, 1847; Menzies, 1854; Murray, 1869; Elliott, 1874; Davis 1879, who resigned in April, 1885, since which time there has been no settled minister.

It will be observed that the Rev. Thomas Hickington died in the year 1754, aged 82, having been minister for many years, and it was a coincidence that the Rev. Peter Hickington died in the same year, aged eighty, he having been Vicar of the parish for fifty-two years.

REV. ROBT. TODD, M.A.

On the passing of the Act of Uniformity, above referred to, there were three clergymen at Leeds who were unwilling to conform, namely, Mr. Todd, Mr. Sales, and Mr. Nesse. Of these three, two were natives of this district, Mr. Todd being born at South Cave in 1594, and Mr. Nesse at North Cave in 1621.

REV. CHARLES BARFF.

South Cave was the birth-place of Charles Barff, who for about half-a-century spent an active and useful life in the South Pacific, as a missionary in connection with the London Missionary Society. Mr. Barff was born September 11th, 1791, and was the son of Robert and Jane Barff. Little is known as to his youthful days, but when about twenty-four years of age he devoted himself to missionary work. When in London preparing for his future career he was a member at Surrey Chapel, then under the ministry of Rowland Hill, and he married a Miss Sarah Swain, who was a member of the "Tabernacle" where Matthew Wilks was then the minister. Mr. and Mrs. Barff sailed for the South Seas in July,

1816, and in July, 1818, Huahine became their permanent station. They visited England in 1847, and returned again to Huahine in 1849. They finally retired from mission work in March, 1864, and on their voyage to Sydney, in the "John Williams," were wrecked at Danger Island on the 17th May, 1864. The passengers and crew all escaped safely to the shore before the vessel went down, and in a few weeks were all landed in safety at Samoa, from whence they got a vessel to take them on to Sydney. Mr. Barff died there on the 23rd June, 1866, and Mrs. Barff about the year 1870. Mr. Barff left a son, Rowland Hill Barff, who still resides at Huahine.

WESLEYAN CHAPEL.

The Wesleyan Chapel was erected in 1816. A few years ago the interior was re-seated and greatly improved; a neat little room for the Sunday School being added at the same time.

PRIMITIVE METHODIST CHAPEL.

In the year 1819 the Rev. William Clowes, one of the founders of the Primitive Methodist Connexion, preached at South Cave, and in his "Journal" we find the following entries :—"On Sunday, February 28th I rode eight miles, walked ten, preached three times, and heard two sermons. The places officiated at were Elloughton in the morning, South Cave in the afternoon, and North Cave in the evening. In the afternoon, at South Cave, in the open air the congregation was very great." Later in the same year we find another entry, "At South-Cave I administered the Word in a large yard belonging to Mr. Pickering, who kept an inn, and whose kindness and hospitality to me were very great." A Society having been formed, a chapel was built behind two cottages in Church Street. The old chapel and cottages were pulled down in the year 1876, and a commodious chapel, with school-room and vestries, erected on the same site at a cost of about £600.

CAVE CASTLE.

Cave Castle, the residence of the Boldero-Barnard family, is pleasantly situated between the Market Place and the West End of the town. The park contains some very fine old timber, and the grounds were laid out with great taste by William Emes, in 1787, for Henry Boldero-Barnard, Esq. According to an old paper, in the handwriting of Leuyns Boldero-Barnard, great grandfather of the present owner, the house stands on the site of an old castle, and the fact that some portions of the walls have been pronounced, both from their construction and thickness, to be of very ancient date, and also the discovery, a few years ago, of a subterranean arched passage leading from the house to the church, seem to bear out this tradition. The house, as we now see it, is comparatively modern, having been partly rebuilt and enlarged by Henry Boldero-Barnard, Esq., in 1791, and contains an excellent library, and a choice collection of pictures (principally of the Dutch School), amongst which the following are considered very fine specimens of the masters :—

1. The Traveller and the Satyr, by ... ... *Jan Steen*
2. An Interior, "The Matrimonial Quarrel," a small but very highly finished picture, by ... ... *Jan Steen.*
3. A Village Fair, from the Duchesse de Berri's collection, by ... ... *D. Teniers.*
4. The Mussel Eater, from George IV's collection, and others by ... ... *D. Teniers.*
5. The Head of an Old Man in a red cap, from a collection at Copenhagen—a very fine specimen, by *Rembrandt.*

6. A beautiful large Sea Piece, "Men of War becalmed, bearing the French Flag," by... ... *W. Vandervelde.*

7. Very fine and large Landscapes, by   *Zuccarelli.*

8. A River Scene with Cattle, by   *A. Cuyp.*

Dort in the Morning Light, by   ...   . *A. Cuyp.*

9. The Battle of Neerwinden, with a Portrait of King William III., by   ...   *Hughtenberg.*

10. A Storm at Sea, by   ...   .   *Backhuysen.*

11. Small cabinet picture, "Inn Yard," by   *Wouvermans.*

12. A Drunken Carouse, by the rare artist,   *Adrian Brauer.*

and landscapes by Pynacker, Jacob and Solomon Ruysdael, Berghem, Vanderneer, Hobbema, De Konigh, Van Goyen Wynants, Guardi, and Palma Vecchio : as well as by Gainsborough, Richard Wilson, and George Moreland. Also two very large pictures, "Moonlight on the River Eske, and Reslyn Castle," and "An English Landscape," by G. Arnald, A.R.A., who was brought into notice by Mr. Barnard's grandfather, and took numerous views of Cave and its neighbourhood. Amongst the portraits is a very fine one of James I.; others of the Lord Protector, Edward, Duke of Somerset; Bishop Nicholas Ridley; Sir George Lyle; Lord Leicester, &c. Amongst the more modern portraits are : George John, Earl of Spencer, K.G., by Sir Martin Archer Shee, F.R.A. ; Sir John Mitford, Speaker of the House of Commons, First Lord Redesdale, by Sir Thomas Lawrence, F.R.A.; Garrick, by Gainsborough An original portrait of Napoleon I., by Gobeau, authenticated by his brother Joseph, ex-King of Spain. There is also a copy by Freemen, of Cambridge, of a portrait of the President Washington, in the full uniform of Commander-in-Chief of the American Forces. The original portrait had been sent as a present to the Prince of Orange Stadtholder of the Dutch Republics, but the vessel being captured during the war by the

English frigate, "Alarm," the Hon. Captain Kepple, who was in command, presented it to his uncle, the fourth Earl of Albemarle, by whose permission Lord Spencer, First Lord of the Admiralty, had it copied for his friend Mr. Boldero-Barnard.

On succeeding to the estate, in 1872, the present owner at once began the restoration of the Castle. The work was brought to a conclusion in January, 1875. Early in the morning of the very day on which the scaffolding was to have been removed, a fire broke out, considerable damage being done to the building and its contents. The fine collection of china, which was valued at £10,000 (and which included, among other treasures, a Sevre tea service, made for Queen Marie Antoinette, each piece bearing her initials and the name, " Petit Trianon "), was almost entirely destroyed.

THE SCHOOL.

" Endowment, 9a. 1r. 6p. of land which, in 1797, were demised for thirty years on a nominal rent in consideration of £300 which was applied in building a market-house, with a schoolroom above, and a house for the master. The school, at the time of the report, was conducted on the National plan ; about fifty scholars. The master's salary arises from voluntary subscription, and 1s. 6d from each child per quarter." *

GIRLS' SCHOOL.

In the year 1841, a girls' school was established and maintained by the late Mrs. Elizabeth Mary Barnard.

In 1862, she built the present school, and schoolmistress's house, which are entirely maintained by the present Mrs. Barnard, the school being under Government Inspection.

* Commissioners' 10th Report.

Mount Airey.

Mount Airey is a commanding elevation of the Wold Hills, overlooking South Cave, and rises to the height of about five hundred feet. A footpath from the Beverley Road brings the visitor to the hill, the ascent of which is in one part somewhat steep, but any difficulty that may be experienced in reaching the summit is amply compensated for by the goodly view which lies before him. At his feet is South Cave, with the Castle rising just above the trees ; to the left is the village of Ellerker, with its windmill ; beyond this is the broad estuary of the Humber, with the Rivers Ouse and Trent joining it under the shadow of the lofty promontory of Alkborough. To the right, and stretching westwards, is a fine open country extending as far as Howden, with its church, forming a conspicuous object some thirteen miles distant. To the north-west is Brayton-Barff Hill, two miles from Selby, with its wood-covered top ; to the right of it is Hemingbrough Church with its lofty spire, and still more to the right is the beautiful Vale of York, with the Cathedral rearing its lofty towers above every other object. In the same direction, but nearer, is Holme Church. The whole forming a charming view, which, for extent and diversity, is seldom met with.

The New Burial Ground.

The churchyard having become greatly over-crowded, Mr. Barnard, in 1872, gave 1a. 1r. of land for a new burial ground, which was opened in 1873, and the first interment therein took place on November 15th, in that year. The Rev. Digby S. Wrangham, on resigning the living in 1875, gave an endowment of £5 per annum towards keeping the new burial ground in order. In 1880 the old churchyard was closed by an Order in Council.

MANOR AND BAILIWICK of SOUTH CAVE 1759.

REDUCED FROM A MAP OF SURVEY MADE BY GELDART IN 1759 FOR L. BOLDE[RO]

ESQ.   THE ORIGINAL IS NOW IN THE POSSESSION OF C. E. G. BARNARD, ESQ.

OLD LANDMARKS, &c

The quaint looking building to the left-hand in the view of the Church, was formerly the "Bay-Horse" Inn, but Mr. Barnard bought it some years ago and allowed the license to lapse. The old house has been recently pulled down and a new cottage erected on the site.

In the parish there is a farm called "Provence," belonging to the Dean and Chapter of York, and it affords an illustration how ancient names linger in connection with land. The farm, shortly after the conquest, was the property of Roger de Poitou, who gave it the name of "Provence" (after his native district in France), and his widow, in 1154, granted it to the Church of St. Peter's, at York.

In 1431, Sir Henry Bromflete had in Bromfleet one messuage and thirty acres of land ; in Brantingham, one toft and twenty acres of land and ten acres of meadow ; and in South Cave twenty acres of meadow called Bagflete.

On referring to the copy of the old Parish Map, it will be seen that in 1759 the vicarage was then on the south side of the church. The map also gives us the names of open lands, some of which occur in a deed dated April 27th, 1689, whereby Christopher Bayles, of Selby, conveyed to Philip Thomlinson, of York, draper, certain estates, including :

"All those several parcells of arable meadow and pasture ground comonly called Firby Lands lying and being in the Townefields and territories of South Cave, in the said County, and heretofore in the tenure or occupation of Edward Galland or his assigns (that is to say) one Milbut Headland, one Carr Daile, one Broad Rangham, one Narrow Rangham, one North Wrangland, one Broad Santon Land, one Narrow Santon Land, one Becktoft, two Beane lands, one Broad Moore land, one Hammer land, one Skell land, one other land beyond Coney Garth, one other land called a Greenegate Moorland in the Newfield, one Arras dale, in the same field ; one Land within the Newfield Gates, one Lyne Butt,

F

one high Howdale, one low Howdale, one fracrow, one Land under Raven flatt side, one Land on the North Wald, on the Daile Side, one Wandale, one land att Moungy Nooke, one acre of Meadow lying in a certain place called the South Cave Inggs; also all that Moyety, or half of two acres of meadow or pasture ground lying within South Cave field, in a certaine place there called twixt closes between the lands formerly of Sr. Thomas Metham, on the South, and of Nicholas Girlington, Esqre., on the North. Together with all Buildings, Barnes, Gardens, Backsides, wayes, common of pasture, beast gates, and appurtenances to the said premises belonging."

In 1774, " Frog Hall" and a considerable quantity of land in South Cave belonged to a Captain Newmarch.

On May 23rd, 1751, there was an admission in the Faxfleet Manor of William Wilkinson, the elder (butcher), and Elizabeth, his wife, on a surrender from John Newton, to "a messuage in the Markett place, abutting upon a messuage of John Moorhouse on the south, a road called the Pouter hole towards the north, the Townfields towards the east, and the Markett-place on the west."

Early in the last century, the roadway leading from the Town Street to the Congregational Church was called "St. Katherine's Yard ; " and the lane at the West End, leading to the farm now occupied by Mr. Jewitt, was called " Langthorne Lane."

On the old Parish Map it will be observed that opposite Mr. Lloyd's Manor House is the Nunnery Field, where, according to tradition, there formerly stood a religious house dedicated to St. Katherine, the foundations of which are still supposed to remain under the ground.

St. Helen's Well is a fine, clear spring within the park, said to have been formerly used by the inhabitants from time immemorial.

Previous to the enclosure, a farmhouse stood against the north wall of the Churchyard, and four roads crossed the ground, one to the farm, another to the Castle, a third to the West End, and a fourth

to the Market-place, which passed over a stile at the south-east
corner. All, however, are now removed.

The road from the Market-place to the West End formerly
made a turn near Frog Hall and went by the side of St. Helen's
Well. The beck, also, had a different course from the present.
It then passed by the well and flowed through an arch under the
road on the south side of the present lodge-entrance to the park.

In an old book containing the accounts of the late Mr. George
Petfield, joiner, from 1815 to 1838, we find the following entry in
1821 : " Robert Marshall, Constable, To pair of Stocks and two
oak Posts, £1 14s. od." The Parish Stocks formerly stood in
the Market-place, between the main street and the footpath, nearly
opposite what is now Mr. Anderson's shop, but were removed
some years ago.

NORTH CAVE.

A a distance of two-and-a-half miles from South Cave, in a north-westerly direction, is the village of North Cave. The parish includes Drewton and Everthorpe, the total area being 4,684 acres, with a population of 1,135 inhabitants.

In Domesday Book it is referred to as "another Cave," and the owners of the land were Robert Malet, who had seven carucates and two oxgangs; the Archbishop of York, one carucate and six oxgangs; the Earl of Moreton, six carucates and two oxgangs; and Hugh, son of Baldric, two oxgangs.

The Robert Malet referred to in Domesday was the son of William Malet, also mentioned therein. William is described as Sheriff of Yorkshire, and, it is added, "the whole County testifies that William Malet held, in his own demesne, the whole land which

Norman, the son of Malcolumbe, had in the East Riding, so long as he held land in Yorkshire." He held lands in Holderness "until the Danes took him." Robert Malet's name appears in a list of those who held land in Yorkshire "of the King," which included land in Cave, Drewton, Hotham, Houghton, and Sancton ; and the jurors "affirm that Robert Malet ought to have all the land of Asa, because she held her land separate and free from the power and controul of Bernulf, her husband, even whilst they lived together, so that he could neither grant, sell, nor forfeit it. But after their separation, she retired with all her land, and kept possession of it as owner. But the County (Jurors) have seen or recollected William Malet siezed, as well of that land, as of all her land, until the castle was besieged. This they affirm of all the land which Asa had in Yorkshire." *

In the reign of Stephen, the famous Roger de Mowbray, Earl of Northumberland, held lands here, but being a rebel against that monarch's authority, his estates were forfeited. It would appear, however, that they were afterwards granted to Nigel Albini, who had married his daughter, and who took his name. This Nigel de Albini richly endowed the Order of Knights Templars with lands in Lincolnshire and Yorkshire, including lands in North Cave. History records that during the Crusades he had the misfortune to be taken prisoner by Saladin, in 1187, and having been ransomed by the Templars, he shewed his gratitude to the Order by the rich donations which he made them.

Leland, in his *Itinerary* of Yorkshire, in the reign of Henry VIII., has the following quaint reference to North Cave :—" From Walkington Village to Northcave Village V. miles by fair cham-

---

* Bawdwen's Translation of Domesday, pp 9, 237 and 238.

pain corn ground. There rennith a Broke by Northcave and so into Humbre."

The following Fines and other proceedings, relating to this parish, supply many interesting facts connected with its early history.

"Fine between Brother Robert De Saunford, Master of the Knights Templars, Plaintiff, and Ralph de Vermeles and Joan, his Wife, deforciants, concerning two bovates of land and one messuage, with appurtenances, in North Cave. The right of the Master is acknowledged."—*Feet of Fines, 24, Henry III., 89.*

"Fine between Walter de Heydon, plaintiff, and Hugh le Bygot and Joan, his wife, deforciants, concerning the advowson of the Church of North Kave. The right of Walter, by the gift of the ancestors of the same Joan is acknowledged."—*Feet of Fines, 28, Henry III.*

"Fine between John, son of Geoffrey de Thorntoft, plaintiff, and William de Kelyngthorp, of Overhemelseye, and Matilda, his wife, Deforciants, concerning one messuage, two tofts, three bovates of land, a third part of one mill, and 14d. of rent in Northcave. The right of John is acknowledged."—*Edward I., 37 (old No.).*

"East Riding.—An assize comes to acknowledge whether German Hay, Robert de Meynill, and Alice, his wife, Peter Hakun and Cecily, his wife, Walter de Kylpun and Beatrice, his wife, and Thomas de Iverthorp, unjustly disseised William de Kava of his free tenement in North Kava, viz., of three roods of land with appurtenances. And none of them appear except Alice and Cecily. German was attached by Robert, son of Geoffrey de Seton, and Thomas Mathegrey, of Kava. Thomas de Iverthorp was attached by Ralph Mathegrey, of Kava, and Richard de Gringeley, of the same. Therefore let them be amerced. Robert Meynil was not attached because he was not found, &c. Alice and Cecily only say that William [de Kava] was never in seisin. The Jurors say that Robert de Meynil and Alice, his wife, previously arraigned an assize of novel disseisin, concerning the same tenement, against the said William, whereupon, by agreement, Robert and Alice withdrew from their writ for 100s. paid by William (the rest of the entry is mutilated). It seems that Robert, notwithstanding, remained in possession, and that German and others ploughed and sowed the land against the will [of William]. Judgment, that William shall recover seisin, all the Defendants being amerced, except Peter Hakun, who was sick." *Assize Rolls, 52, Henry III. York, No. 1-2, 1 m. 18.*

" North Riding. Master William Passemer presented himself against John de Stamigrave, in a plea, wherefore he came to the field of North Kave, and took away the corn and hay of the same. Master William there found, to his damage of 15*l.* John failed to appear. The Sheriff was ordered several times to distrain him and ' have his body ' at certain days, but nothing further is recorded."—*Assize Rolls, 52, Henry III., York, N. 1-2—1 m. 41.*

" East Riding. An assize comes to acknowledge whether Master William Passemer unjustly disseised John de Stanygrave of his free tenement in North Cave, viz., of four bovates and twelve acres of land with appurtenances. Master William does not appear : he was attached by Ralph le Wyte, of North Cave, and Robert de Meynhill of the same : therefore let them be amerced. Roger de Wetewang, " bailiff of the same Master " comes, and says that John was never in seisin as of his free tenement. Verdict and judgment for John. Damages 10s." —*Assize Roll, 52 Henry III., York, N. 1-2, 1 m. 54d.*

" East Riding. Roger de la Wodehall, who brought a writ of mort d' ancestre against Robert, son of Thomas de Danthorp, concerning two bovates of land with appurtenances (except one toft and two acres) in North Cave, and one-and-a-half acre in Irenthorp, does not prosecute : therefore let him and his pledges be amerced, viz., John Thothe, of North Cave, and Richard le Butillier, of Yverthorp."—*Assize Roll, 52 Henry III., York, N. 1-2, m. 63.*

" Nicholas de Stapleton and Elias de Bekingham are appointed [Justices] to take the assize of mort d' ancestre which John [son] of Thomas de Newbald has arraigned against Constance, daughter of Arnald de Wyghton, and William, son of Peter de North cave, concerning one messuage five bovates of land, and a moiety of one mill with appurts. in Wyghton and Northcave."—*Patent Roll, 2 Edward I. m. 9.*

" Roger de la Wodehalle. next Beverley, before the Justices in Eyre, demanded against Thomas de Danthorp and Agnes, his wife, two bovates and one acre-and-a-half of land with appurtenances in North Cave and Iverthorpe (except two acres in North Cave), of which Geoffrey de Askewy, Kinsman of the said Roger, whose heir he is, was seised in fee. He alleges that the said Geoffrey died seised thereof without issue, whereupon ' the fee ' reverted to one William, as Kinsman and heir of one Isabel, grandmother of the said Geoffrey, and from William it decended to this Roger, as son and heir. Thomas and Agnes vouch to warranty, Peter, son of Roger de Santon, of Suthe Cave, who warrants to them, and says that after the death of Geoffrey, one, Guy, son of Ellen, sister of the said Isabel, was seised of the premises. Roger says he is son of the said William, brother of the said Ellen, mother of Guy, by the same father and mother. Guy was rather an intruder into the premises than his

(Peter's?) ancestor [therein]. Peter says that one, William de Land, had two wives, by one of whom he had one, William, father of the said Roger, and by the other, two daughters, Isabel and Ellen. Isabel had issue Geoffrey. and Ellen had issue Guy, who enfeoffed him (Peter). He asks, therefore, whether Roger, who was born of another mother, can have any claim. Roger says that William was brother of Isabel, and Ellen by the same father and mother. Issue was joined thereupon. Afterwards, before W. De Burton, at York, a Jury found that William was brother of Isabel and Ellen by the same father and mother. Judgment, that Roger shall recover against Thomas and Agnes, and they shall have of Peter's land to the value, &c. And Peter was amerced. Damages, ten marks."—*De Banco Roll, Mich. 10 Edward I. m. 115d.*

"Whereas the King's beloved yeoman, Walter de Teye, and Isabella his wife, lately in the King's Court at Westminster, acknowledged certain Manors in various Counties, including the Manor of North Cave, in co. York, to be the King's right, and rendered them to the King and his heirs, as appears in a certain Fine ; the King now grants the said Manors to the same Walter and Isabella and the heirs of their bodies, with remainder to the right heirs of Isabella : to hold of the King and other chief lords of those fees. Witnesses : A. Bishop of Durham, and others. Dated at Canterbury, 3rd June."—*Charter Roll, 25 Edward I. No. 11.*

"Fine between Richard Santon, of Northcave, plaintiff, and John Buketon, of Greneake, and Ellen, his wife, deforciants, concerning one messuage, and one bovate of land with appurtenances in North Cave. Deforciants release to Plaintiff."—*8 Henry V.*

" Fine between John de Hothum, Bishop of Ely, plaintiff, and John de Cave, of Northburgh, deforciant, concerning one messuage, ten tofts, eleven-and-a-half bovates of land, and £4 13s. 4d. of rent in Northcave, Hothum, Iverthorp, and Drewton. The right of the Bishop and his heirs is acknowledged."—*Feet of Fines, 12 Edward II., 123 (old No.).*

"Fine between Sir Marmaduke de Lomley, Knight, and Thomas, son of Marmaduke de Thweng, Deforciants, concerning lands and rents in many places, including Northcave" (this is a lengthy document).—*Feet of Fines, 22 Edward III. 54 (old No.).*

"Fine between John, son of William Tothe, of Northcave, plaintiff, and John Tothe, of Northcave, and Emma, his wife, deforciants, concerning three messuages, four tofts, two carucates of land, three acres of meadow, 5s. 1d. of rent, and a moiety of one carucate of land in Northcave and Iverthorp. The right of plaintiff is acknowledged, except as to five acres. Plaintiff shall also have the reversion of one toft, which William de Malton holds for life, and of the said five acres which John Warde holds for life, in the said Vill of North-cave."—*40 Edward III. 58 (old No.).*

" Fine between William, son of John de Fereby, plaintiff, and William de Feriby, Canon of the Church of St. Peter, of York, deforciant, concerning messuages, lands, and rents in sundry places, including North Cave. Defor-ciant grants to Plaintiff and the heirs of his body, rendering yearly one rose to Plaintiff. Several remainders are set out, &c."—*Feet of Fines 49 Edward III.. (old No).*

" Fine between John Brakele, Vicar of the Church of Wolaston, and William Heryot, chaplain, plaintiffs, and William Kyngesman, of Wolaston, and Elizabeth, his wife, deforciants, concerning the Manor of Esthorp, and lands, &c., in Touthorp, Lannesburgh, North Cave, and Everyngham. Defor-ciants release to plaintiffs and the heirs of John."—*Feet of Fines, 14 Henry IV.*

THE CHURCH.

The Church of All Saints is an ancient cruciform building in the decorated style, overgrown with ivy ; it consists of a chancel,

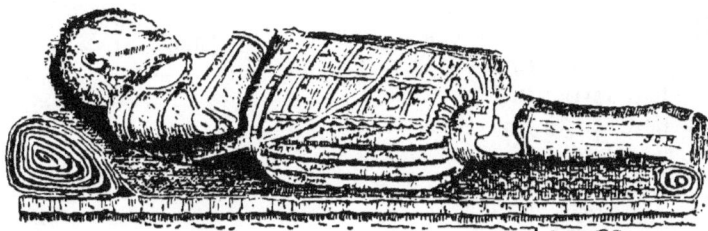

MUTILATED EFFIGY OF A KNIGHT, IN ALL SAINTS. NORTH CAVE.

nave, aisles and transept, with a tower in the perpendicular style. In recesses on either side of the chancel are alabaster recumbent figures ; the inscriptions are entirely lost, but they have been sup-posed to be to the memory of members of the Metham family, former owners of the manor.

The following particulars and list of Vicars are from "Torre's":

" The town of North Cave hath therein eight carucates of land, held of the fee of Stuteville, whereof five oxgangs belong to the Knts. Templars, and one carucate was held of the liberty of St. John of Beverley; also the heirs of Brus. held here two carucates of land, and the Flamvill's held other two carucates of William de Percy, of Kiddall, who held of Brus.; also the Lords Manley held here five carucates of land, and in the 18th of King Stephen, Roger de Mowbray, that he himself, also his wife and children might be admitted into the fraternity of the Canons of York, with his own hand offered upon the high altar of the same £10, and land in N. Cave, viz., four carucates of land. The Manor of N. Cave hath for many generations belonged to the Methams, Knts. The Church of All Hallows, of N. Cave having been newly built on the 7th December, 1318, a Commission issued out to John, Bishop of Ely to dedicate the same. It was an ancient rectory belonging to the Patronage of the Meauxs, Kts., till William De la Pole got it appropriated to the House of Carthusians, of Hull."

List of the Rectors.

Temp Instit.	Vicarii Eccle.	Patroni.
21st Feb., 1234...	Will Maulimet	....
5th Nov., 1248...	Will Passmore	Isabella, dame of Walter de Hedon.
16th Oct., 1272...	Will Passmore	Joh de Melsa ....
16th June, 1280...	Gilbert de Melsa	....
22nd July, 1311...	Galfrid de Cave.....................	....
15th July, 1345...	Joh de Place	....
17th Oct., 1356...	Johe de Melbourne	....
10th May, 1364...	Johe de Cottingham	....
14th May, 1373 ..	Robt. de Dyghton.....................	Mic. de la Pole ....

List of Vicars.

Temp Instit.	Vicarii Eccle.	Patroni.
	Nic Dyghton	Prior and Convent, St.
16th April, 1399...	Nic de Newton	Michael's, juxta,
31st Dec., 1410...	Thos. Elleston	Hull. ....
24th July, 1416...	Geradus Whitelosse	....
10th June, 1418...	Joh Aclom	....
17th Oct., 1450...	Hen. Strynger	....
4th July, 1468..	Will Talbot	....
9th Dec., 1482...	Johe Watson, M.A.	....
1st Mar., 1484...	Alan Braytoft.....................	....

Temp Instit.	Vicarii Eccle.	Patroni.
7th Oct., 1505...	Wm. Spalding	....
10th Dec., 1521...	Robert Wade	....
29th April, 1531...	Thos. Marshall	....
4th Nov., 1531...	Rich. Browne......	....
	Robt. Hall	....
18th July, 1572...	Ed. Browne	Wm. Elleker ....
10th Dec., 1578...	Thos. Billard	Robt. Elleker ....
20th June, 1606...	Joh Terry, B.A...................	Assignee of Christopher Broke
14th Oct., 1606...	Will Bearclyff, M.A.	Thos Metham ....
17th May, 1644...	Wm. Metham	....

CONTINUATION SINCE TORRE'S.

Temp Instit.	Vicarii. Eccle.	Patroni.
29th Oct., 1646...	Thos. Forge	....
7th Sept. 1681...	Dan Thorsvell, M.A.	....
15th Aug., 1684...	John Mould	....
1722...	John Clark, M.A.	....
23rd April, 1728...	Anth. Almond, B.A.	....
21st Oct., 1773...	Ric. Gee.....................	....
7th July. 1807...	Joh Petch	H. Burton ....
1819...	Wm. Craven	....
15th May, 1820...	Robert Todd, B.A.	.................-...........
22nd Oct., 1830...	John Jarratt, M.A., Canon of York (died Nov. 30th 1890).	....
6th April, 1891...	Walter Michael Tomlinson, M.A., Cantab	....

TESTAMENTARY BURIALS, &c.

4th January, 1421. Will Frankys to be buried in the Church.

17th August, 1423. Thomas Waldley, of S. Clyff, to be buried in the Church.

29th Jany., 1432. Richard Santon, of N. Cave, esq., to be buried before the Altar of St. Thomas.

18th August, 1466. Symon Strynger, Vicar, dying intestate, administration was taken.

27th June, 1521. William Spalding, Vicar, to be buried in the upper part of the Church.

10th March, 1564.   Robert Constable, of Hotham, to be buried in the Church before his wife's stall and his cousin Banke's stall, under a stone there already laid.

14th May, 1555.   Marmaduke Monkton, of Drewton, gentleman, to be buried within the high Quire.

10th Nov., 1615.   John Skearne, of Drewton, Gent., to be buried in the Church.

19th May, 1571.   Sir Robert Hall, Vicar, to be buried in the Chancel.

2nd Nov., 1646.   Dame Mary Metham, of N. Cave, to be buried in the Church.

24th July, 1606.   Thos. Bellard, Clerk, to be buried in the Chancel.

By his will, dated 12th May, 1552, John Watson, of London, "bruer," made a bequest to the Church of Cave, and to Clyf Chapel, within the parish of North Cave, where he sometimes went to school.

COATS OF ARMS, &c.

Glover, in his "Visitation of Yorkshire," in 1584, gives the following coats of arms, &c., as being then in the church.

"In the east end these seven :—

XXIII.   "Azure a cross of sixteen points or."

XXIV.   "Argent, fesse azure, over all six fleur-de-lis, 2, 2 and 2, countercharged."

XXV.   "Quarterly, 1 and 4 sable, a bend flory; 2 and 3 or, a cross sable, over all a label of 5 points."

XXVI.   "Sable, a bend engrailed or."

XXVII.   "Sable, on a bend flory or 3 escallops gules, 'flory sans nombre."

XXVIII.   "Quarterly 1 and 4 azure fretty argent, 2 and 3 sable, on a bend flory or 3 escallops gules."

XXIX.   "Argent on a bend flory azure 3 fleur-de-lis or."

These six Escocheons following stand together :—

XXX.   "Or a bend gules."

XXXI.   "Gules a bend or."

XXXII. and XXXIII.   "Argent 2 chevorns gules."

XXXIV.   "Blank."

XXXV.   "Barry of 6 or and gules, in chief 3 torteaux."

XXXVI. " Argent on a bend flory azure 3 fleur-de-lis or."

XXXVII. " Metham impaling, quarterly and verrey over all a bendlet. **Ibic jacet Thomas Metham miles, qui obit vicissimo die Anno Domini** MDVIV., **Fc.**"

XXXVIII. " Azure a fesse dancettée between 10 billets 4 and 6 or.

XXXIX. Argent, a fesse dancettée between 10 billets 4 and 6 or (sable).

THE FOLLOWING MONUMENTS AND INSCRIPTIONS ARE NOW IN THE CHURCH.

SOUTH SIDE OF CHANCEL.—"Here lies the body of Francis Metham, Gent., youngest son of George Metham, of North Cave, Esq., who departed this life March 2nd, 1721 ; and of Margaret, his wife, second daughter of William Pearson, of Stokesley, Esq., who departed this life, August 17th, 1723."

ON FLOOR OF CHANCEL.

" In the Vault lies Barbara,
Hugh Montgomery, Esq's. Wife,
Who ne'er was Angry in her life :
As Daughter, Sister, Wife, or Mother,
You'l rarely hear of such another.

She died the 26th of May, in the 59th year of her age, 1747."

Also on the floor of Chancel :—

" Near this Monument of Sir Thos. Metham lies Geo. Metham, Esq., and Cath., his wife, daughter of Lord Fairfax. They died 1672 ; and Geo. Metham, Esq., their son, with Mag. Harcourt, his wife. She died 1697. He 1716. Also Phil. Metham, his son, he died 27th March, 1732.

My Father a North Briton,*
My Mother Rutlandshire.†
From Dublin their Son
Hugh Montgomery, Esq
When my race is run
Shall rest me in this Choir,
In hope, as he began,
God will raise me higher.

Ætat 68, A.D. 1748.

* Eglinton, }
† Green,   } Vide Camden."

On South Wall of Chancel.

"Under this stone lies two grandsons of George Metham, of N. Cave, Esq., by Barbara, his daughter . . . . . "

East Window of Three Lights.

"John Christie Clitherow, born 26th December, 1809 ; died 30th May, 1865." Christ enthroned, four Evangelists, St. Peter, St. Paul.

"Near this place lies the body of Richard Burton, Esq., of Hull Bank, late a Captain in His Majesty's 74th Regiment, who died October 1st. 1784, æt 26."

In the Chancel.

A marble tablet on the wall "To the memory of George Burton, Esquire, of Hotham and North Cave, eldest Son of General Christie Burton, and late Representative for Beverley, in this county, who died at Paris, 13th April, 1822, aged 57 years. This tablet is erected by his affectionate Sister, Sarah Burton Peters."

Tablet—"To the memory of Mary Christie Burton, wife of Major General Burton, Lieutenant-Colonel of the 3rd Regiment of Guards, and Representative for Beverley, by whom this monument was erected, and who ever must lament the loss of so excellent a woman. She died 13th April, 1801, aged 37 years."

Tablet – "To the memory of Colonel John Christie Clitherow, late of the Coldstream Guards, who died 30th May, 1865, aged 56 years. This tablet is erected by his affectionate mother, Sarah Burton, of Hotham Hall."

"In memory of Sarah Burton, of Hotham Hall, who died February 11th, 1869, aged 82, wife of Henry Burton Peters, Esq., and eldest daughter of the late General Napier Christie Burton."

South Chapel.

In the South Chapel is a stained glass window of three lights, bearing the following inscription :—

"In reverence to God, to the memory of the family of Mr. John Medcalf, this window is dedicated A.D. 1885.

Beneath the window is a brass as follows :—

John Medcalf died December 27th, 1845, aged 88 years. Mary, his wife died January 5th, 1841, aged 67 years.

Children of the above.—Mary died June 6th, 1813, aged 13 years. Ann died March 1st, 1822, aged 20 years. Elizabeth Ellen, died October 20th,

1827, aged 21 years. George died January 5th, 1834, aged 38 years. John died December 16th, 1874, aged 76 years. Henry Calvert died March 13th, 1885, aged 72 years.

This window is erected by Henry Calvert and Jane, son and daughter of John and Mary Medcalf."

TABLET ON WALL. —" In memory of Sarah Baron, of Drewton, born 24th January, 1766 ; died 28th April, 1844."

TABLET ON WALL.—" In memory of Nathan Jowett Baron, of Drewton. He was educated at Ch. Cl., Oxford, and received in that University the degree of B.A., born April 4th, 1796 ; died 10th Ocbert9, 1841.

TABLET ON NORTH WALL OF NAVE.

" To the memory of John Foster, who died 18th October, 1816, aged 82."

IN NORTH AISLE.

" Jane, the wife of James Pinkerton. The above James Pinkerton lieth at her left hand."

BRASS PLATE ON FLOOR OF CENTRE AISLE.

" Rev. John Petch, Vicar of North Cave, died June 29th, 1818, aged 45 years."

SOUTH WALL, NAVE—TABLET.

" To the memory of the Rev. Robert Todd, M.A., ten years Vicar of this parish, cum cliffe, obit. 4th June, 1830, ætat 34 ; also of Alice, his wife, obt. 7th December, 1824, ætat 32.

Their remains are deposited in the family vault at North Ferriby."

MARBLE TABLET ON PILLAR IN NAVE.

" Sacred to the memory of George Baron, Esquire, of Drewton Manor, died 29th July, 1854, aged 62."

ON FLOOR SOUTH AISLE.

" Rd. Baley, obt. A.D. 1691, æt. 60."

FLOOR CENTRE AISLE.

" J. W. Jarratt, died December 22nd, 1855, aged 17 years ; Margaret Jarratt, died August 22nd, 1872, aged 70 years."

IN THE CHURCHYARD.

" In affectionate remembrance of Thomas Blossom. As an ambassador for Christ he laboured amongst the heathens of Tahiti and Eimei, in Polynesia, for twenty-three years, in connection with the London Missionary Society, and after a long life, characterized by Christian consistency, having served his own generation, by the will of God he fell on sleep in this parish on the 5th of Feb., 1855, aged 77 years."

THE REGISTERS.

The following extracts are from the registers, which begin in 1678.

MARRIAGES.

1713. Hugo Montgomery and Barbara Metham, nupt., 23 Octr.

1679. Thomas Foster and Frances Meadlye, nupt. 29th April.

,,   Johannes Hickington et Ellonor Rotheram, July.

,,   Richardus Patdgett et Allice Richmond, Novr.

BAPTISMS.

1678. Hannah Howdle, filia Thomœ, bapt. primo die Septr.

1679. Elizabeth Foster, filia Thomœ, bapt. Feby.

1696. Jeremias, filius Timothei Newmarch, bapt. July.

1738. Josephus filius Josephi Stickney, bapt 16 die July.

1716. Georgius filius Hugonis Montgomery, armiger bapt. 6th Feb.

BURIALS.

1706. Anna Metham, 22nd Jany.

1716. Georgius Metham, armig. Sepult decimo 8vo. die Aprilis (18th April).

1746. Hannah, wife of John Blossom, Dec. 23rd.

1772. Thomas son of Thomas Richardson, buried July 11th.

The following memorandum is inserted in the registers :—

"In the year 1746, Hugh Montgomery, Esq., the Patron of North Cave, did build a new Pew adjoining the pulpit on the East, for his Tenant of Druton and such others as the said Patron should think fit to sit therein at any time, and for the Vicar's family. Antho. Almond, Vicar."

TERRIER.

From an old Terrier (undated) it appears that the tithe on every messuage and cottage was "one henne at Christmas." For every skep of bees, two pence per annum; for every cow three-half-pence which renews, and for every cow which does not renew, one penny. For every man and woman above the age of sixteen years, for their oblations at Easter, twopence. "For every mill, two shillings." In the same terrier the Communion Plate is described as follows : " A Flaggon for the wine with this inscription upon it, 'The Gift of the Patron, Hugh Montgomery, Esq., to the Church of North Cave, 27th March, 1754 ;' a Patten with this inscription upon it, 'The gift of George Montgomery Metham, Esq. to the Church of North Cave, the 24th day of May, 1754 ; High Sheriff and Knighted, 1756 ; chose Member of Parliament for Hull, 1757 '; a Chalice with this inscription, ' North Cave."

Pedigree of Metham.

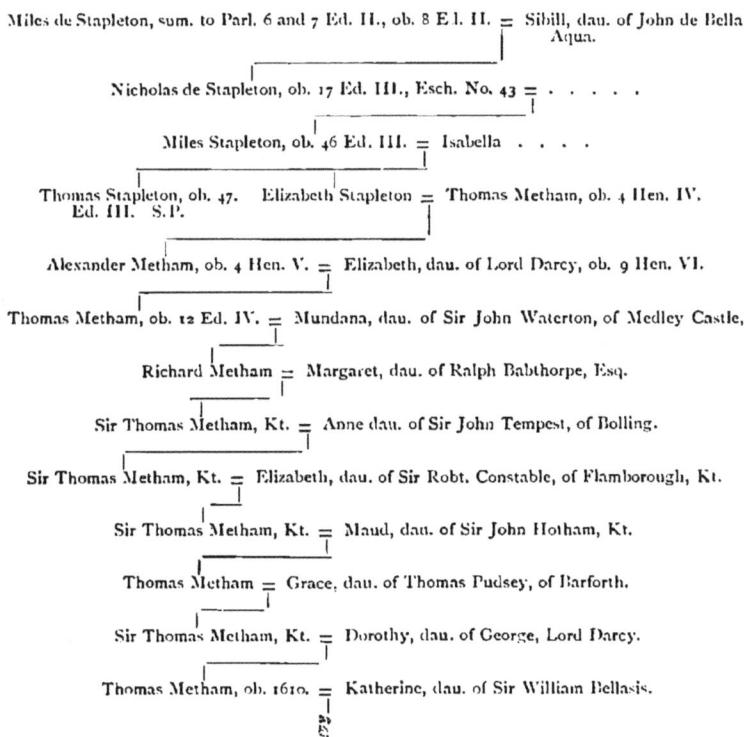

Miles de Stapleton, sum. to Parl. 6 and 7 Ed. II., ob. 8 E I. II. = Sibill, dau. of John de Bella Aqua.

Nicholas de Stapleton, ob. 17 Ed. III., Esch. No. 43 = ...

Miles Stapleton, ob. 46 Ed. III. = Isabella . . . .

Thomas Stapleton, ob. 47. Ed. III. S.P.   Elizabeth Stapleton = Thomas Metham, ob. 4 Hen. IV.

Alexander Metham, ob. 4 Hen. V. = Elizabeth, dau. of Lord Darcy, ob. 9 Hen. VI.

Thomas Metham, ob. 12 Ed. IV. = Mundana, dau. of Sir John Waterton, of Medley Castle,

Richard Metham = Margaret, dau. of Ralph Babthorpe, Esq.

Sir Thomas Metham, Kt. = Anne dau. of Sir John Tempest, of Bolling.

Sir Thomas Metham, Kt. = Elizabeth, dau. of Sir Robt. Constable, of Flamborough, Kt.

Sir Thomas Metham, Kt. = Maud, dau. of Sir John Hotham, Kt.

Thomas Metham = Grace, dau. of Thomas Pudsey, of Barforth.

Sir Thomas Metham, Kt. = Dorothy, dau. of George, Lord Darcy.

Thomas Metham, ob. 1610. = Katherine, dau. of Sir William Bellasis.

G

Sir Thomas Metham. (æt. 10 anno 1565), slain at = Barbara, dau. of Philip Constable. Esq.
                Marston Moor.

Thomas Metham, ob. cælebs.   Catherine, sister   Barbara, sister = Thomas Dolman, Esq.,
                               and co-heir.   and co-heir ob.   of Babsworth and Pock-
                               m.   1626.   lington, Co. York.
                               Ed. Smith, Esq.

Robert Dolman, of Pocklington, Esq. = Catherine, dau. of Edmund Thorald, of Hough, Co.,
                                                      Lincoln, Esq

Two sons, ob. S.P.   William Dolman, only surviving son and heir = . . .

Robert Dolman, of Pocklington, Esq., son and heir = Anne, dau. of Richd. Brigham, of
                                                     Brigham, Esq.

Robert Dolman, of Pocklington, M.D. = Peggy, only dau. of Thomas Reynolds, of Mauraugh,
                                                     Co. Notts.

Thomas Dolman, Esq., died 1841. = Martha Leach, dau. of John Griffith, of St. Briavels,
                                                     Co., Glouc.

John Thomas Dolman, son and heir nunc., 1844.[*]

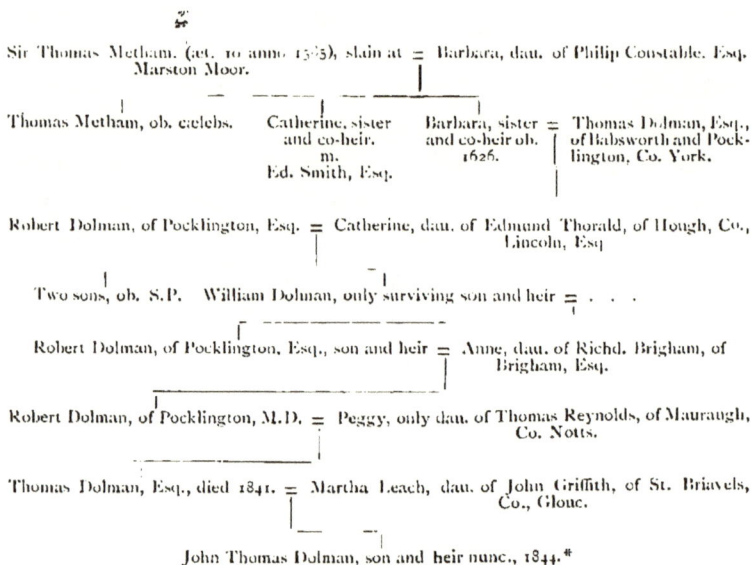

The Methams were an opulent and wide-spread family. One
branch was located at Metham, near Howden, and another at
North Cave, where several members of the family are buried. As
will be seen from the pedigree, they were connected by marriage with the Stapletons. The latter family was "of very great note,
and assumed their surname from the Lordship of Stapleton, upon
the River Tees, in the Bishoprick of Durham. Anno Dom. 1159,
about the 6th Henry II., Robert de Stapleton was witness to a
Charter of Henry de Lacy, Baron of Pontefract, and in the 33rd of
Henry II. the same Robert was a benefactor to the Priory of
Monks Bretton in Yorkshire."[†]

Referring to Elizabeth Stapleton, who married Thomas

[*] *Baronia Anglica Concentrata.*
[†] Banks's *Extinct Baronage*, Vol. I. p 409.

Metham, Sir Harris Nicholas says "the Barony is now vested in
her representatives, of which representatives, Mr. Dolman, a gentleman at York, is the heir, and has accordingly presented a petition
to Her Majesty and obtained an order of reference thereon to the
Attorney General. It is to be observed that this Barony, though
dormant, is not in abeyance, Mr. Dolman being the sole heir
representative of Miles de Stapleton, the first baron summoned to
Parliament."

Thomas Metham was High Sheriff of the County of York in
the year 1443, and again in 1460.

A very long Will of Francis Metham, of Wiganthorpe, dated
"the foure-and-twentieth daie of October, in the year of Our Lord
one thousand five hundred nynetie five," contains the following
bequest :—

"Unto my well-beloved nephew, Thomas Metham, of Metham, Esquier,
all those parcells belonging to the house of Wigginthorpe, viz. :—All the wain-
scot and sealinge in the hall, and in both the parlors, the glasse in all the
wyndowes in and about the house, with all the doores, lockes, and knies, and
all frames and shelves fastened vnto the walles or grounde. All the brewinge
vessellys theire stand now in the brewhouse, all the stable heckes, mangers, and
hayes, with all the oxstalls and heckes together with all the pales and rayles about
the house, and all the stoops and rayles of stacke garthes in the groundes. I give
vnto my good neece, Katheren Metham, his wife, the best breedinge mare
which I have, and one spurre ryall, * as a token of remembrance of my good
will towards her." †

THE CHARITIES.

"The school endowment, 1a. 1r. 11p. of land. The school house was
erected many years ago at the expense of the inhabitants. which, together
with an allotment of 2r. 32p. of land in lieu of common rights, and 2r. 19p.

* Spurr royal, a handsome gold coin. On the obverse a figure of the Queen
in her royal robes; on the reverse, the star-pointed figure of a spur in the centre,
value 15s.

† Yorkshire Archæological Journal, viii., p 368.

of land, the gift of Sir George Montgomery Metham, the Lord of the Manor, were in March, 1772, conveyed to new trustees, in trust to nominate a schoolmaster to teach the children of the parish, reading, writing, and vulgar arithmetic. The schoolmaster has the house and land, for which he teaches four poor children as free scholars, besides others who are paid for by their friends." *

The poor have, by deed of gift from the late G. Baron, Esq., between £40 and £50 annually, from money invested in railway shares, which is distributed in coals on the 23rd of January.

WESLEYAN CHAPEL.

The Rev. John Wesley, in his "Journal," under date of Thursday, July 2nd, 1761, says, "I set out early for North Cave, about twenty computed miles from York. I preached there, at nine, to a deeply serious congregation, and was much refreshed. At two I preached to such another congregation at Thorpe, and concluded the day by preaching and meeting the Society at Pocklington." The chapel, a neat and commodious structure, erected at the beginning of the present century, and restored a few years ago, is in Church Street.

PRIMITIVE METHODIST CHAPEL.

This chapel was built in 1819 near the Friends Meeting House, and was supposed to be the oldest Primitive Methodist Chapel in Yorkshire. The building is still in existence, though in a very delapidated condition. A new chapel was erected a few years ago in West-gate.

PARISH CLERK.

Mr. Hicks, the Parish Clerk, who has been a ringer at the Church for more than half a century, assisted in ringing the bells on her Majesty's Accession to the Throne in 1837, and at her Jubilee in 1887. On both occasions sermons were preached by

* Commissioners' 10th Report, p 655.

the Vicar, the late Canon Jarratt. Mr. Hicks had a great-grand-mother named Sarah Barker, who died in 1849, aged 104 years and nineteen days, and is buried in the churchyard.

VICAR ACCUSED OF HERESY.

In 1534, the then Vicar of North Cave was accused of heresy. It seems probable that the crime committed by the vicar occurred in Hull, as the penance for it was to be undergone there. Probably some of Luther's works, or an edition of the New Testament, in English (then recently imported from Antwerp), may have been found in his possession : or, he may have preached some unorthodox ser-mon. Whatever was the ground of offence, the vicar was sentenced to make public recantation of his errors in Hull, both on Sunday and on a market day ; he was also bare-footed, bare-legged, and in his shirt, to carry a great faggot in his arms round the Holy Trinity Church. The latter church was also placed under an inter-dict ; the windows and doors were closed with thorns and briars, the pavement torn up, and the bells "curbed" or taken down. The vicar might consider himself fortunate in getting off so easily, as on the 21st of April in the same year, seven persons had been hanged at Tyburn for daring to express opinions, upon doctrinal points, different from those entertained by their Sovereign.

CHRISTOPHER NESS.

Christopher Ness, an eminent divine and voluminous theo-logical writer, was born at North Cave, December, 26th, 1621. He was the son of Thomas Ness, and "was educated under Mr. Seaman, in grammar learning, till he was sixteen, when he was sent to Cam-bridge," where he graduated. "Having spent seven years there he retired, at the age of twenty-three, into the country, in the time of the Civil Wars, and preached for a while at Cliffe Chapel under the inspection of his uncle Brearcliffe, an eminent divine, Vicar of North Cave. From thence he received a call into Holderness, and, after a few years, to Beverley, where he taught school and preached occasionally." In 1650, he was presented with the living of Cottingham, and was subsequently appointed lecturer to Mr. Styles, at Leeds. He was ejected by the Act of 1662, and preached for some time in private. The Five Mile Act of 1665, drove him to Clayton, and thence to Morley, when he preached in the villages about Leeds. Afterwards, he opened a school at Hunslet, and preached there; and in 1672, when the persecution raged less fiercely, he ministered publicly in the Riding-house, Leeds. He was four times excommunicated; and upon the fourth there was issued out against him a writ "De Excommunicato Capiendo," to avoid which he removed to London, in 1675, and there preached to a private congregation in Fleet Street. He died on December 26th, 1705, aged eighty-four years to the day, and was buried in Bunhill-fields, having been upwards of sixty years in the ministry. Mr. Ness wrote several books, the principal of which was "A History and Mystery of the Old and New Testaments" (four volumes folio).

SOCIETY OF FRIENDS.

The Society of Friends had formerly numerous adherents in this neighbourhood. The old chapel adjoining their burial place in Church Street, was pulled down about three years ago, and a cottage has since been erected on its site. John Richardson, an itinerant preacher of some note amongst the Society, was born at North Cave, in 1666. His father, who bore the same christian name, was born there in 1624, and, after enduring the usual share of suffering which in those days fell to the lot of members of the Society of Friends, died in the year 1679, leaving a widow and five children, with a small farm for their support. After his father's death, John worked upon the farm and helped his mother to maintain the family. In the course of a few years his mother re-married, and the step-father, having no sympathy with John's religious convictions, treated him harshly, and eventually turned him out of doors. After casting about for some time, John apprenticed himself to William Allon, a weaver, at South Cliffe, who treated him as his own son. He had commenced preaching occasionally in the villages at the age of eighteen, and had met with much opposition, but, being a fluent speaker, and having a robust frame, he was capable of enduring fatigue and privations which would have appalled most men. He made two voyages to America, one in 1700-3. and the other in 1731-3, and travelled over a considerable portion of what are now the Eastern United States, as well as in the West Indies, and met with many perils by sea and land. He visited Ireland in 1722 ; and travelled through a great portion of England and Southern Scotland, preaching the tenets of George Fox. He was twice married, first to Priscilla Connely, and secondly to Anne Robinson, both of whom pre-deceased him. With the latter, who was a preacher in the Society, he obtained a small property at Hutton-in-the-Hole, near Lastingham, where he went to reside in after life, and where he died.

PARISH APPRENTICES.

The following is a copy of an apprenticeship indenture, during the period when each parish maintained its own poor, and pauper children were apprenticed with farmers or trades-people in the parish.

"**This Indenture,** made the eighth day of July, in the Twelfth year of ye Reign of or. Soveraigne, Ld. William ye third, by ye grace of god, King of England, Scotland, France and Ireland, and Anno ye Dni 1700, Witnesseth that Thomas Dunn, Overseer for the poor in ye towne of North Cave, in ye County of Yorke, and Mr. Richard Bayley and Allan Bayley, Churchwardens of the same Towne, by and wth ye consent and allowance of two of his Majesties Justices of ye peace for ye same County, have placed, and by these prsents do put, place, and bind Thomas Barlow as an apprentice with Timothy Newmarch, of North Cave, to dwell from ye day of ye date of these prsents untill ye sd Tho. Barlow shall come to and attain ye age of twenty-four years, according to ye statute, in yt case made and provided. During wch time and terme ye sd Tho. Barlow shall ye said Timothy Newmarch, his Mastr, well and faithfully serve in all lawfull Business as ye sd Tho. Barlow shall be put unto, according to his power, will, ability, and honesty, and obediently in all things shall behave himselfe towards the sd Timothy Newmarch, his children and family. And ye sd Timothy Newmarch, for his part, covenanteth, promisseth and agreeth during all ye sd terme to find and allow unto his said apprentice sufficient meat, drinke, linen, woollen, shooes stockings, washing, lodging, and all other things necessary or meet for such an apprentice. In witness whereof ye parties abovesaid to these prsent Indentures their hands and seals interchangeably have set the day and year first above written.

Sealed and delivered in the prsence of ⎫
  Robert Walker, John Mell, ⎬ Timothy Newmarch
    Tho. Baley. ⎭

  We, whose names are subscribed Justices of ye peace of ye Queen, do consent to ye putting forth of ye aforesaid Thomas Barlow apprentice according to ye intent and meaning of ye Indenture abovesaid.   Fra. Warton.
                    Tho. Alured."

An Old Will.

In the following Will we have references to open lands in various parts of the parish, some of which still retain the names they then bore.

"In the name of God, Amen, the fifteenth day of July 1747, I, Richard Padgett, of the North Cave, in the County of York, being long sick and weak of body but of perfect mind and memory, thanks be given to God therefore, calling unto mind the mortality of my body and knowing that it is appointed for all men once to die, do make and ordain this my last will and testament ; that is to say, principally and first of all I give and recomend my soul into the hand of Almighty God that gave it, and my body I recomend to the earth, to be buried in decent christian burial, at the discretion of my executors, nothing doubting but at the general Resurrection I shall receive the same again by the mighty power of God ; and as touching such worldly estate wherewith it has pleased God to bless me in this life, I give, demise, and dispose of the same in the following manner and form : Also I give and bequeath to Richard Padgett, my eldest son, two oxgang of land in North Cave field, William Roberts on the east, and William Burton, Esq. on the west, and a Broad and Narrow lying in the Wode field ; also a piece of land in the East field called Dam. Also I give to William Padgett, my son, a certain cottage in a lane commonly called Saint Ellen Lane ; also one broad land at Thomas Walker's garth end, also four broad lands in a place commonly called Open Close. Also I give to John Padgett, my son, a cottage in North Gate ; also two oxgang of land in North Cave field, Padley on the south side and John Gelder on the north ; also a Gare lying in the West Field, and a narrow in the South Ings ; also west end of a narrow at Cave Gates ; also a narrow at Law Drewton Gates ; also a narrow at Baley Rawside ; also a Broad land at Moles Garth, and also a narrow in the New Close."

STAGE COACHES.

The following advertisement in the old stage-coaching days (and about five years before the opening of the Hull and Selby Railway), forcibly reminds us of the great changes which have taken place since then.

"Hull and Cave New Coach. R. J. Chafer respectfully informs his Friends and the Public that he has this day commenced running a new Four-In-side Post Coach, which leaves the White Hart, North Cave, every morning (Sundays excepted) at a quarter-past-seven, and the Fox and Coney, South Cave, at a quarter before eight ; calls at the Half Moon, Brantingham ; Green Dragon, Welton ; Duke of Cumberland, Ferriby; and the Granby Inn, Hessle ; and arrives at Mr. Lyons, the Black Horse, Carr Lane, at half-past-nine ; from which it returns each afternoon at half-past-four. R. J. C. begs to return his sincere thanks for the liberal encouragement he has received since his commencement, and trusts that his future exertions will secure to him a continuance ; and hopes that the above coach and arrangement will prove to be that accommodation so long wanted ; no coach having hitherto run between North Cave and Hull. Hull, May 4th, 1835."

DREWTON.

Drewton forms the western portion of the parish, and runs up to the Wold Hills. The houses are few and scattered. The township is a very ancient one, and has doubtless been associated with many important and stirring events connected with the history of this part of Yorkshire.

In Domesday Book, we find the following reference to Drewton : —"In Drowetone, Chetel and Norman had four carucates of land to be taxed, where there may be two ploughs. Robert (Malet) has now there two ploughs, and six villanes and five bordars with two ploughs. Value in King Edward's time, forty shillings, now thirty-two shillings." *

A little to the north-east of the South Cave Railway Station is the entrance to Drewton Vale, with the beck gently winding its way along the bottom, and the railway following the course of the valley. On turning into this road, in the corner field on the left hand, there were, until a few years ago, foundations which were said to be the remains of a church, and a small stream rose out of the gravel at a short distance from the eastern corner of the remains of the churchyard wall. This stream, after being covered up for some years, has recently been opened out again.

In a retired position in the valley stands Drewton Manor, belonging to Mr. James Atkinson Jowett, and occupied by Mr. Gray. It was formerly the residence of Mr. George Baron, who took considerable interest in the neighbourhood and who was said to have in his possession (in 1841) several articles which he had dug up, viz., "a silver ring in the form of a snake, brooches, spear heads, arrow heads, leaden balls, a piece of Roman pottery resembling the head of a deity, a hand-mill for grinding corn, Roman coin, and a lachrymatory."

Human bones are frequently found in the neighbourhood. About half a century ago the skeletons of seven persons were found near to Mr. Baron's residence, one of them without a head : and when the new railway was being made a few years ago, several skeletons were dug up.

Mr. George Baron, the owner of Drewton Manor, died July 29th, 1854, leaving estates at Drewton, Faxfleet, North Cave, and at several places in the West Riding, the value of the whole being estimated at about £8,000 a year. He was a bachelor, without any near relations, and, as he had derived the greater part of his property from a Miss Jowett, he determined to devise it so that it would revert to the Jowett family. Having no intimate knowledge of their whereabouts, he left his real estate in a vague manner, " To his Trustees upon trust for the heir male of Nathan Atkinson, of Bolton, near Bradford, whose mother was a Jowett of Clock-house." As may be supposed, a general devise of this kind opened the way for a number of claimants, and the estates became involved in litigation which lasted for about six years, being finally carried to the House of Lords, where judgment was given in favour of Mr. Nathan Atkinson Jowett, as the rightful claimant, and he lived in the quiet enjoyment of his unexpected wealth for several years. On his death the estates descended to his son, the present owner.

St. Austin's Stone.

This stone, around which many traditions have gathered, stands in the vale about half a mile to the north-east of Drewton Manor. It is a mass of rock projecting from the side of a hill, and in its longest part, extending from the hill side to the face of the stone, measures about sixty feet. By some it is supposed to have formed a centre for Druidical worship, and that the adjoining township took the name of Drewton (or Druid Town) from this fact. When St. Augustine came to England, at the instance of Pope Gregory, to mission the country, he is said to have visited this part of the East Riding ; and that this stone took its name from his visit.

KETTLETHORPE.

Kettlethorp is a farm adjoining Drewton Manor. The house stands in an elevated position overlooking the South Cave Railway Station, which lies at its foot, to the south. It is referred to in Domesday Book, under Drowetone (Drewton), as follows:—"Manor. In Torp (Thorp) Chetel (Ketel) had two carucates of land to be taxed, and there may be one plough there. Robert (Malet) has it, and it is waste. Value in King Edward's time, thirty shillings."

EVERTHORPE.

Everthorpe, a pleasant hamlet, stands upon somewhat elevated ground between North Cave and South Cave, and commands delightful views of the Humber and the Lincolnshire Hills.

In the early part of the present century, Mr. Eggington, a Hull shipowner, lived in the village, and one of his whaling ships was named the " Everthorpe." A harpoon used on board this ship and marked " Everthorpe, 1822," is now in the possession of Mr. W. Richardson, of South Cave.

When the Hull and Barnsley Railway was being constructed the greater portion of Everthorpe-Hill, which consisted of a bed of good gravel, was removed, and during its removal several skeletons were met with.

* Bawdwen's Translation, p 154.

THE FAMILY OF CAVE.

HE history of this Knightly Family dates back to the time of William II., and some of its members appear to have played prominent parts during several generations, not only in local, but also in national affairs, two at least having been judges of the land.

Jordan de Cave, the founder of the family, held land in both North Cave and South Cave, but the family connection with the latter place seems to have been much closer than with the neighbouring village.

Sir Alexander de Cave, during the reign of Edward II., occupied an important position in the district; and the family became connected by marriage with the ancient county families of St. Quintin, Metham, Broomflete, Hotham, Sturmy and Ellerker.

The family removed into Northamptonshire, the present owner of the title being Sir Mylles Cave-Brown-Cave, whose seat is at Stretton-en-le-Field, county Derby.

Lord Braye is descended from this ancient family, through his grandmother, Sarah, daughter and heiress of Sir Thomas Cave, Bart. His Lordship has assumed the name and arms of Cave

The pedigree of the family was certified by Sir William Segar, the Garter King of Arms, in 1632. This document is now in the British Museum*— and a very beautiful specimen of the genealogical work of the 17th century it is. Unfortunately, it lacks, like almost all the work of Heralds of that date, references to the authorities which were consulted by the compiler. We know, however, that a great part of the pedigree was recorded at Heralds' Visitations of Yorkshire† and Leicestershire, much before 1632. It is now to be seen in Burke's "Peerage" as the lineage of Sir Mylles Cave-Brown-Cave, Bart., but the statement given in some genealogies, that the elder brother of the founder, Wyamarus de Cave, died without issue, does not seem justified by anything stated by Sir William Segar. On the contrary, Wyamarus de Cave, can scarcely have been any other than the powerful steward of the still more powerful and wealthy, Alan, Earl of Brittany and Richmond. Wymar, or Wyamarus, held much land in the neighbourhood, and he is supposed to have been the founder of the Priory of Marryke, near Richmond, Yorkshire : at any rate he was a liberal donor to this and other religious houses.‡ In the confirmation of one of these gifts, namely, the township of Engelby, given to the Abbey of Jervaux, he is joined by his brother, Garnarus, or Jordan, who was the forefather of the Cave family. From the records of these religious houses, we are able to construct the following pedigree :—

* Add. M.S., 18, 667.

† Will. Flower, Norroy K. 1564 (Published by Harl. Soc., 1881).

‡ Burton's *Monasticon Eboracense.*

Guiomar.
|
Warner.   Roger de Gumpuar.

Wymar, forefather of the Askes of Aske.   Jordan, forefather of the Caves of Cave.

To return to the work of Sir William Segar, which is known as the "Weston Pedigree," it was evidently compiled for the Earls of Portland, who were descended from Henry Weston, and his wife Mary, daughter and co-heiress of Anthony Cave, of Chichley. It is written on vellum, and beautifully illuminated by the emblazonment of the arms of every person mentioned, and handsomely bound as a large folio volume : every page bears the signature of Sir William Segar. It passed into the possession of the second Earl of Denbigh by his marriage with Lady Anne Weston, and was presented to the British Museum, by the seventh Earl of Denbigh.

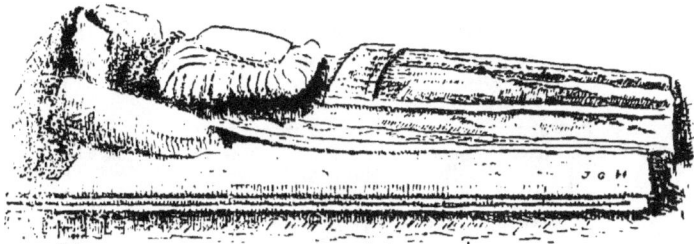

MUTILATED EFFIGY OF A LADY IN ALL SAINTS, NORTH CAVE.

The Caves of Cave, Co. York.

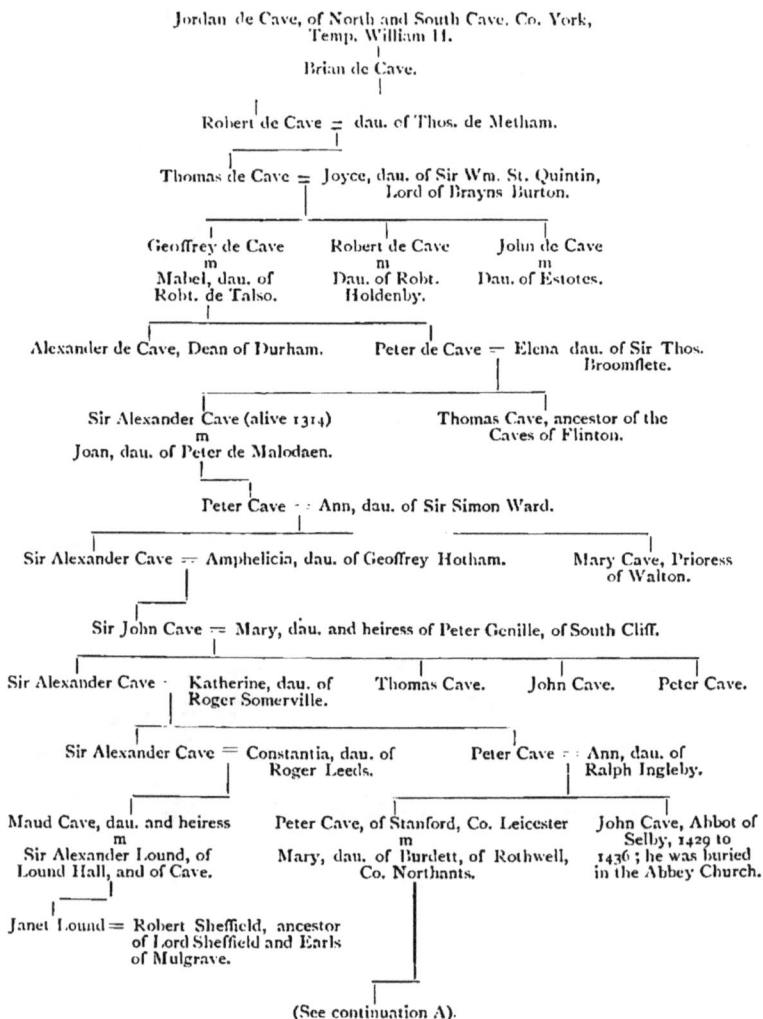

Jordan de Cave, of North and South Cave, Co. York,
Temp. William II.

Brian de Cave.

Robert de Cave = dau. of Thos. de Metham.

Thomas de Cave = Joyce, dau. of Sir Wm. St. Quintin,
Lord of Brayns Burton.

Geoffrey de Cave	Robert de Cave	John de Cave
m	m	m
Mabel, dau. of	Dau. of Robt.	Dau. of Estotes.
Robt. de Talso.	Holdenby.	

Alexander de Cave, Dean of Durham.   Peter de Cave = Elena dau. of Sir Thos.
Broomflete.

Sir Alexander Cave (alive 1314)   Thomas Cave, ancestor of the
m   Caves of Flinton.
Joan, dau. of Peter de Malodaen.

Peter Cave -- Ann, dau. of Sir Simon Ward.

Sir Alexander Cave = Amphelicia, dau. of Geoffrey Hotham.   Mary Cave, Prioress
of Walton.

Sir John Cave = Mary, dau. and heiress of Peter Genille, of South Cliff.

Sir Alexander Cave - Katherine, dau. of	Thomas Cave.	John Cave.	Peter Cave.
Roger Somerville.			

Sir Alexander Cave = Constantia, dau. of   Peter Cave = Ann, dau. of
Roger Leeds.   Ralph Ingleby.

Maud Cave, dau. and heiress	Peter Cave, of Stanford, Co. Leicester	John Cave, Abbot of
m	m	Selby, 1429 to
Sir Alexander Lound, of	Mary, dau. of Burdett, of Rothwell,	1436 ; he was buried
Lound Hall, and of Cave.	Co. Northants.	in the Abbey Church.

Janet Lound = Robert Sheffield, ancestor
of Lord Sheffield and Earls
of Mulgrave.

(See continuation A).

The Caves of Stanford, Co. Leicester.

Continuation A.

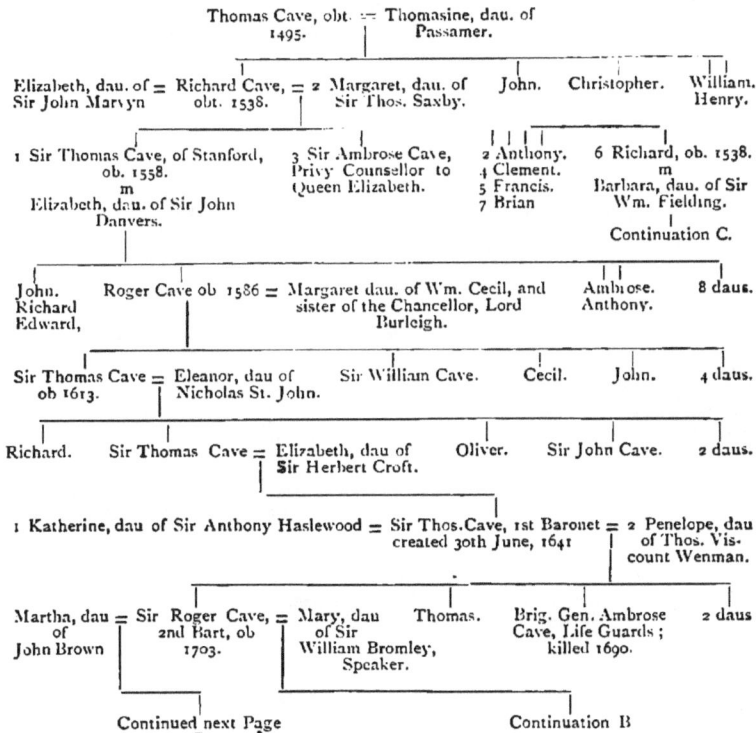

Thomas Cave, obt. = Thomasine, dau. of
1495.   Passamer.

Elizabeth, dau. of = Richard Cave, = 2 Margaret, dau. of   John.   Christopher.   William.
Sir John Marvyn   obt. 1538.   Sir Thos. Saxby.   Henry.

1 Sir Thomas Cave, of Stanford,   3 Sir Ambrose Cave,   2 Anthony.   6 Richard, ob. 1538.
ob. 1558.   Privy Counsellor to   4 Clement.   m
m   Queen Elizabeth.   5 Francis.   Barbara, dau. of Sir
Elizabeth, dau. of Sir John   7 Brian   Wm. Fielding.
Danvers.

                                                          Continuation C.

John.   Roger Cave ob 1586 = Margaret dau. of Wm. Cecil, and   Ambrose.   8 daus.
Richard   sister of the Chancellor, Lord   Anthony.
Edward,   Burleigh.

Sir Thomas Cave = Eleanor, dau of   Sir William Cave.   Cecil.   John.   4 daus.
ob 1613.   Nicholas St. John.

Richard.   Sir Thomas Cave = Elizabeth, dau of   Oliver.   Sir John Cave.   2 daus.
                              Sir Herbert Croft.

1 Katherine, dau of Sir Anthony Haslewood = Sir Thos. Cave, 1st Baronet = 2 Penelope, dau
                                created 30th June, 1641   of Thos. Vis-
                                                         count Wenman.

Martha, dau = Sir Roger Cave, = Mary, dau   Thomas.   Brig. Gen. Ambrose   2 daus
of   2nd Bart, ob   of Sir   Cave, Life Guards ;
John Brown   1703.   William Bromley,   killed 1690.
                             Speaker.

Continued next Page   Continuation B

H

Continued from previous Page

Sir Thomas Cave, 3rd Bart. ob 1719   John   Charles   Oliver   2 daus
m
Margaret, dau of John Verney, Visct
Fermanagh, and Earl of Verney.

Sir Verney Cave, 4th Bart, obt 1731, unmarried   Sir Thomas Cave, 5th Bart, obt 1778
m
Elizabeth, dau of Griffith Davies.

Sir Thomas Cave,   The Rev Sir Charles Cave,   6 daus
6th Bart, ob 1780,   8th Bart
m
Sarah, dau of John Edwards.

Sir Thomas Cave, 7th Bart, ob 1792. s.p.   Sarah Cave, ob 1862
m   m
Lucy, dau of the Rt. Hon the Earl of   Henry Otway, Esq,
Harborough.   of Otway Castle, ob
                                                1815.

Henrietta Otway Cave, 4th Baroness Braye, = The Rev Edgell Wyatt Edgell,
ob 1879.   ob 1888.

Edmund Verney-Wyatt-Edgell,   Henry Adrian,   Alfred Thomas Townshend Verney Cave,
Captain 17th Lancers, killed in   ob unmarried.   Baron Braye, in the Peerage of England,
Zululand, at Ulundi, 1879.   J P., D L., &c., &c., of Stanford, Co
                                                       Leicester
                                                       m
                                                       Cecilia Henrietta, dau of William Gerard
                                                       Walmsley, of Westwood Hall, County
                                                       Lancaster.

Verney-Adrian,   Thomas Florian,   3 daus.
b 1874.   b 1885.

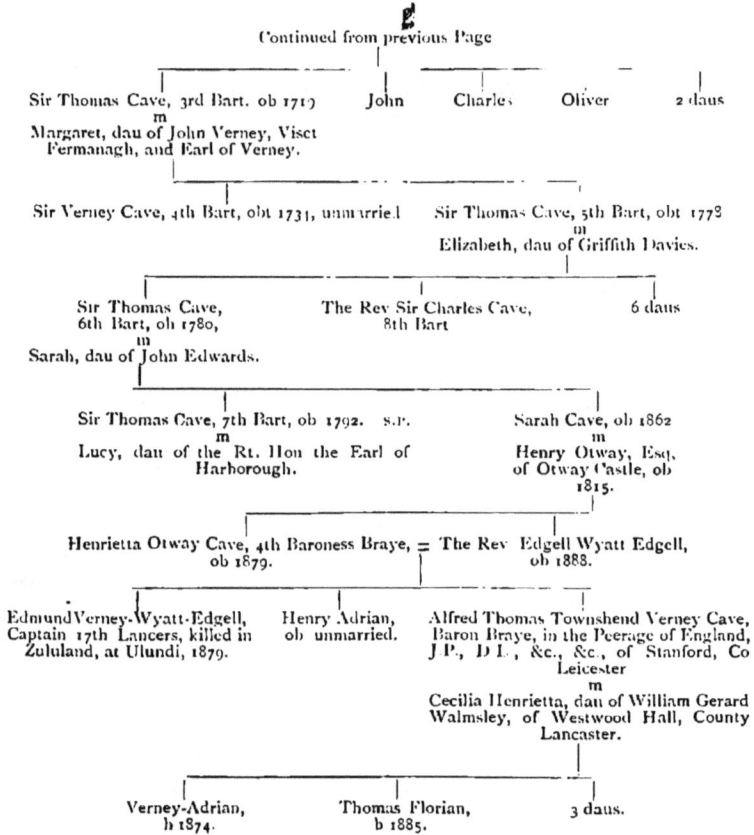

Arms of the late Baroness Braye.

The Caves of Stretton=en=le=Field, Co. Derby.

Continuation B.

Issue of the second Marriage of Sir Roger Cave, 2nd Baronet.

Roger Cave, Esq, of Eydon, Co Northants; = Catherine, dau and co-heiress of William Brown,
and Raunston, Co Leicester; ob 1741.   Esq, of Stretton Hall, Derby.

William Cave, ob   Frances, dau of Theodosius = John Cave, Esq, of = Catherine, dau and
unmarried, 1738.   Wm. Inge, s.p.   Stretton Hall, took   heiress of Thos.
                            the name of Brown   Asteley, of Wood-
                               in 1752.   eaton, co. Stafford.

Sir William Cave-Brown, 9th Baronet, = { 1 Sarah, dau Thos. Prinsep, Esq, who ob. s.p.
took the name of Cave and became Cave-   { 2 Louisa, dau of Sir Robert Mead Wilmot.
Brown-Cave of Stretton Hall, ob 1838.

Sir John Robert Cave-Brown-Cave,   The Rev Wm. Astley C. B. Cave,   Thomas C. B.
10th Bart, of Stretton Hall, ob 1855   Rector of Stretton, ob 1799; twice   Cave.
m   married, and had issue.   Wilmot C. B.
Katherine Penelope, dau and co-   Cave.
heiress of Wm. Mills, Esq, of Barl-   Edward Sache-
eston Hall, Staf.   verell C. B. Cave.
                                                                All three married
                                                                and had issue.

Sir Mylles Cave-Brown-Cave, 11th Bart, of   The Rev Verney C. B. Cave.   3 daus.
Stretton Hall, Major Derbyshire Yeo-   The Rev Ambrose, C. B. Cave.
manry, formerly Lieut 11th Hussars. D.L.   Captain Bowyer Wenman C. B. Cave
m
Isabelle, dau and co-heiress of John Taylor, Esq, of The Newark, Leicester.

Geoffrey Lisle Cave-Brown-Cave, born   Genille Cave-Brown-Cave, born 1869.   2 daus
1857, ob 1880.

ARMS.—Quarterly: 1st and 4th az., fretty, ar.; 2nd and 3rd az,, a chev. between 3 escallops, or.
CREST.—1st, a greyhound, current, sa., to which, on an escroll, the word Gardez, for motto; 2nd
     a stork ppr., beaked and membered, gu.

The Caves of Yateley, Co. Hants.

Continuation C.

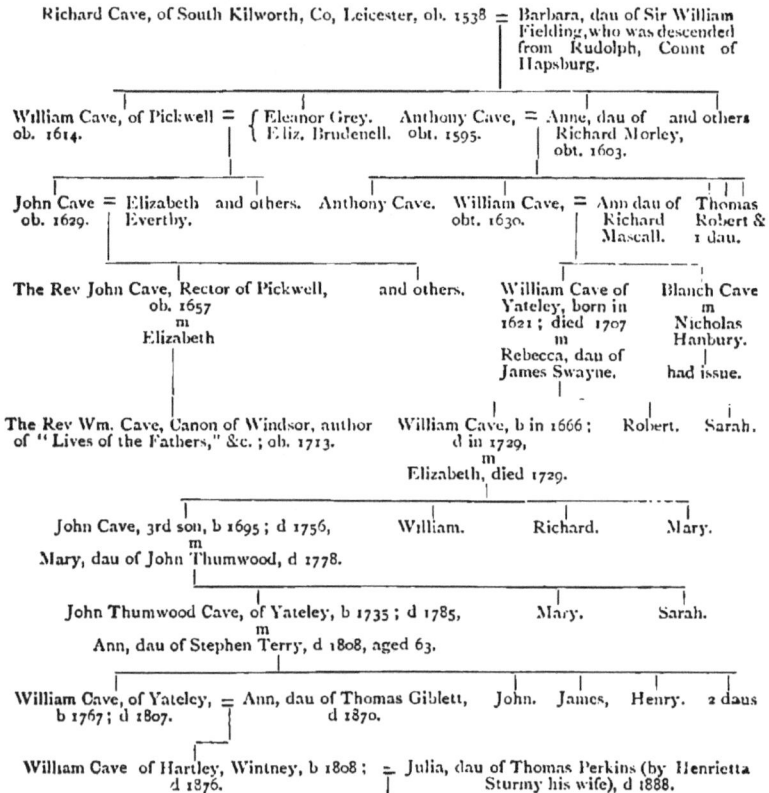

Richard Cave, of South Kilworth, Co, Leicester, ob. 1538 = Barbara, dau of Sir William Fielding, who was descended from Rudolph, Count of Hapsburg.

William Cave, of Pickwell = { Eleanor Grey.   Anthony Cave, = Anne, dau of   and others
ob. 1614.   { Eliz. Brudenell.   obt. 1595.   Richard Morley, obt. 1603.

John Cave = Elizabeth   and others.   Anthony Cave.   William Cave, = Ann dau of   Thomas
ob. 1629.   Everthy.   obt. 1630.   Richard   Robert & Mascall.   1 dau.

The Rev John Cave, Rector of Pickwell,   and others.   William Cave of   Blanch Cave
ob. 1657   Yateley, born in   m
m   1621 ; died 1707   Nicholas
Elizabeth   m   Hanbury.
                                       Rebecca, dau of   had issue.
                                       James Swayne.

The Rev Wm. Cave, Canon of Windsor, author   William Cave, b in 1666 ;   Robert.   Sarah.
of " Lives of the Fathers," &c. ; ob. 1713.   d in 1729,
                                       m
                             Elizabeth, died 1729.

John Cave, 3rd son, b 1695 ; d 1756,   William.   Richard.   Mary.
m
Mary, dau of John Thumwood, d 1778.

John Thumwood Cave, of Yateley, b 1735 ; d 1785,   Mary.   Sarah.
m
Ann, dau of Stephen Terry, d 1808, aged 63.

William Cave, of Yateley, = Ann, dau of Thomas Giblett,   John.   James,   Henry.   2 daus
b 1767 ; d 1807.   d 1870.

William Cave of Hartley, Wintney, b 1808 ; = Julia, dau of Thomas Perkins (by Henrietta
d 1876.   Sturmy his wife), d 1888.

Continued next Page.

Continued from previous Page.

3 Thomas Sturmy Cave, of Yateley, Twickenham, Col. 1st. Vol. Bat. Hampshire Regiment, b 1846; m. 1878 to Beatrice Maria, dau. of Edward Carlile, b 1854.	5 Herbert Cave, b 1859, M.A.	Emma Henrietta, m. 1872 to Peter John de Carteret, of Jersey. ‖ has issue.	Catherine Louisa m. 1870 Robert Hewett, of Leckford. Captain, 1st Vol. Bat. Hants. Reg. Has issue.	Louisa m. 1st to John Geffrard Pirouet of Jersey, and m. 2nd, the Rev. Edmomd Jos. Fra. Johnson, M.A. ‖ has issue.	Fanny Blanche, m. 1886 to Rev Edward R. Mosley, M.A. ‖ has issue	Julia. Janet. Georgiana.

Julia Mary Sturmy Cave, born 1879.   Ann Barbara Carlile Cave, born 1891.

ARMS. 1. Cave, az fretty argent.
2. Broomflete sa on a bend betw. 6 fleur de lis or 3 escallops gu.
3. Genille, er on a bend sa 3 pikes' heads ar.
4. Cliff arg a chev. between 3 paraquets vert.
5. Morley sa a leopard's face or. jessant de lis ar.
6. Cave as 1.

The following particulars respecting members of this old county family are selected from a mass of material which we have collected bearing on the subject.

" A Fine was made in the King's Court at York, on Sunday after St. Clement, between William de Santon, demandant, and Roger de Cava, tenant, concerning half a carucate of land in Cava. William released to Roger, who released to Peter, brother of William, all claim which he had in two bovates of land in Cava ; and Matilda, mother of the same Roger, released all her right therein, by name of dower, to Peter and his heirs."—*Feet of Fines, York, 4 John, No. 31.*

John de Cave was a judge in the reign of Henry III., and Fines appear to have been acknowleged before him from December, 1254, till Michaelmas, 1260.*

" Hugh de Cave presents himself against Alan de Sancto Jacobo, of Dreuton, Arnold de Arreynes, of Dreuton, Thomas de Arraynes, John, son of William de Suth Kave, and Peter, son of Ralph Fitz Gerard, on a plea wherefore they forcibly depastured cattle on a certain meadow in Dreuton, which is in the custody of the said Hugh, to his damage of 100s. They did not appear, &c. Some of them had been attached by certain other persons (named). Adjourned till Easter term. (The heading shows that it belongs to Hilary term ; year not stated)."—*Coram Rege Roll, Mich. 2-3 Edward I. m 32d.*

"Thirteen Knights, including Robert de Cave, having been chosen [to serve on a jury], were amerced 100s. each 'for contempt.' "—*Pleas of Juries at York, 8-9 Edward I.*

In 1295, Hugh de Hotham gave certain freeholdings in Hotham and North Cave to John de Cave, a Priest. Agnes le Fevre, the sister of Hugh de Hotham, disputed the validity of this gift, and the case was accordingly tried at York Assizes, in Trinity Term, 1298. John de Cave, contended that Hugh de Hotham enfeoffed him by deed, dated at Northbury, in the County of Leicester, and made Thomas de Cave, Parson of the Church of Plumpton, and Richard le Prestman, of North Cave, his attorneys, to put the said John in seisin. Agnes replied that Hugh de

* Dugdale's *Orig. Juria* p 43.

Hotham was her brother, that she was his heir, and entered into possession of the said tenements of which she was unjustly disseized by the said John de Cave. The jury found that the deed was given as John de Cave contended, and gave a verdict for him accordingly.*

On November 7th, thirtieth Edward I. (1303), Alexander de Cave and Geoffery de Hotham were appointed Collectors for Yorkshire of the Aid for marrying the King's eldest daughter, and in connection with the same Aid, we find in the Nomina Villarum, "Suth Cave, Petrus de Eyvill et Alexander de Cave." †

In 1310, a license was granted to Alexander de Cave, to give four bovates and three acres of land, and two and a half acres of meadow, and five shillings of rent in "Suth Cave," to a chaplain to celebrate divine offices in the Church of South Cave, for the souls of the said Alexander and his ancestors ; dated at New Minster, 9th September.‡ And by a Charter (2 Edward II. X, 15). there is a grant to Alexander de Cave and his heirs, of free warren in all his demesne land of South Cave, Ripplington, Howmn, and Kyplingcotes, in County Yorks.

Neither Sir William Segar nor any of the subsequent genealogists who have worked on the Cave Pedigree give the christian name of the daughter and heiress of Sir Thomas Broomflete, by whose marriage with Peter de Cave the right to quarter the Broomflete Coat of Arms was achieved. This quartering § has figured very prominently as the second in the Cave Coat of Arms for nearly six centuries. The lady's name was Elena, as appears from an Indulgence granted by the Bishop of Durham, which runs as follows :—

* Coram Rege, 26 Edward I., Trin. m 36.
† Parl. Writs, 1-133.
‡ Pat. Roll, 4 Edward II. p. 1 m 10.
§ Sa. 3 escalops gules on a bend between 6 fleur de lis or

" Indulgence of forty days to those contributing to the fabric, &c.
of the Chapel of St. Mary, in the Church of South Cave, dated
24th September, 1314 — . . . And who pray for the good
estate of Alexander de Cave and Joan, his wife, while they live,
and for their souls after they depart from this life ; and for the
souls of Peter de Cave, formerly father of the same Alexander, and
of Elena, mother of the same Alexander, whose bodies rest in the
Church of All Saints, South Cave * " This interesting document
gives us also the name of the wife of Alexander, the son of Peter and
Elena, that is to say Joan (another name which had been left out
of the pedigree), and enables the identification of the Alexander de
Cave, and Joan, his wife, whose monument Glover saw in the
Church of South Cave, in 1584.

In 1315, a mandate † was granted by Edward II. to Alexander
de Cave and William de Bevercote, constituting them the keepers of
the temporalities belonging to the Archbishopric of York during a
vacancy which occurred after the death of the Archbishop, William
de Grenfeld. They rendered a lengthy account of their steward-
ship, ‡ which seems to have lasted about eighteen months. The
account, of which there are two copies preserved at the Record
Office, states that they received the charge from the King's
Escheator, on 30th December, ninth Edward II., and they retained
the charge until the Feast of St. Michael, in the eleventh Edward
II., and from that said feast to the 8th October next following,
when they delivered the temporalities up to master William de
Melton, who was then appointed Archbishop by the Pope.

Another mark of the King's confidence in Alexander de Cave

---

* *Registers of Durham*, pub. by Longman, 1873, Vol I. p 609.
† Orig. Roll 9 Edward II. m 6.
‡ Bishop's *Temporalities*, York, 579 and 582.

was shewn by a mandate * to the said Alexander and Robert de Ancotes, who are described as keepers of the lands which formerly belonged to the Templars in the County of York, to re-seize the Manors of South Cave and Etton, which the King had granted to David, Earl of Athol, because he 'has adhered to Robert de Brus, the King's enemy and rebel."

In Commissions to choose horsemen and footmen in divers Wapentakes of the County of York, to oppose the agressions of the Scots, Alexander de Cave was one of four Commissioners in the Wapentake of Herthill, "except the parts of Holdernesse."—*Rotuli Scotiæ I. 130 a, 8 Edward II. (1314.)*

A Commission to Alexander de Cave and three others, to raise "the people" in the same Wapentake of Herthill, in the East Riding, between the ages of twenty and sixty, to be ready to attend the King at York.—*Ibid. 12 Edward II.*

Another commission to the same persons to raise "the people" in the same Wapentake, between the ages of twenty and sixty, against the Scots.

A Commission to Alex. de Cave and others, to choose 2,000 footmen in the East Riding, and conduct them to the King at Newcastle against the Scots.

In ninth Edward II., "John de Doncaster, Peter D'Eyvill and Alexander de Cave, were assigned to enquire of the defaults in repair and cleansing of certain ditches in the parts of Spalding-more, within the Bishop of Duresme's liberty of Houedone, whereby the low grounds then were overflowed, and in the same year the said John and Alexander, together with Hugh de Louthre, Adam de Midleton, and Adam de Hopton, had the like assignation for the view and repair of those banks upon Ouse betwixt Rikhall and Houedon-dyke ; and again in 14 Edward II had Alexander de Cave, Thomas de Howke, and Hugh de Pikworth, for those betwixt Faxflete and Cawode ; and again in 17th of Edward II. had Alexander de Cave, and others, the like commission for the view and repair of those betwixt Suth Cave and Barneby, near Houedon, then broken in divers places, and in case that they who

* Orig. Roll 6 Edward II. m 12.

had thus diverted and obstructed these water courses were not able to repair them again, then to distrain all such to give assistance therein, as by such reducing them to their former channels and de-obstruction of those stops, should receive benefit and safeguard." *

In 1316, Alexander de Cave was returned joint Lord of South Cave, North Cliff, and South Cliff. He occurs as a Commission of Array for the Wapentake of Harthill, in 1318, and was elected a Knight of the Shire for Yorkshire in the same year. †

In 1317, an inquisition was taken at Pokelington, Yorkshire, on Saturday before St. Margaret's the Virgin, at which it was decided that it was to the King's damage if he should grant to Geoffrey de Cave to give one messuage, six tofts, and four bovates of land in Esthaytfelde to a certain chaplain to cele-brate for the souls of the said Geoffrey de Cave and his Ancestors at the Altar of St Mary's, in the Parish Church of All Saints, of North Cave, because, if the said Geoffrey should commit any felony, the King would lose the year and waste, and the mesne lord would lose his escheat, and the wardships and marriage during the minority of any heirs of the said Geoffrey. The said tenements were held of Walter de Faucanberge, by Knight's service, and he held of the King as of the honour of Albemarle. Geoffrey de Cave also held at this time, in the Vill of North Cave, one messuage and fourteen bovates of land worth yearly twenty marks, and these he held of Roger del Hay by Knight's service, the said Roger held of Peter de Maulay, who held of the King. Also Geoffrey de Cave held in the Vill of Esthorpe, eight bovates of land, worth yearly £6, and the said land was held of Richard Sturmy, by Knight's service, and the same Richard Sturmy held of the heirs of Henry de Percy, who holds of the King." (In this Inquisition it is many times mentioned that sixteen carucates of land made one Knight's fee). ‡

"At an Inquisition § Post Mortem, taken at Middleton, on Sunday, the mor-row of St. Gregory, the Pope (1323), it was ruled that Nicholas de Cave, of Beverley, deceased, had jointly with Christiana, his wife, who survived at this date, held to them and their heirs one capital messuage, one windmill, and eight bovates of land in Brantyngham and North Cave, of John de Faucanberge, son and heir of Walter de Faucanberge, by Knight's service. The

* Dugdale's *Embanking and Draining*, p 115.
+ Parl. Writs ii., 651.
‡ Inquisition Ad Quodandum, 11 Edward II., 2 n 84.
§ Inquis. Post. Mort., 16 Edward II., N. 17.

messuage was worth yearly in the profit of the herbage 3s. 4d., the windmill 13s. 4d., and each bovate 6s. 8d.; also one capital messuage and twelve bovates of land in Middleton of William de Roos, Lord of Hamlac, by Knight's service, the messuage being worth 5s. and each bovate 6s. 8d. per annum. John de Cave, his son and heir, was aged fourteen years and upwards."

"In the year 1350, by an Inquisition post mortem * taken at York, on the Wednesday before Easter, it was found that John de Cave, of Middleton, next, Watton, held one messuage and four bovates of land in Middleton of the heir of William de Roos, of Hamlak, who held of the King in chief by the service of one twenty-fourth part of a Knight's fee. Each bovate of land had formerly been worth the yearly rent of six shillings, but owing to the great mortality among men that has just taken place (this was doubtless the great plague of 1347, known as the black death, which had carried off all the tenants) the land was lying wasted and untilled. At one time the said John de Cave had been seized of one messuage and eight bovates of land and one Windmill in Middleton, but he granted this property, seven years before the date of his death, to Richard de London and John Levene, Chaplains, who re-granted the same to the said John de Cave and Isabella, his wife, and the heirs of their bodies. Isabella died before the said John, and John, the son of the said John and Isabella, is their next heir. These last premises are held of the same William de Roos by the service of a twelfth part of a Knight's fee and by homage; six of the said bovates are in tillage and are worth the yearly rent of 30s., and two lie untilled on account of the recent mortality; the said Windmill was worth 4s. and no more, its value being also depreciated on account of the mortality. John de Cave held as well ten bovates of land in Kibelyngcote, of the Chapter of St. John's, of Beverley, by fealty and 12d. yearly. Each bovate of this land used to be worth a yearly rent of 12s., but they had at this date lain waste and untilled for many years for want of tenants, owing to the unproductiveness of the land."

* Inquisition Post Mortem, 24 Edward II. 1st n 103 RO.

NEWBALD.

EWBALD is a Parish comprising the townships of North and South Newbald, four miles south-by-east from Market Weighton, and about two and a half miles from South Cave Station, on the Hull and Barnsley Railway. The area of the entire parish is about 6,000 acres, and the population is 799. The principal landowners are Lord Galway and W. H. Harrison-Broadley, Esq.

Ulphus, the son-in-law of Canute, Governor of West Deira, and Lord of a great part of East Yorkshire, possessed land at Newbald, and, in order to prevent his two sons quarrelling over their inheritance, he vowed that he would make them equal. Taking with him his drinking horn, made of an elephant's tusk, curiously carved and polished and ornamented with gold mounting, he went to the altar of the Cathedral at York, filled the horn with wine, drank

it off, and dedicated all his lands to God and St. Peter, thus dis-
inheriting his family. The gift included Newbald, Goodmanham,
Aldborough, and other places.*

In Domesday, Newbald is referred to as follows : --" Land of
the Archbishop of York. In Niwebolt are twenty-eight carucates
and two oxgangs to be taxed, where there may be sixteen ploughs.
Eldred, the Archbishop, held this for one manor. The Canons of
St. Peter, under Thomas, Archbishop, now have in the demesne
two ploughs, and seven villanes with two ploughs and a half, and
four mills paying thirty shillings. There is a Church and a Priest
there. The whole manor is three miles long and two miles broad
value in King Edward's time, twenty-four pounds, at present ten
pounds." †

Torre gives us the following particulars respecting this parish,
and a list of the vicars.‡

"The Church of St. Peter's, York, held in Newbald twenty carucates of
land given by Ulphus, which is now shared among the following Prebends, viz. :

The Prebend of Ricall hath in Newbald one Capital Messuage of his
demesne manor and eight oxgangs of demesne land, and other tenants holding
25 oxgangs of land by suite of court and certain services.

The Prebend of Warthill hath one Capital Messuage and two oxgangs
of demesne land held by rent and services.

The Prebendary of Osbaldwick hath one Hall or Capital Tenement and

---

* This horn, a valuable relic of ancient art, forms the title by which the
Chapter of the Cathedral still hold several of their estates, and is deposited in
the vestry. During the Civil War, this famous horn disappeared from the
Minster, and fell into the hands of Sir Thomas Fairfax. His son, the next
Lord Fairfax, restored it to the Cathedral, and in 1675 it was re-decorated by
the Dean and Chapter, who bestowed on it the following inscription (in Latin) :
" Ulphus, Prince of Western Deira, once upon a time bestowed this horn,
together with all his lands and revenues. It having been lost or stolen, Henry,
Lord Fairfax, at length restored it. The Dean and Chapter decorated it anew,
A.D. 1675."

† Bawdwen's Translation, p 46.

‡ Torre's Peculiars, p 809.

sixteen oxgangs of land in demesne with nine tenements and fourteen oxgangs of land.

The Prebendary of South Newbald is Lord of the whole town, having therein his manor and fourteen oxgangs of demesne land, and jurisdiction over the inhabitants from the Beck under the Churchyard side as far as the South-end of the town, on both sides of the highway, excepting two tenements lying together.

The Prebend of Husthwaite hath one Capital Messuage at the South-end of the street called Gaylgate, and ten oxgangs of demesne land ; also twenty-two tenants holding twenty-four oxgangs three acres of land, and jurisdiction over them all.

The Prebend of North Newbald hath twenty-four oxgangs of demesne land and eighteen other tenants, and a manor-house and mill and jurisdiction over all his tenants.

'The Prebend of North Newbald is Rector of the church thereof, and receiver of the great tythes thereunto belonging."

CATALOGUE OF THE VICARS OF NORTH NEWBALD.

Temp Instit.	Vicarii.	Patron.	Vacat.
27th Jan., 1349....	Joh de Hayton	Prebend of	....
13th Oct., 1385....	Robt. de Stoke	North Newbald.	Mort.
8th Oct., 1397 ...	Walt. de Gode............	....	....
	Edmd. Pall		Res.
28th Sept., 1410...	Will Andrews	....	Mort.
7th Feb., 1417...	Thos. Woolone		....
13th May, 1426 ...	Will Ellys..............		Mort.
1457 ...	Thos. Ellerker........ ...		Res.
20th Dec., 1460...	Ric. Small		Mort.
18th April, 1470...	Johe Walker.............		Res.
25th May, 1471 ...	Thos. Burton		Mort.
6th Nov., 1479...	Joh Santon		Mort.
23rd Dec., 1479...	Ric. Walker.............		Mort.
12th Feb., 1509...	Will Hobson		Res.
15th Nov. 1522....	Johe Watson		Res.
10th Dec., 1523...	Thos. Coke		Mort.
25th Nov., 1545...	Geo. Atwell.............		... ...
6th April, 1573...	Geo. Gibson		....
Oct., 1577	Johe Coke		Mort.
23rd Dec., 1592...	Xtopher Croper		Mort.

Temp Instit.	Vicarii.	Patron.	Vacat.
10th Nov., 1606...	Thos. Sugden		Res.
22nd Nov., 1620...	Xtopher Ware		Mort.
16th Nov., 1638...	Saml. Casley		Mort.
Nov., 1668	Reginald Hopwood		Mort.
1680..................	R. Dolman		Mort.
1684..................	Herbert Teryman		

Testamentary Burials.

13th Aug., A.D. 1458. -Alice Hotham, late wife of Stephen Hotham, of Newbald, made her will, proved 2nd November, 1458, giving her soul to God Alm., St. Mary, and all Saints, and her body to be buried in the Psh. Church of Newbald.

20th May, A.D. 1457—Will Ellys, Vic of the prebendal Church of Newbald, made his will, proved the 16th of October, 1459, giving his soul (ut Supra), and his body to be buried in the said church.

On Monday, after the Feast of St. Michael the Archangel.—Robert Burton, of Newbald, made his will, proved, giving his soul (ut Supra), and his body to be buried in the Church of St. Nicholas, of Newbald.

27th February, A.D. 1545.—Thos. Cooke, Vicar of Newbald, had his will proved.

December, A.D. 1509.—Ric. Walker, Vicar of Newbald, made his will, proved 25th January, 1509, giving his Soul (ut Supra), and his body to be buried in the Quire of St. Nicholas, Newbald.

19th February, A.D. 1571.—Richd. Small, Vic. of Newbald, dying intestate, his goods were granted to Ric. Owersby.

21st May, A.D. 1606.—Xtopher Croser, of Newbald, Clerk, made his will, proved 29th January, 1606, giving his soul to God, his creator, and his body to be buried in the Church of St. Nicholas, of Newbald.

The Church.

The Church, which stands on a slight elevation, is dedicated to St. Nicholas, and consists of a nave, chancel, north and south transepts, with a large square tower in the centre, and is, without doubt, the finest among the many fine parochial edifices in the East Riding which were built in the Anglo-Norman period ; indeed, it

has been asserted by architectural critics that this church is
one of the most perfect Anglo-Norman parochial edifices in the
kingdom. The late Archbishop Thomson termed it his Norman Cathedral. The date of its foundation is the latter part of
the twelfth century, and of this period there are still existing, the
large nave, except the west window ; the transepts, except the

ST. NICHOLAS, NEWBALD.

triple lancet window, in the south face ; and the tower as far upwards as the roof of the present nave. It is extremely probable
the east end of the nave terminated in an apse, where the chancel now stands, and from the beautiful circular-headed arches
in the interior of the transepts (which have now windows of the
perpendicular period inserted within them), two other apsidal

terminations also formerly existed. About the time of Henry III. the church was re-roofed, the former roof having been destroyed by fire; and at the restoration of the church, a few years ago, there were evident marks of fire discernible in the south transept. The new roofs were raised to the height of the water mark on each face of the tower, which would then be too low, hence the upper part of the tower with its two lancets in each face, dates from this period —as also the triple lancet window in the face of the south transept. The font is of the early English period, with clustered columns and stiff ornamental foliage round the bowl. The present chancel is of the Tudor period, it has on its south side three pointed windows of three lights, with cinquefoil heads and perpendicular tracery in the sweep of the arch; in the east end is a similar window of five lights; and on the north side of the chancel is a chapel now used as a vestry. In the south wall is a cinquefoil-headed piscina; and on the north side of the east window a niche of considerable proportions for an image or statue. The nave is lighted by circular-headed windows, with the exception of the large west window of the perpendicular period, of four lights. The doorways of this church are very fine, especially the one on the south side of the nave, the walls of which are built thicker in order to receive the arch; it consists of five receding arches springing from an impost, which is broken at each arch, and serves as a base to four columns attached to each jamb; the capitals of some of the columns are leaved; the outer arch is formed of plain keystones; the second shews a cabled torus; the third has a cavetto above a torus; the fourth, several rows of chevron work; and the fifth is plain like the first. Above the arch, enclosed in the vesica piscis, is a statue of the patron saint, which is surrounded by chevron and other mouldings. In the south transept is another good circular-

headed doorway; also two smaller ones on the north side of the
nave and transept.   The massive tower rests on four semi-circular
arches which have bold chevron mouldings resting on columns
with bold capitals.   On various parts of the outside of the building

THE FONT, ST. NICHOLAS CHURCH, NEWBALD.

are tiers of sculptured blocking courses, some of which are
extremely ludicrous.   The church is spacious, the dimensions
being: nave, 63ft. long by 21ft. wide; chancel, 34ft. long by 18ft.

wide ; north transept, 22ft. long by 17ft., wide ; and south transept, 22ft. long by 17ft. wide. In the tower are three bells with the following inscriptions :—

> 1st—"Venite Exvltemvs Domino, 1667, F. P., W. B., E. B., Church-wardens."
> 2nd—"Soli Deo Gloria Pax Homnibvs, 1663. R. K., P. H.——S. S."
> 3rd—"Hec Campana Sacra Fiat Trinitate Beata, 1610."

The living is a Vicarage, valued at £285, with a residence and sixty acres of glebe land, in the patronage of the Archbishop of York, the Rev. S. J. Soady, M.A., being the present Vicar.

Monuments in the Church.

A tablet on the north wall of the chancel bears the following inscription :—

"To the memory of Sir Philip Monckton, Knight, buried in South New-bald Church, 21st February, 1678. This zealous Loyalist was the eldest son of Sir Francis Monckton, Knight, and grandson of Sir Philip Monckton, Knight, of Cavil Hall and Newbald ; who were all sequestered at one time for their loyalty to King Charles the First, whom they not only supplied with large sums of money, but supported with active service. Sir Philip Monckton, the younger, at the breaking out of the Civil War, was senior Captain of Sir Thomas Metham's Regiment of Foot, when the King went against Hull. He was at the battle of Adderton Moor, and for his conduct at Corbridge, near Hexham, in 1644, was Knighted by the Marquis of Newcastle, who commanded the army sent against the Scots. At the fight of Bowden Hills, at the disastrous Battle of Marston Moor, and in the relief of Pontefract, he assisted. Three horses were shot under him at Naseby Field, and at Rowton Heath, near Chester, he was severely wounded. While commanding Sir Marmaduke Langdale's Brigade, in 1648, Sir Philip was taken prisoner at Willoughby Field, with the whole of his little army, by the much superior force of Colonel Rossiter, and in the returns made to Parliament was styled General of the Pontefract Forces. After being sent a prisoner to Belvoir Castle he was banished, and for some years he lived in France and the Netherlands with other English exiles. While he was at York, in 1658, he, at great hazard of his life, was plotting the restoration of King Charles II., and materially contributed to a right understanding between General Monk and Lord Fairfax, and obtained the admission of the latter into the

City, New Year's Day, 1659, for which Sir Philip received the thanks of the Mayor and Aldermen in 1669, when he was High Sheriff of the County. In 1670, he was elected one of the Members of Parliament for Scarborough, and was then residing at Newbald Hall, where it is probable he wrote his interesting memoir and other manuscripts, proving that he feared God as well as served his King. Sir Philip Monckton married in 1658, Anne, eldest daughter of Robert Eyre, Esq., of Highlow, Derbyshire, by whom he had one daughter and two sons; William, the youngest, was in the navy, and slain before Barcelona, in 1706; and Robert, the eldest son, was the father of the first Viscount Galway."

On the floor of the chancel is a stone inscribed as follows :—

"Here lies the body of Mary Gunby, the onely daughter of Mr. Robert Gunby and Susanna, his wife, who was buried the 19th day of November, 1683, being the sixteenth year of her age.

Here also lies the body of Mrs. Grace Burton, widdow, her Grandemother, who was buried the 11th day of September, 1684, being the 71 year of her age.

Here also lyeth the body of Mr. Robert Gunby, of this Town, who departed this life the 3 day of July, 1709, being the 69 year of his age."

On the north wall of the nave is a monument bearing the following inscription :—

"This monument, erected in memory of Mr. William Gill, who was born at North Newbald, and died near Fort William, in Bengall, and by his will, dated 26th of July, 1723, left thirty pounds per annum for ever to the poor of this parish. Pursuant to whose will, land of inheritance to the yearly value of thirty pounds, were, by decree in Chancery, purchased at Cherry Burton, called Rainthorpe Closes, and settled to Trustees for the use aforesaid." [The Testator also left six shillings a year to the parish clerk for cleaning his monument in the churchyard].

Also on the north wall of the nave :—

"Sacred to the memory of Michael Duckett, of the Town of Kingston-upon-Hull, who died 20th December, 1799, aged 54 years, and lies interred in the Parish Church of Drypool.

Also of Ann, his wife (daughter of the late Joseph Kirby, of Monckton-walk, in this parish), who died 15th September, 1836, aged 84 years, and whose remains are deposited in the aisle of this Church.

Michael Matthew, son of the above, died at Kingston, Jamaica, on the 4th June, 1814, aged 28 years.

And eight of their children who died in their infancy."

On the South Wall of the Chancel.

" In remembrance of the Rev. Francis Metcalfe, Vicar of Righton, in this County, and a Magistrate for the East Riding, also Rector of Kirkbride in the County of Cumberland. He died on the 20th of October, 1834, in the 40th year of his age ; his remains are deposited in a vault within the rails of this altar."

A slab on the north wall, within the altar rails, has the following inscription :—

"Sacred to the memory of John William Clough, Esqre., who died at Newbald, October 15th, 1842, aged 69 years."

On a Brass over the Altar.

" To the Glory of God, and to the loved memories of Georgiana Maria Clough ; her son ; and Edmund Clough. This chancel was restored A.D. 1864."

Monument on the North Wall of the Chancel.

" Sacred to the memory of Georgiana Maria Clough, youngest daughter of William Ford Hulton, of Hulton Park, Co. Lancaster, and beloved wife of William, eldest son of John Clough, of this parish ; she died after child birth, April 6th, 1864, aged 21 ; and sleeps with her infant son in the chancel of this church."

On the Floor of North Transept.

" In memory of Mary Frances Anne Blyth, the beloved wife of the Rev. George B. Blyth, B.D., Vicar of this parish, who died November 20th, 1861, aged 60 years ; also of Emily Popham Blyth, daughter of the above, who died September 28th, 1855, in her 17th year ; also of the Rev. George Blanshard Blyth, B.D., twenty-eight years Vicar of Newbald, who died February 4th, 1863, aged 64 years."

In the south transept are stones to the memory of Richard Kirby, gentleman, and William Hall, gentleman ; and in the floor of the nave, a stone to Thomas Kirby, gentleman.

Parish Registers.

The Registers commence in 1600. There are no entries from 1642 to 1654, nor from 1679 to 1709, inclusive. Transcripts are in the Prebendal Court at York.

The Registers do not appear to contain any entries having special antiquarian interest, but the names of Galloway, Pearson, Howson, Stevenson, Atkinson, Hall, Young, and Barff, frequently occur therein. In the Register of Marriages we find the following. entry :—

"A marriage, intended between John Faukiner, of the parish of Beverley, single man, aged thirty years, and Elizabeth Todd, of the parish of Newbald, widow, aged thirty-three years, was published in the Market Place of South Cave, on the 21st day of January, 1655, betwixt the hours of one and two of the clock, and noe prson did alledge any thinge to the contrarie. The said intended marriage was published the second time the 28th day of January, 1655, and noe pson did alledge any thinge to ye contrarie. These were againe published ye third time the fourth day of February, 1655, and noe pson did alledge any thinge to the contrarie.

Be it remembered that John Faukiner and Elizabeth Todd, above named, were married at Etton, the 28th day of Febuarie, 1665, in the presence of Thomas Waudby, James Andrew.   By me, J. Smedlye."

The churchwardens' books contain the following entries : —

"October 24th, 1658.—Collected for the fire at Bridlinton, in the Kirk of Newbald, the sum of three shillings and sixpence."

		£	s	d
1738.	Spent when Dr. Sterne * viewed the church	0	1	0
1741.	For killing a Fox	0	1	0
	Spent the 5th of November	0	10	0
1803.	Journey Northallerton, two men and horses after a			
	man for a bastard child, and expenses ...	6	1	9
1747.	Paid for Perambulations	1	0	0
1748.	Do. do.	0	15	0
1772.	Do. do.	1	10	0
1798.	Base string and allowance	0	6	6
1799.	Base string	0	1	4

An old Poor-Rate Book, relating to the parish, commencing in 1722, contains many interesting entries. The overseers had drifted into a slovenly way of keeping their accounts, and in the

* Laurence Sterne, the author of "Tristram Shandy," as Prebend of York, visited the Church in this year.

year 1797 we find that instead of giving details of their expenditure they simply say :—

	£	s	d
Sess Bill and in Purse	77	14	8
Disbursements to Poor People	77	6	3
In Purse	0	8	5

The Prebends evidently refused to sign such a bald statement of accounts, as the rate is unsigned, and on the next page they appended the following warning :—

"N.B.—The future Overseers of the Poor are to take Notice that no Accounts will hereafter be allowed unless the particulars of the Expenditure are all inserted in this Book—and they are liable to be sent to the House of Correction untill they do account."

In the next year's account the overseers accordingly give full details, the following being amongst the entries :—

	£	s	d
23rd April—Paid to the poor house for two paupers, 4s. weekly	5	12	0
For Mark Tindle, 28 weeks at 2s. weekly	2	16	0
For Hannah Skelton, 1s. 6d. weekly	2	15	6
Cloth for two Petty Coats, four shifts for two paupers in the poor house, and one Handkerchief, and spent at two Meetings	1	4	0
For two Militia Men's Wives	2	14	0
Richd. Tindall, Bill for Shoes	0	14	0
Two orders for Benson wife, and Letter from Kilpin	0	2	7
For 24 Metts of Coals	1	11	0
Thos. Hornsey, for repairing the Poor House...	1	1	0

CHAPELS.

In the village there are chapels belonging to the Baptists, Wesleyans, and Primitive Methodists.

THE CHARITIES.

"Mr. Gill's charity, rent of land (quantity not stated), let at the time of the report for £113 10s. per annum, and dividends on £216 12s. three per cent. consols, and interest of £15 in Savings Bank ; the sum of £1 per annum is paid to a receiver, and 6s. a year to the parish clerk for cleaning the donor's monument in Newbald Church. The residue of the rents and dividends is distributed among twenty poor persons of the parish who have never received parochial relief.

Gunby's, Wilson's and Burton's rent-charges, £2 12s. 6d. per annum, for educating six poor children, and £1 6s. per annum laid out in weekly bread.

Payment by J. W. Clough, Esq., £1 per annum to the poor out of an estate at Newbald, supposed to be an acknowledgement for taking in part of a public road.

Payment by H. B. Barnard, Esq., an ancient charge of 10s. per annum.

Payment by Mr. Peter Lyon, 10s. per annum, an ancient charge to the poor.

Payments by Richard Burgess and Saml. Dawson 6s. 8d. and 3s. 4d. per annum, respectively, to the poor.

Some small donations left to the poor of the parish appear to have been lost." *

A TOLL-FREE LICENSE.

From its connection with York Minster, Newbald enjoyed immunity from toll, and the following is a copy of an old Toll-Free License, the original being now in our possession.

" LIBERTY OF ST. PETER OF YORK.—**Whereas** the Dean and Chapter of the Cathedral and Metropolitical Church of St. Peter, in York, and their Successors, and the Men and Tenants, and all other the Inhabitants within the Liberty of the said Dean and Chapter, by custom before the reign of King Edward the Confessor, had and enjoyed several remarkable Liberties and Immunities, and were acquitted of and from payment of all and all manner of Tolls, Tonage, Pontage, Menage, Podage, Smallage and Stallage whatsoever in all Fairs and Marketts within the Realm of England, Ireland, and the Dominion of Wales, which the Charter made to the Dean and Chapter of the said Church by King Henry the First ratifys and confirms, and the same, as well by several other Charters made since as by several Acts of Parliament have been ratified and confirmed, as by the same Charters and Statutes do fully and at large appear. **Now know ye** That I, William Stables, Esquire, Steward of and to the said

* From the Commissioners' 11th Report, p 719.

Dean and Chapter, Do, by the authority incident to the said office of Steward, hereby certify all whom it may concern, That the Bearer hereof, John Edwards, Yeoman, is an Inhabitant within the Liberty of the said Dean and Chapter, and is to have and enjoy the benefit of all franchises and privileges within the said Charters contained, to the Men and Tenants of the said Liberty appertaining, and is to be Toll Free in all places in England, Ireland, and Wales. In Testimony of which I have hereunto set the Seal of the said office, the tenth day of July, in the second year of the Reign of our Sovereign, Lord George the Third, by the Grace of God, King of Great Britain, France, and Ireland, Defender of the Faith and so forth, and in the year of Our Lord, one thousand seven hundred and sixty two."

OLD LANDMARKS.

In a grass field to the south of the blacksmith's shop, in south Newbald, there are distinct traces of a terrace, which may have formed the front of a mansion, and a tradition exists that here was the site of the Manor House where Sir Philip Monckton "wrote his interesting memoir and other manuscripts."

Newbald Hall, in North Newbald, formerly belonging to the Clough family, was sold a few years ago to Mr. W. H. Harrison-Broadley, and, after being unoccupied for sometime, was pulled down.

SANCTON.

HIS village is about two miles, in a south-easterly direction, from Market Weighton, on the western edge of the wolds, and on the old Roman Road from Brough Ferry. It is pleasantly situated in a deep valley, and, although in itself containing little of special interest, its surroundings have proved a prolific source of antiquarian and archæological research, as almost every field in and around the parish is rich in relics of the Britons, Romans, and Saxons, who, in their turn, lived and died here, and have left, in antiquities which are still being constantly found, distinct evidence of their existence. The food jar of the Ancient Briton, with his implements of flint and stone; the cinerary urn of the Imperial Roman, with coins of that people; the bronze arms and substantial pottery of the Anglo-Saxon, with coins of the Heptarchy, and down to the time of Elizabeth, have all been found in the neighbourhood. A few months ago we visited the locality, and, with Mr. Foster, of Sancton, for our guide, we proceeded to an eminence about half a mile from the village, where many urns and other antiquities had previously been found. After digging for some little time we were successful in finding an urn, almost entire, of the early British type, filled with cinerated bones, and among them part of a bone comb. Portions of other urns with varied markings were also found.

The page of history is almost silent as to the manners and customs of the ancient Britons, and perhaps very little reliance can be placed on any account we have prior to the conquest of the island by Cæsar. We are given to understand that they had their dwellings in the interior of woods and forests, that they dwelt in huts and formed ramparts by felling trees for defence, and thus entrenching themselves, their families, and their cattle. They are described by Strabo and others as being naked, their bodies covered all over with curious devices, and the skin punctured and stained with the juice of wood. Their hair, which was of a red colour, was worn long, and altogether they presented a terrible appearance in battle.

The greater part of the Wold district contains memorials of these ancient people, and in the neighbourhood of Sancton we have entrenchments and a great number of tumuli, many of which, thanks to the antiquarian zeal of Canon Greenwell, the late Professor Rolleston, Mr. Mortimer, Mr. Foster and others, have been opened, the explorers being rewarded by discoveries of skeletons, urns, bronzes and flints.

The following interesting description of the Sancton antiquities, and of the amphitheatre at Hessleskew, near Sancton, is from the pen of Mr. M. Foster :—

"About a mile from the village there is a piece of ground,

about one hundred and fifty yards in length, by fifty yards in
breadth, which had been nearly filled with urns, but, being near the
surface, most of them have been destroyed by cultivation.   In a

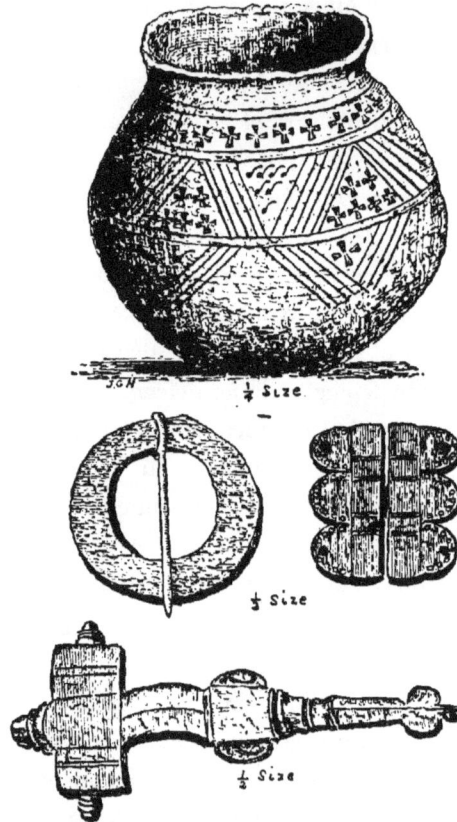

URN AND ANGLO-SAXON BRONZE ORNAMENTS FOUND WITH THE
BODY OF A FEMALE AT SANCTON.

space of three yards I counted eleven urns, all broken to fragments.
In a bank by the side of a hedge several were found entire ; some
very plain, hand-made, and rudely marked : others lathe-turned

and elaborately finished. In one place I found one broken in pieces, and in searching the bottom of the hole I found the upper rim of another. Further excavation revealed a complete urn, which I succeeded in taking out entire. This was full of burnt bones, amongst which were two bone needles about four inches long. In others several articles of bronze, flint, and bone were found. In another place nearer the village, in walking over a piece of newly ploughed land, I found a fragment of an urn. On digging down about nine or ten inches I found numerous fragments of urns and burnt bones, extending over a considerable portion of ground. On removing a flat stone I found a hole had been scooped out in the hard sand and filled with burnt bones. On extending my investigations a little further southward, I came upon an urn bottom upwards. This was found to be resting on the head of a skeleton, laid on its side, doubled up, the knees forming an acute angle towards the head. On removing the urn it crumbled to pieces. Inside were the following articles:—A bronze pin, about four inches long, with a circular loop at the end; three bronze fibulæ, a clay spindle whorle, several beads of very hard stone, and a small flint knife. A little southward of this I found another skeleton, extended to its full length, the head to the north-west. Amongst the bones were several fragments of urns and charcoal. The leg bones presented a series of indentations, as if they had been bound together by a cord for a considerable length of time. They are now in the Museum at Oxford. Not far from this was another, laid face downward, and doubled up. With this I found an iron spear about eighteen inches in length, also the remains of an iron knife, a socket, some fragments of urns, and charcoal. Near this was another skeleton, also much contracted. With this I found two bronze armclasps, one belt clasp, three circular fibulæ, one long circular fibulæ, twenty-three amber beads, one curious inlaid amber bead, also fragments of urns and charcoal. This had evidently been a lady of rank, resplendent with jewellery. The bronze articles were all perfect, highly ornamented, and in good preservation. Shortly afterwards I found another skeleton, more extended, lying on its side. The left temple of the skull presented a deep indentation, as if from a blow. I sent it to Oxford, where it was examined by the late Professor Rolleston. He supposed the injury had been inflicted early in life and recovered from, but that the person had been a great sufferer. Nothing was found with this, except portions of urns and charcoal. On making a trench across a portion of ground three more skeletons were found, all more or less contracted. Over the head of one was a very fine Saxon urn full of the fibres of the roots of a neighbouring tree. The urn was profusely marked, and in good preservation. With another were several beads of glass and amber, a fine leaf-shaped flint arrow head, fragments of urns, and charcoal. I may here remark that I never found a decayed tooth. Some had been much worn, but they fitted even and close all round."

THE AMPHITHEATRE AT HESSLESKEW.

"The Amphitheatre at Hessleskew is about two hundred yards in circumference, and appears to have been about ten or twelve feet in uniform depth. The arena is now a plantation of trees of about sixty years growth, and when these trees were planted, numerous animal bones were found in the floor of the pit. Near the pit, in the middle of a field, is an ancient well, now partly filled up, which, fifty years ago, was sounded to a depth of three hundred feet. Near the well are some old foundations,

which can be traced continuously for about fifty yards. Taking
the pit as a centre, in a radius of about one mile, more antiquities
have been found at different times, which mark a longer period
of time than perhaps any other uninhabited part of the country—
over two hundred tumuli, stone, bronze, and iron weapons and
ornaments, remains of harness, chariot wheels, swords, spears, and
coins, the earliest of the latter which I have seen being of the time
of Constantine, the latest that of Elizabeth. From the above facts
I draw the following inferences : —' That the pit was excavated by
the Romans for the purpose of bull-baiting, and other similar
sports ; that an annual carnival has been held, when horse, chariot,
and other races and games have been practised ; the well had most
probably been dug for a supply of water for the visitors, biped and
quadruped : the foundations near the well suggest a series of sheds,
one section of which, from the cinders, &c. found, had been a
smith's shop ; that the immense mass of chalk excavated from the
pit and well had been used in levelling the ground for a considerable distance round the pit, which now forms one of the most
extensive plateaus to be found on the Yorkshire Wolds.' "

DOMESDAY,

In Domesday we find the following references to Sancton :—

"Land of the King. In Santone (Sancton) and Wiluelai twelve carucates of land are to be taxed. Land to eight ploughs. There is one villane
there and one sokeman and one bordar with two ploughs and one acre of meadow. Turchill held it in the time of King Edward, and it was valued at three
pounds, now ten shillings."

"Land of Robert Malet. Soke in Santum (Sancton) four carucates of land
and a half, it is in Wieftun (Weighton)."

"Land of Gislebert Tison. Manor. In Santune (Sancton), Norman had
fifteen carucates of land to be taxed. There is land to eight ploughs, three
Knights have of Gislebert themselves there one plough and a half, and six

Villanes and five Bordars, having two ploughs and a half. There is a priest and a church, and six acres of meadow. Three miles long and one broad. Value in King Edward's time, eight pounds, now fifty shillings."

The following references to the church are from Torre's manuscript.

"The Church of All Hallowes, of Saunton, was a rectory of mediates till 5 Ides of October, 1251, that Walter Gray, Archbishop of York, by reason of diversity of patrons, cessions of incumbents frequently happened, inasmuch that the rights of patronage did entirely devolve upon the priors, canons, and nuns of Walton, did consolidate the two heads into one church, and made the same presentible by the said prioress and convent of Walton for its future, and forasmuch as one mediety was then vacant by the death of Robert, the late rector thereof, and the other mediety was in the hands of Thomas de Stretton. The Archbishop then admitted to him the whole church, reserving out of it to the said nuns of Walton an annual pittance of five marks, payable by the rector for the time being at Pentecost and Martimas, by equal portions, which pittance of five marks was granted by the Archbishop to the said prior for ever. Afterwards, the Church of Saunton, being appropriated by Pope Clement to the prior of Walton, on 5 Ides July, 1310, Wm. de Grenfield, Archishop of York, ordained this vicarage therein, viz., that the portion thereof do consist of ten marks per annum, payable by the prior and convent to the vicar for the time being, being by them presentible at Michelmas and Easter by equal portions, and the vicar have assigned for his habitation a house with cartelge, and a croft adjoining containing one acre of land nigh the church, and on the west side of the rector's mansion, and that the said religious do as oft as need requires, repair and new build the chancel of the church, and find books and ornaments at their own cost, and pay ten shillings per annum to the archdeacon in the name of his procuration, the vicar bearing all other burdens, and these extraordinary to be divided between the said religious and vicar, according to the rate of their respective portions.—*Torre's Manuscript, p 1,123.*

LIST OF THE RECTORS OF SANCTON.

Temps Instit.	Vicarii Eccle.	Patroni.
1237	Thos. de Stretton	Prioress and Con-
1246	Ric de Saunton	vent of Walton.
1306	Roger de Heslarton	....

LIST OF THE VICARS.

Temp Instit.	Vicarii Eccle.	Patroni.
1310	Will Gere de Middleton	
1314	Girl de Beverlac.................................	
1325	Adam de Driffield	
	Adam de Craume	
1349	Johe de Birdsall............................	
1349	Will de Humandby	
1371	Patric Scott.................................. ...	
1383	Joh de Atte Brigg	....
1392	Robt. Hawton	
1398	Johe de Clarke	
1406	Rad. Hovton	
1420	Johe Day........................... ...	
	Thos. Selby.....................................	
1472	Thos. Kurr	
	Roger Garrard	
1512	Ed. Baxter	
1538	Thos. Norman	
1549	Rog. Lockwode	Archbishop of York

A CONTINUATION OF THE VICARS.

1661 ...	... R. Witty, B.A.
1663 ...	Ric Langdale
1673 ...	... R. Hopwood
1676 ...	... Joshua Daubney
1691	... ... Johe Bland
1704	... Joh'e Moold
1721 ...	... Jno. Clark
1768	... Tho. Stanton
1794	Thos. Atkinson
1835	Thos. Mitchell
1858	Andrew Ker
1865	C. K. Holt, B.A.

TESTAMENTARY BURIALS.

29th January, 1408.—John Langdale, of Houghton, to be buried in the Church

K

25th September, 1421.- William Cliff, of Cliff, to be buried against his parents in the church.

7th March, A.D. 1445.—John Day, Perpetual Vicar, to be buried in the Quire.

19th June, 1487.—Richard Langdale, Esq., of Sancton, to be buried in the church.

19th March, 1502.--Anthony Langdale, of Holton, Esq., to be buried in the church.

5th June, A.D. 1505. -Beatrix Greystoke, of N. Clyff, widow of Robert Constable, Serjant at Law, to be buried in the Quire.

7th November, 1509.—Thomas Kerr, Vicar, to be buried in the chancel, on the north side, by the wall side opposite to the horn of the altar.

21st October, A.D. 1540.—Thomas Nevill, of Saunton, to be buried in the church.

29th February, A.D. 1541.--Marmaduke Peter, of N. Clyffe, to be buried in the churchyard.

14th July, 1556.—Anthony Langdale. of Houton, Esq., to be buried in the church.

14th October, A.D., 1571.—Roger Lockwood, Vicar, to be buried in the church.

18th June, 1617.—Peter Langdale, to be buried in the church.

18th November, 1639.—Sir Marmaduke Langdale, of Dalton Knight, to be buried in the chancel amongst his ancestors.

The Church.

The church is situated on rising ground at the north end of the village. A few years ago it was rebuilt, in the early English style, with the exception of the tower, which is octagonal, and is of the perpendicular style of architecture. In the church are memorials of the Langdale family, and in the tower are three bells with the following inscriptions :—

" 1.　Sca trinitas unus deus.

2.　Gloria in altissimus Deo 1719.
　　Thos. Wauldby,　⎱
　　　　　　　　　　⎰Churchwardens.　　E. Seller.
　　Will Marshall,　　　　　　　　　　　Ebor.

3.　Gloriosa Post Tenebras Lvsem
　　Esg in Conspectv d m mors Sanctorvm Eive."

The pulpit and stalls are of oak, and the font is an octagon. The dimensions of the church are, nave 41ft. by 20ft 3in., chancel 28ft. 4in. by 21ft.

Houghton Hall is the seat of C. Langdale, Esq., J.P., the Lord of the Manor, who is a descendant of an ancient family. The mansion is spacious and stands in a well-wooded park ornamented by a fine sheet of water.

Sir Marmaduke Langdale, was knighted in the tenth year of Charles II., for the eminent services rendered by him to the King's father. Dugdale informs us that he raised three companies of foot, and a troop of seventy horse at his own proper charge, and engaged the Scots in Northumberland and put them to the worst. Afterwards he was Commander-in-Chief of those troops which the King sent from Oxford against that great rebel of Lincolnshire, Colonel Rossiter. After marching against Lord Fairfax and putting him to the rout, he retired to Pontefract Castle, at that time beseiged by a numerous body of the northern rebels. He adhered to the King's cause until the Parliamentary party became all powerful, when he was taken prisoner, but effected his escape and went beyond the sea, where, with great loyalty, he attended Charles the II. in his most low and desperate condition. In consideration of these services he was, by Letters Patent, bearing date at Bruges, in Flanders, upon the 4th of February, in the tenth year of His Majesty's reign, which was about two years preceding his restoration, advanced to the degree and dignity of a Baron of the Realm, by the title of Lord Langdale, of Holme-in-Spalding-Moor, and to the heirs male of his body. He married Lenox, the daughter of Sir John Rhodes, of Barlborough, in County Derby, Knight, and left by her, issue two sons, Marmaduke and Philip, the rest dying young, as also two daughters, Lenox and Mary, and departing this life at his house at Holme, 5th August, 1661, was buried at Sancton.*

THE JACKSON FAMILY.

In 1829, Thomas Jackson, a labourer, died at Sancton, aged 83, leaving behind him eleven children, three of whom (Thomas, Samuel, and Robert) became Wesleyan Ministers, and one the mother of the Rev. Jackson Wray, a popular minister in London. Thomas Jackson, one of the three sons referred to above, was twice elected President of the Conference, the highest official position in the Wesleyan Connexion. He was author of several works, and from 1842 to 1861 held the important post of Theological Tutor at the Richmond Theological Institute. From a most interesting volume of " Recollections of My Own Life and Times," by the Rev. Thomas Jackson, we make the following extracts :—

"In the days of my boyhood, the labouring people in Sancton were generally rude, ill-informed, profane, and superstitious. A young man, who died of consumption, remained several hours in his la t conflict, his mother being almost distracted. It was believed that his dying agonies were prolonged by feathers of pigeons in the bed upon which he lay ; and it was suggested that he would linger in a state of intense suffering till they were removed. The wife of a labouring man in the village was for several months in a declining state of health ; her husband and some of their confidential friends thought that she was bewitched, and suspected that a poor old widow, who lived in the neighbourhood, was the author of all the mischief. Having been instructed by some persons whom they thought to be wiser than themselves, as to the means by which they might detect and punish the witch, and effectually relieve the afflicted woman, they purchased of a butcher the heart of a slaughtered ox ; stuck as many pins into it as it could well contain ; used a form of incantation which they had carefully learned ; and then placed the whole close to a blazing fire. The process of roasting the heart full of pins was begun early in the evening, and continued till midnight ; and all this while it was supposed the witch felt as much pain

* Dugdale's *Baronage*, Vol. II., p. 476.

as if her own heart were full of pins, and burning before a fire. At twelve o'clock it was believed the witch could bear her pain no longer, would come to the house of the bewitched woman, beg in the most earnest manner for admission, confess her sin and ask forgiveness of the injured family. While the beast's heart was all but dried up before the fire, the hearts of all the party who were engaged in the punishment of witchcraft were full of wrath against the offender, whom they supposed to be in agonies of pain, and whose penitent confession they expected soon to receive. At last the desired hour arrived ; the incantations were finished, the clock struck twelve, and all listened to hear the shrieks and entreaties of the poor old widow at the door. No voice was heard. The aged woman, whom I distinctly remember, and who was as innocent of witchcraft as those who suspected her were of wisdom, was, I presume, fast asleep in her bed. So after several hours spent in high mental excitement, the party confessed themselves to be disappointed, and, like children who are afraid of ghosts and apparitions,

> ' To bed they creep,
> By whistling winds soon lull'd asleep.'

This account is no fiction ; for, as I happened to be in the confidence of the afflicted woman's husband, though I was then a youth, he related the whole to me as a profound and awful secret."

"It is a remarkable fact, that amidst all this ignorance and irreligion some vestiges of ecclesiastical discipline still lingered in the village. Two examples of public penance I remember to have witnessed. A farmer's son, the father of an illegitimate child, came into the church at the time of Divine service on the Lord's day, covered with a sheet, having a white wand in his hand ; he walked barefoot up the aisle, stood over against the desk where the prayers were read, and there repeated a confession at the dictation of the clergyman ; after which he walked out of the church. The other case was that of a young woman,

> ' Who bore unhusbanded a mother's name.'

She, also, came into the church barefoot, covered with a sheet, bearing a white wand and went through the same ceremony. She had one advantage which the young man had not, her long hair so completely covered her face, that not a feature could be seen. In a large town few persons would have known who she was ; but in a small village everyone is known, and no public delinquent can escape observation and the censure of busy tongues. These appear to have been the last cases of the kind that occurred in Sancton The sin was perpetuated, but the penalty ceased ; my father observed that rich offenders evaded the law, and then the authorities could not for shame continue to inflict its penalty upon the labouring classes."

PARISH REGISTERS &c.,

The Registers commence in 1538, but are deficient from 1641 to 1717.

The living is in the gift of the Lord of the Manor and is at present vacant.

The old Grammar School had an endowment of £20 annually. It was founded in 1610, by Marmaduke, First Lord Langdale, Baron of Holme-on-Spalding-Moor.

A new school was erected in 1872, at a cost of £600, as a memorial to the Rev. Thomas Jackson, who, as previously mentioned, was born in the parish.

There is also a small Wesleyan Chapel, built in 1840.

NORTH AND SOUTH CLIFF.

The townships of North and South Cliff (the former being in the parish of Sancton, and the latter in North Cave) are situated a little to the west of Sancton. There is a small church at South Cliff, which was built a few years ago at the expense of the late Samuel Fox, Esq.

From Domesday, it would appear that the land here belonged to the King, and it is stated that, to the Manor of Weighton belonged "the soke of one carucate in Clive (Cliff) which one plough might till."

We have no record of the owners immediately succeeding Domesday, but from Post Mortem Inquisitions we find that in fifty Henry III., Roger Merely died seized of the Manor of Cliff.

The present Lord of the Manor of South Cliff is Mr. C. Langdale, J.P.; Mr. W. H. Fox being Lord of the Manor of North Cliff.

HOTHAM.

OTHAM is a township, parish, and picturesque village, five and a half miles south-by-east from Market Weighton, and six miles from Brough.

Prior to the Norman Conquest, the Saxon owners of this parish appear to have been Grim, Ingrede, Turchil, Orme, Basin, and the Bishop of Durham, the latter holding three carucates of land. The Bishop afterwards continued to hold his portion; the King, one carucate; the Earl of Moreton, five carucates; and Robert Malet, three carucates. According to the pedigree of the Hothams, Sir John de Trehous, who fought with William at the battle of Hastings, had a grant of the Manor of Hotham. His descendant, Peter de Trehous, married Isabella de Turnham, by whom he had two sons, Peter and John, the former receiving his mother's estate at Mulgrave, and John, that of Hotham ; from that time the name of Trehous was abandoned, Peter taking the name of Maulay, and John that of Hotham. John de Hotham married a daughter of Baldwin de Wake, and had three sons, the youngest married a Grindall, and had a son, Geoffry de Hotham, who, in 1331, founded the monastery of St. Austin, called the Black Friars, in Hull.

The second son, William, was Prior Provincial of the Friar Preachers, and was a person of great piety and learning. He died at Dijon, and was buried in the Church of the Dominicans in London.

John, the younger, was ordained priest at York, in 1274, and held the living of Rowley, and that of Cottingham ; he was afterwards made Bishop of Ely, Treasurer of the English Exchequer, and, in 1319, became Lord High Chancellor of England. He died in 1336, and was buried in Ely Cathedral.

Peter, the eldest son of Sir John, married a daughter of Thomas Staunton, by whom he had several children. His eldest son, John, was created a Knight of the Bath, and he was also summoned as a Baron of the Realm, eighth Edward II. (1296). His grandson, John, married into the family of Stafford, and had an only child, Alice, who married twice. Her second husband was Sir John Trussel ; her first, Hugh le Despenser, son of Edward Despenser, who was executed by order of Queen Isabella, wife of Edward II., in 1326, and the family tradition is that Hugh, the husband of Alice, was also executed the same year. There were two children of this marriage, Hugh and Anna. The son Hugh died in the 48th of Edward III, and among the possessions which he held at the time of his decease, was the Manor of Hotham.* Our space will not

* Post Mortem Inquis.

permit of us following this noble family through their various
vicissitudes, but the history of Sir John and his connections with
the siege of Hull during the Civil War are well known.   The
direct line of the Hothams failed at the death of Sir John Hotham,
who died without issue in 1691, and it then reverted to a distant

The Effigies of the Right Worshipfull Sr John Hotham of
Hotham Governer of Hull A member of the Honble
House of Commons

SIR JOHN HOTHAM.
(From an Old Engraving).

cousin, Charles Hotham, but the whole of the property had been
left by the last Sir John to his mother at her free disposal.
Whether Sir John had any quarrel with him, or whether he regarded
half blood as no relationship, we are not able to say.   Fortunately, Lady Hotham was both high principled and unselfish,

and she immediately sent for Sir Charles, and told him she felt the
great responsibility laid upon her, and was anxious to do the best
for the family honour, as for her own immediate kith and kin. If,
therefore, he would marry her grand-daughter, Bridget Gee, she
would make over the whole estate to him, only retaining an
annuity of £300 for her life.

Sir Charles, who was a young officer of Dragoons, at once
acceded, not doubting of his success with the young lady, but,
to his surprise, on communicating to her his wishes, he was quietly
but firmly refused. Perplexed and crestfallen he returned to Lady
Hotham and told her what had occurred. She replied that she
learned, with great regret, the failure of what had been the cher-
ished wish of her heart, but, as she could not control another's
affections, and as he had shewn himself ready to comply
with her wishes, she was determined that the family should not
suffer, and therefore would make over the estate to him without
that condition, leaving him free to marry whom he pleased. But he
had a real affection for his young cousin, and, venturing to make
another appeal, he was at once accepted, in what language we cannot say, but in words which told him that while she would not
be his wife for mere mercenary considerations, she cordially
reciprocated the love which he so evidently entertained for her.*

The present Lord of the Manor is Colonel Clitherow, of
Hotham Hall, who is also principal owner of the soil.

The living is a rectory in the patronage of the Crown, and the
incumbency of the Rev. W. Cole, M.A.; it is rated at £10 0s. 7½d.,
and returned at £328 per annum. The tithes were commuted in
1839 for about £44, and there are about four hundred acres of
glebe land.

* *Heraldy of York Minster*, by the Very Rev. E. Purey-Cust, D.D., p. 199.

The church is dedicated to St. Oswald, and is of ancient foundation, the tower being of Norman work : round the lower stage is a belt of chevron work ; in the west face is a circular-headed doorway, and on the east side one of a similar type now hid by a gallery. The other parts of the church consist of a nave, chancel, and north chapel, but they have been so modernised as to merit little notice. The tower contains two bells inscribed as follows :—

1. " Gloria in Excelsis Deo."
2. " Gloria in Altissimus Deo, 1730."

MONUMENTS IN THE CHURCH.

" Sacred to the memory of the Reverend James Stillingfleet, M.A., nearly fifty-six years Rector of Hotham, lineally descended from the eminent Dr. Edward Stillingfleet, Bishop of Worcester. Unambitious of worldly distinctions, though a gentleman and a scholar, he made an early and entire consecration of his various talents to the sacred office of the Christian Ministry. To proclaim the glad tidings of salvation through the Cross of Christ, to inculcate sound doctrine, as it respects both faith and practice, and to discharge the arduous duties of his function, were at once his object and delight. Placed by the providence of God in this retired parish, he ministered nearly to the close of his life with fidelity, zeal, and affection, leaving his impressible discourses and his disinterested benevolence, and persevering efforts to promote the temporal and eternal welfare of his flock, to their grateful and lasting remembrance. He ended his pious life in peace, relying only on his Saviour's merits, December 19th, 1826, aged 85 years."

" Sacred also to the memory of Elizabeth, his wife, daughter of William Taylor, Esq., of Great Hadham, Herts, sister and co-heiress to William Taylor How, Esquire, of Stondon Place, Essex. The law of kindness written on her heart, the ornament of a meek and quiet spirit and the christian graces of humility and charity testified her sincere and unaffected piety, and endeared her in no ordinary degree to her friends during a protracted earthly pilgrimage : she died March 12th, 1832, aged 91 years, looking for the mercy of God unto eternal life, through the merits of her Redeemer. This tablet is erected by their only son, as a just tribute of filial affection and gratitude."

" Also a tablet to the memory of the Rev. Edward William Stillingfleet,

B.D., of Lincoln Coll., Oxford, 30 years curate of Hotham, and 10 years vicar of South Cave, died May 3rd, 1866, aged 84 ; and to Dorothy Cordelia, wife of the above, died 25th November, 1857, aged 54 years."

The following monuments are in the churchyard :—

"Here lies the body of Ann Fife, who died of three children, aged 34, which was the wife of Stephen Fife, and departed this life November the 13th, 1739."

"To record the pious life and impressive death, the steady churchmanship, and consistent conduct of Joseph Fife. A blind pauper but rich in faith, and exemplary in good works, who died February 13th, 1832, aged 86 years. This stone is erected by the Rev. E. W. Stillingfleet."

" In loving memory of John Edward Brooke, who died January 5th, 1858, aged 65. Also of Mary, his wife, who died April 12th, 1882, aged 80."

" In most loving remembrance of Elizabeth Denton, the dearly beloved and devotedly affectionate wife of William Denton, who entered into rest after a happy married life of forty years, on the 19th of January, 1874, aged 72 years."

"Also in loving memory of the above William Denton, who entered into rest, April 23rd, 1877, in the 77th year of his age."

" In loving memory of Elizabeth Cross (daughter of John and Rebecca Denton, and niece of Major General Cross, C.B.), who died November 22nd, 1877, in her 80th year."

LIST OF THE RECTORS, &c.

Torre gives the following list of rectors, with the testamentary burials :—

"In the town of Hotham were four carucates of land, held of the fee of Stuteville, whereof the Abbot of Meaux held five oxgangs, whereof St. John of Beverley held one carucate and one oxgang, and the Prior of Watton half a carucate, and the Templars one oxgang, and the Lord Manley the residue. The Church of St. Oswald, of Hotham, is an ancient rectory belonging to the patronage of the family of the Hothams, Kts., and is endowed with half a carucate of land."

RECTORS.

Temp Instit.	Vicarii Eccle.	Patroni.
1282	Will de Norfolkehin	John de Hotham ....
1308	Ric de Insula....................	....

Temp Instst.	Vicarii Eccle.	Patroni.
1319	Mansers de Marymion	....
1322	Robts. de Cotun......................	....
1340	Rich. de Wathe	....
1348	Johe de Wombewell	....
1350	Thos. de Melton	....
1351	Johe Mariscott de Ferriby	....
1362	Robt. de Sedgebrooke	....
13 ·	Thos. de Scardeburgh	John Trusils ....
	Rad Vel Ric Bursell	
1398	Thos. Martyn....................	Johanis Aske...............
1405	Robt. Biggesdill.......................	....
1425	Will Wright	Ric de Bellacomps ....
1431	Thos. Garlike...	Earl of Warwick ....
1434	Thos. Maskfield..	....
1436	Ric Whiteleaf.........................	....
1477	Thos. Oustby	Ric, Duke of Gloucester ...
1483	Thos. Atkynson	Ric III. ....
1512	Joh de Jordan Worsley...............	Hen. VIII. ....
1517	Thos. Worsley	... .
1539	Joh Loney	....
1606	Phil Lengs, B.A.	Jac Rex ....
1609	Rad Rokeby	....
1626	Robt. Lodington, M.A.	Chas. I. ....
1661	Joh Norton, M.A.	Chas. II.... . ...

CONTINUATION OF RECTORS TO THE PRESENT TIME.

Temp Instit.	Vicarii Eccle.	Patroni.
1670	Walt. Blakestone, B.A.	Charles II. .. ..
1709	John Reid, M.A.	Anne Reg. ....
1722	William Key, B.A.	Geo. I. ....
1752	John Branfoot, M.A..................	Geo. II. ....
1771	Jas. Stillingfleet, M.A.	Geo. III. ....
1826	Wm. Horne	Geo. IV........................
1844	Archer Thompson, M.A.	Victoria Reg....................
1857	Wm. Sabine, B.A........................	....
1868	G. A. Willan, M.A	....
1873	W. Cole, M.A.	....

TESTAMENTARY BURIALS.

31st October, 1431.—William Wright, Rector, to be buried in the church.

24th January, 1462.—Thomas Dobson, to be buried in the church.

5th September, 1498. —Rich. de Wressel, to be buried in the church.

28th July, A.D. 1554.—Job Moncton, of Hotham, to be buried in the church.

24th January, 1565.—Edmd. Skerne, of Hotham, Gent, in the church, near his brother.

4th May, 1620.—Nic Coplin, of Hotham, Gent, in the church.

6th April, 1670.—John Norton, of Hotham, Clerk, giving his soul, that particle of Divine breath, to Jesus Christ, and his body to be buried under the pulpit at Hotham.

PARISH REGISTERS, &c.

The Parish Registers for baptisms commence in 1706; for burials in 1709, and for marriages in 1711.

In the church is a board with the particulars of Anthony Rotherham's Charity, who, in A.D. 1653, gave to the overseers of the poor and their successors for ever, forty shillings for the use of the poor of Hotham, out of certain houses and lands in Hotham.

CHAPEL.

The Primitive Methodists have a neat little chapel in the village.

WALLINGFEN.

WALLINGFEN is a township on the Market-Weighton Canal, two miles west of North Cave, and eight miles east of Howden.

By an order of the Local Government Board, dated 21st December, 1880, detached parts of the parish of Balkholme, Bellasize, and Gilberdyke were amalgamated with the parishes of Newport, Wallingfen, and New Village, the newly created village taking the name of Wallingfen, containing 2,409 acres, and having, in 1881, a population of 862.

The ancient district called by the same name appears to have been of considerable extent, and to have comprised the greater portion of the low lands in this part of the country. Leland says "that this Fenne is communely caullid Waullyng Fenne: and hath many Carres of Waters in it: and is so bigge that a 58

Villages ly in and butting of it, whereof the most part be yn Houghden Lordship longging to the Bishop of Duresme : and part yn Harthil Hunderith. The Fenne is a sixteen miles in Cumpace, and is all of Houghdenshire." *

It would be interesting to know by whom these low lands were first reclaimed. Probably it may have been the work of the Romans, who, it is well-known, took great delight in agriculture, and were always anxious to instil the same fondness for this pursuit amongst the different people brought under their control ; and we have historical evidence of the great drainage works in some of the other fen districts of the country which were accomplished by the skill of the Roman Generals and Commanders. Dugdale tells us that " the Romans wore out and consumed the bodies and hands of the Britons in clearing woods and banking the fens."

The first notice we have met with referring to the drainage of this district is in the 23rd of Edward I. (1295), when Hugo de Cressingham and Jno. de Lithgreines were commissioned to view and repair the banks and ditches upon the River Ouse, from Cawode to Faxflete ; and in the 28th of the same reign, " upon information made by the land-holders of Brunkflet and Faxflet, that one, Peter Betard, and the townsmen of Beleby, had diverted the stream of Beleby Wathe out of its ancient channel, into the water course of Fulnathe ; and, likewise, that the inhabitants of Eastringtone and Portingtone had turned the course of those such waters, as passed near those towns, by several trenches, so variously, that upon any great rain they drowned the greatest parts of the lands adjacent : so that neither passengers could travel in the common road betwixt Beleby and Pokelington, nor the said men of Brunkflete and Faxflete, till and sow their low grounds,

* Leland's *Itinerary* (temp. Henry VIII).

or dig turf in the moor of Wallingfen, or depasture their cattle in the parts thereabouts; the King therefore assigned the before mentioned John de Lythegreyns, and Robert de Boulton, to view those places, and to redress the said nuisances." Dugdale also refers to many other commissions relating to this district, (which appears to have required almost constant attention), and amongst the names of the Commissioners occur those of Alexander de Cave, Peter d'Eyvill, John de Hotham, William de Vavasour, Peter de Saltmarshe, Thomas de Metham, Sir Robt. Constable, Thomas Bromflete and Henry le Scrope.

Dugdale further says "that the Commissioners had directions to do all things therein according to the law and custom of this realm, and the custom of Romney Marsh (which custom or ordinance was made in the 35th of Henry III), also to impress so many labourers upon competent wages to be employed in that work, as should be necessary for the same, considering the great and urgent necessity in expediting thereof, for preventing of further damage." *

From an old manuscript, in the possession of C. E. G. Barnard, Esq., of Cave Castle, the following interesting extracts from the rules relating to the government of the Fen are taken:—

"Anno 1425.—The Rules and Ordnance of ye Comon of Wallingfen, made in ye 3rd year of the Reign of K. Henry ye Sixt, as followeth:—

'Be it remembred that upon Tuesday, in ye first week of June, in ye year aforesaid, at ye hill called Yand Hill, on Wallingfen, in ye presents of Sr. Robt. Babthorp, Knt., Sir Henry Bromfleet, Kt., Thos. Metham, Jno. Aske, Thomas Portington, and John, his son; Thos. Saltmarsh, Alex. Lound, Edmond Lound, Wm. Moston, Richd. Santon and Robt. Santon, Esqrs., and all others, the comoners, of Wallingfen, there at that time assembled for the comonweal and good government of ye said Comon of Wallingfen. There was at that time Redd in old record written in these words, that is, that every comoner shall come on St Hellen's even, by noone, or a man for him, to take a reasonable place or

---

* Dugdale's *History of Imbanking and Draining*, p. 115.

L.

peice for Graving Torves in to serve him for that whole year within the aforesd. Comon, and if there be any man sicke or masterfise, or any reasonable excusation had wherefore he may not come after ye ordnance aforesaid, Let him come then to Four of the same pish, and let them Lymitt him a reasonable peice or place wch. is not taken in before, and that none shall grave but one torfe deepness in ye earth upon pain of every default, 3s. 4d., and also if any shall grave in the cart-gaits shall loose for every default, 3s. 4d., nor to grave within 40 foot of any highway or cart-gaite, as ye ordnance is, but he shall loose 3s. 4d. and that none shall grave any Peates, but he shall loose 3s. 4d. and his Peates, and that no man hold any Ballocked Horse on the said Common but he be above the age of two years and be 14 hand-fulls high, and that he payes 10 pence upon pain of forfeiture. And also that no outen men shall have any horse bease or sheep going upon ye said Common of Wallingfen upon pain of every Horse 12d., every bease 12d., and every five sheep 12d., and every swine so often as they are taken 4d., and that none shall grave any torves on ye Comon of Wallingfen, to sell the same upon pain to forfeit his torves, and for every loade 3s. 4d., and that none shall grave any torves or mowe any seaves upon Wallingfen after mid-summer and the 2nd of August upon pain of his Sithe and Spaid and 3s. 4d., and if any man shall . . . . any cattle or horses but his own he shall loose for every horse and for every bease 3s. 4d., also if there be any escape from Holme, Bursay, or Hotham, or from any other place they shall pay a penny to the drivers, and also if there come any Ballocked horses from whence soever they shall likewise pay a penny for them. And because this evidence was profitable, and of old time used without disturbance, as well in the tyme of Thomas Davill, John Davill, and Roger Davill, and others, their ancestors, as followeth, therefore it was ordered and fully concluded in the presence of ye abovesaid parties, that ye said old ordnances shall be kept confirmed, and in ye more plain Execution the sd. Thoms. Metham, Alexander Lound, Thos. Saltmarshe, Wm. Moston, and Richd. Santon were assigned surveyors of ye said Common, and other eight-and-fortie men of the 5 parishes belonging to the same to be governers of the sd. fen, as it is well knowne to all the comoners there.' "

At another meeting of the Commissioners held in the 8th year of the same reign (1430), the names of the Eight-and-forty Governors, with their several parishes, are given as follows :—

NORTH CAVE PARISH.

Robt. Canbuaye	Thos. Bridgisle	Gerrarde Webster	John Cooke
Thos. Ellerker	Thos. Mawer	John Jackson	John Comyn.

SOUTH CAVE PARISH.

Richd. Croppe	John Croft	Wm. Webster	Jno. Leadell
Will Pinder	Pet. Robinson	Rich Dudding	Jno. Webster
Rich. Elenor	Petr. Barnett	Robt. Tomlinson	Thos. Robinson.

HOWDEN PARISH.

Jno. Robinson	Thos. Mason	Allan Proudfellowe	Alex. Person
Thos. Barker	Thos. Johnson	Jno. Pigas	Thos. Maurod
Richd. Nelson	Abm. Person	Richd. Nelson	Jo. Proudfellowe

BLACKTOFT PARISH.

Jo. Harison	Rd. Harison	Jo. Williamson	Wm. Pinover
Jo. Jackson	Rd. Jackson	Thos. Skin	Rog. Carter

EASTRINGTON PARISH

Rd. Northabie	Thos. Cattell	Jo. Gofer	Wm. Cooke
Rd. Beadall	Wm. Smithson	Jno. Sowle	Wm. Taylor.

Regulations then follow much the same as those of the year 1425, with the addition " that no one shall gather any wool on ye common before sun rise nor after sun set, in pain of every default 6d., and who shall make any afray, or comit any blode wyte upon ye said common shall be amerced for an affray, 3s. 4d., and for blood wite, 6s. 8d."

In the sixth year of King Edward IV. (1467), the following cases were reported to the "Commissioners, and the forty-eight assembled for the weale of ye said Common."

"One, Henry Lounde, of South Cave, Gent., presumpteously pretended a title, and did make claim to be Chief Lord of Wallingfen, insomuch as he made a drift and did drive ye said Comon and wrongfully took away divers men's cattle, amongst whom he took away a Whye of one Jno. Brockels-bies, of Linton, that he witheld and kept wrongfully and delivered all other men's chatles again without any suit or pence paying or other charges for ye same, but afterwards, the cause and tytle being opened and made known unto the said Henry Lound, that he had neglegently done great wrong to the comoners. Then ye said Henr. Lound, freely of his own good will, sent into ye next Corte, to the 48 there, ye sum of 6s. 8d. for price and recompence of ye

said Whye, for then she was wanting and could not be found. And afterwards ye
said Whye was found and sent in at ye next Corte holden for Wallingfen, and
delivered to ye 48 to ye use of John Brockelsbie. She was sent in by Jo.
Bellingham. Richd. Darling, and Jo Painter, and those three men did offer to
be bound for ye said H. Lound, that ye said H. Lound, that he should never
pretend any title to ye said Comon any more, and ye said three men at ye
request of ye said H. Lound did openly there desire all ye comoners to for-
give him ye offence yt he had done, for he was very sorry for ye same, and yt
they wd. accept him as a comoner and no otherwaies. And whereas ye said
H. Lound did wrongfully take upon him to take cart-law for passage over a
bridge that lay over Skelfleet, of one, Rd. Tasker, of Gilberdyke, and one,
Richd. Smith, of Benetland, and divers others, ye said H. Lound doth acknowledge himself to have done wrong to ye comoners, and most earnestly
desired Mr. Ro. Sheffield, and one, Alex. Lound, to come to ye 48tie men, and
to deliver to them againe the said monies which he had taken wrongfully for
passage over ye said bridge, and then by them delivered to Edwd. Saltmarsh,
one of ye surveyrs, to ye use of ye said Robt. Tasker and Ro. Smith, who paid
for ye same wrongfully. There was also, in ye said yeare of K. Edward ye 4th,
presented by ye 48, one, Thos. Parker, of Gilberdyke, for that he delivered to ye
bayliff of Howden, two waife Bease that did belong to ye drift of Wallingfen, and
was done contrary to ye orders of Wallingfen, wherefore it is ordered and set
downe at that Corte that they should take two bease of ye said Thos. Parker's,
that he so delivered to ye full values of these two Bease, and moreover did
amerce him for his offence to the Comon.

   And whereas ye aforesaid H. Lound did demand to have duty of every
swine not ringed, and of those that did grave any torves. The said Alex.
Lound, and ye said Ro. Sheffield became sureties shat he shall never hereafter
clayme any tytle to the said Comon of Walling fen, nor covit any thing any way
under pretence of title to the said Comon more, but as all other comoners have."

   The manuscript gives a further account of the meetings of "the
48," held in various years of the reigns of Queen Elizabeth, King
James I , Charles I., and Charles II., but these chiefly refer to drainage, stocking of the common, and fowling and fishing. One or
two are of special interest.

   " Upon ye 18th day of Aprill, in ye 42nd year of Queen Elizth. a pain is
laid. That none shall lead any Turves or Seaves of the common in the night
time, in pain of every load 3s. 4d., and that none shall keep any goods of

Wallingfen but such as are housekeepers and be down lying and uprising within the Liberties for ye space of eight months in the year att ye least, in pain of everyone so offending to forfeit 39s. 11¾d., and yt none shall Raite any Hemp or Flax on any part of ye common, in pain of every default, 10s.

From the following entry it seems that wild fowl were taken by means of the decoy :—

"Att ye Court of ye 48th, holden ye 14th day of May, In ye 44th year of Queen Eliza, was sett down, That no manner of Person shall rob or steall any nett sett to take Fish, or to take any Fowle out of any man's Thinge, or out of any thing sett to take fowls in, in pain of every default 10s. The one third part thereof to the party accusing, an other third part to the party offended, and the other third part to ye benefit of ye Comoners."

There appears to have been a close time with respect to the taking of fish :—

"In ye 10th year of King Charles, att ye Court holden the first day of May, 1634, it was agreed and sett down, and there was a pain laid, That no Comonr shall Fish in ye Marrs before Mid-sumer Even, and that ye Surveyours shall have ye first draught."

The next entry refers to the shepherds and their dogs.

"That all ye Sheppards yt keep Sheep on Wallingfen shall keep their doggs in a string att their Belts, and not to suffer them to goe loose, but to take a sheep, and then to take them up again, in pain of every default, 6s. 8d."

The number of stock for each commoner is set forth in the following :—

"And that no Commoner shall have above ye number of 160 Sheep Gates in Horse, Beasts, and Sheep, one half to be stocked with sheep, ye other half wth mares, geldings, and beasts, according to 7 sheep gates for one horse, and 5 sheep gates to a beast, and that Foals of 2 years old shall go two to a horse gate, and that calves of two yeares old shall go two to a Beast gate. In pain for every horse and two foals more than the sd number, Five Shillings, and every Beast and two Calves, in like manner, 3s. 4d.'"

A case occurs in 1665, where some of the Commissioners were fined for non-attendance :—

"Oct. 9th, 1665, at ye Court, then held before George Metham and Henry Portington, Esqrs.—Phil. Moneton, Kt., Phil. Saltmarsh, Walter

Bethel, and John Belton, esqrs., were all four amerced 3s. 4d. each, for absenting, and having neither sent or shewn their legal excuses—but not having been summoned as by ye orders are beforehand were acquitted."

In 1666 there is a most interesting entry, from which it appears the Court felt no little pride on account of its lengthy history. The minute is as follows :—

"Octr. 8, 1666.—The Court or Congregation of Wallingfen hath been kept after ye same order and form that it now is (as is recorded, anno 1652) ever since ye 4th yeare of K. Henry 6th, wch is this year 240 years in June last past without impeachment or controulment of any person or persons whatsoever, as by ye ancient Rowles, Books, and Proceedings at every Court will appear.

George Belt."

The next two entries refer to commoners who had ceased to reside within the district :—

"31st May, 1681, at ye Court, held by adjournment, it is ordered yt whereas Wm. Bethell, esqr., formerly elected a Surveyor, he having no common right, therefore it is ordered by ye Court, he to have all ye common right his ancestors formerly had or enjoyed."

"9th Octr., 1682, an order was made for Robt. Monckton, Esq,, of Newbald, who was elected ye 8th of May 1679, to have no common right, whilst he lived at Newbld."

The Court had a special method of dealing with bachelors, as will be seen from the next entry :—

"14th Oct., 1754.—That a Bachelor, who is not a housekeeper, shall not stock the Comon, in pain for every horse and Beast and every 5 sheep for every 10 days, each 1s."

By an Act of Parliament, passed in 1777, the Fen (which contained about 3,000 acres), was divided in allotments amongst the commoners of the following forty-eight townships, formerly enjoying right of stray upon it, viz :—

HOWDEN PARISH.—Flatgate in Howden, Skelton, Sand Hall, Saltmarsh, Cotness, Metham, Thorntoffe, Yorkefleet, Laxton, Kilpin, Trandike, Newland, East Linton, West Linton, Balkolme, Duncoats, Belby, and Thorpe. 18.

EASTRINGTON PARISH.—Eastrington, Portington, Burland, Cavill, Owsthorpe, Hithe, Spennffie, Sandholme, Gilberdike, Bennetland, Greenoak, Bellasize, part of Newland et Warwicks.—13.

BLACKTOFT PARISH.—East Blacktoft, West Blacktoft, Staddlethorpe, Clementhorpe, Scalby, Newton, Thornton House, Thorntonland, and Gowthorpe.—9.

SOUTH CAVE PARISH.—South Cave, Provence, Bromfleet, Faxfleet, Faxfleet Hall, Oxmardike, and Boothby Garth.—6.

NORTH CAVE PARISH.—North Cave and Everthorpe.—2.   Total, 48.

Our illustration represents an old house, still standing, which retains the name of " Eight-and-Forty." The upper portion of

THE " EIGHT-AND-FORTY " HOUSE, WALLINGFEN.

this house was re-built a hundred years ago, of brick. The lower portion, which is of stone, is without doubt, part of the house in which the Governors of the Fen formerly held their meetings.

An Act of Parliament was obtained in 1772, for "draining and preserving the commons, low grounds, and cars in the Parish of Market-Weighton, and other adjacent parishes in the East Riding, of the County of York, and for making a navigable cut or canal from Market-Weighton to the River Humber."

The township contains a bed of clay, which is probably

superior to any in the East Riding, and the numerous brick and tile yards, some of which have commodious wharves on the canal, give employment to a large number of the inhabitants.

CHAPELS.

The Wesleyan Chapel, erected in 1814, is a neat and commodious structure, and has a burial ground attached.

There is also a small Roman Catholic Chapel.

The Primitive Methodists are at present erecting a chapel and school-room.

BOARD SCHOOL.

A board school and schoolmaster's house were erected a few years ago, and are substantial buildings.

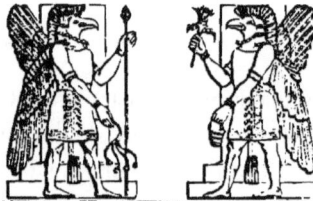

THE WALMSLEY MEMORIAL CHAPEL, NEWPORT-WALLINGFEN.

Primitive Methodist Chapel.

The "Walmsley Memorial Chapel" is situated in the main street, adjoining the board schools, and is an imposing structure.

It is in the Gothic style, built of white bricks and stone dressings, and measures 48ft. by 26ft. inside.

The interior wood-work is pitch pine, with open pews, to accommodate about 250 persons. The entrance is from a side porch surmounted by a tower and spire 65ft. high.

There is a convenient schoolroom, at the rear of the chapel, measuring 26ft. by 18ft. ; and, projecting from the schoolroom, are two class rooms.

The cost of the chapel itself was borne by three brothers, Messieurs John, William, and Benjamin Walmsley, of Leeds, who were born in this village.

The buildings were formally opened December 3rd., 1891

EASTRINGTON.

EASTRINGTON is about three-and-a-half miles east from Howden, and has two railways passing near, the North Eastern Railway on the south, and the Hull and Barnsley on the north.

"The Bishop of Durham held in Eastrington six Carucates of land by Baronage of the King in Capite. The chapel here belonged to the patronage of the Prior and Convent of Durham, together with Ecclesiastical profits of the whole town, which was appropriated to them, with right of Sepulture of the parishoners, in A.D. 1230. And on the 3rd Ides of March, A.D. 1227, the Archbishop of York, by the assistance of Fulke Basset, parson of the Church of Howden, and of the Prior and Convent of Durham, patrons hereof, granted and confirmed unto Walter, of Kirkham, Clerk, all the tythes pertaining to the Chapel of Eastrington, in name of a simple benefice, without cure of Souls and Episcopal burdens, rendering yearly to the said parson of Howden and his successors as a pension. 3 Bezantes on the feast of St. Martin. On the 6th Kal Martii, A.D., 1267, the Archbishop ordained and granted to the prior and convent of Durham this Chapel of Eastrington, and instituted therein a ppetual vicarage for ye vicar thereof to reside, and have for his sustenance a convenient portion out of the fruits of the same. The 1st fruits of the vicarage were £12 9s. 7d." *

CATALOGUE OF THE VICARS OF EASTRINGTON.

Temp Instit.	Vicarii.	Patroni.	Vacat.
14th June, 1318	Robt. de Heyington	Prior and Convent	....
1325	Johe de Misterton	of Durham.	Res.
1325	Hen. de Lymington	Idem	....
1330	Ric de Horton	....	....
	Thos. Skywyn		
1353	Ric de Kyngham		Res.
1353	Tho. de ———		....
1398	Walt. Thurstanton		
1401	Wm. de Almondbury		Res.
1410	Johes Coune		Mort.
1436	Ric Whitgift		Res.
1436	Johes Haryngton		Mort.
1460	Tho. Burneby		Mort.
1474	Wm. Wryght.........		Res.
1479	Tho. Aliceeup		Mort.
1487	Johes Hamylton		Mort.
1491	Richd. Fayrfax		Resig.
1492	Robt. Banys		Resig.
1505	Rogr. Darley		Resig.
1509	Johes Atkynson.............		Mort.
1549	Will Stapulton		....
1554	Ric Yatts	Phillip and Mary ...	Mort.
1587	Wm. Gibson	Reg. Elizabeth	Resig.
1616	Timy. Forde	Miss Warton	....
1620	Jac. Binkes...................	Rex Jac	Mort.
1640	Johes Trotter	Rex Charles	....

TESTAMENTARY BURIALS.

Apud Manet de Portington, 20th November, A.D. 1457.

* Torre's *Peculiars.*

Elene, late wife of John Portington, late one of the Justices of the King's Bench, made her will, proved 22nd April, 1458, giving her soul to God Alm., St. Mary, and All Saints, and her body to be buried in the Church of St. Michael's, of Eastrington, juxta Howden.

1 Jan., A.D. 1562, Robt. Smyth, of Cavill, labourer, made his will, proved 15th Feb., 1562, to be buried in ye psh. Ch. of Eastrington, in the North Isle, near the place where he was accustomed to sit.

3rd August, 1589. Leonard Dent of Eastrington, Merchant, made his will, whereby he bequeathed his soul to God Alm., his Saviour and Redeemer, and his body to be buried in the N. Aisle of the Chu·ch, appointing a large stone set upon 6 pillars, to be laid upon him and his wife, Margaret Dent, buried ye 6th of August, 1589, Merchant Adventurer, and the Arms of the Merchants largely graven with the Posie belonging to them in the midst, and the name of his sister, Alice Wetherall, buried ye 1st Aug., 1589. He bequeathed £20 a year for ever, for to have 4 sermons preached quarterly, the first to be on the 1st Sunday in August.

10th Jany., 32nd of Elizabeth (1590), Richard Aske, of Osthorpe, gent., to be buried in his Chapel, called St. Saviour's Chapel, under the northernmost tomb, where his wife lyeth, which is in the Parish Church of Eastrington.*

THE CHURCH.

The Church is dedicated to St. Michael, and consists of nave, north and south aisles, chancel, north and south chapels, a tower at the west end, and a south porch. The tower is of three stages, and is of good masonry, surmounted by pinnacles and embattled. There are four large belfry windows of two lights each. In the lower stage is a west doorway—now blocked up. On the west face of the tower, on the second stage, are shields of the Aske and Portington families, and other shields on the upper stage. The date of the present church is about the middle of the fifteenth century, and was probably built by Judge Portington, or his father, although there are indisputable proofs in the interior of the building

* Torre gives many more Testamentary Burials which we are obliged to omit for want of space.

that the present church succeeded one of an earlier date, from portions of chevron work which have been used up in the present building, and in the wall of the porch is a sculptured stone of Saxon, or very early workmanship, and we learn from Domesday that a church existed here with a priest, when that survey was made. The interior of the church is spacious, the nave is about forty feet long by twenty feet wide, exclusive of the aisles; the chancel forty-five feet by sixteen feet wide, and the nave is divided from the chancel by a pointed arch. The tower arch is a plain semi-circular one. The floor of the chancel is raised from the other part within the altar rails, which are of oak, and came from Howden Church. An old oak chair and credence table form part of the furniture. On the chair on a brass plate is the following inscription :—"This chair and credence bracket were made out of the remains of an ancient seat, supposed to have been in this parish church upwards of five hundred years, Easter, 1883, G. S. Dunbar, Vicar; Matthew John Nurse, Alfred Hairsine, Church-wardens." A new east window has been placed in the chancel. On each wall are the remains of circular arches, and on the north wall are grotesque carvings of Norman character; probably part of the roof cornice of the old church, before the existence of the Clerestory. The chancel fell down in the early part of the seventeenth century, and, in its fall, partly destroyed the fine monuments of the Portingtons. Between the clerestory windows is a tablet, with the following inscription :—"This chancel fel in, Anno Domino, 1632, and this is bilded the same yeare, by Sir Michael Wharton, of Beverlie high lodge." The restoration spoken of in the inscription was carried out on the north side by a massive pillar of oak, supporting oak beams cut in the form of pointed arches to support the clerestory wall, the oak of which, according to an entry in the churchwardens' account book, came from Spalding Moor. The Aysthorpe chapel is on the north side of the chancel, and has contained some fine brasses, but they are gone Tradition says the spoliation was by Cromwell's soldiers when on their march from Hull to Howden and Wressle, and we met with something of this tradition whilst making the drawing of the tomb of Judge Portington. A little fellow came to us and gravely asserted that the head of the lady was shot off by one of Oliver Cromwell's big cannons, and on our not being willing to believe his account, he turned away very indignant at our infidelity. On the opposite side of the chancel is the Portington Chapel, and on an altar tomb are the effigies of Judge Portington and his lady, the head of the latter being broken away, and that of the Judge considerably damaged. It is of large proportions, measuring nearly eight feet in length, and it is peculiar, the hair being done up in pigtail form, with the end doubled up under the head. It is said that there is only one other pigtailed monument known, and that is in the Cathedral of Chichester. On the floor of the Chapel are some flag stones of alabaster containing figures of Knights and of a lady, about the time of Edward I. Another stone has on it a shield sculptured with steps and a cross, decorated with a fleur-de-lis and supposed to belong to a Battdyle, the heiress of which family married a Portington, about 1250. There is another stone around which is a Latin inscription, much of it is worn away, but sufficient remains to shew that it belonged to one of the members of the Furnival family ; this stone is a palimpset, having been appropriated by one of the Portingtons whose inscription in the centre is : "Here resteth the body of Michael Portington, of Portington, Esq., who married Barbara, the second daughter of Garvis Nevill, Esq., departed this life without issue the 17th of

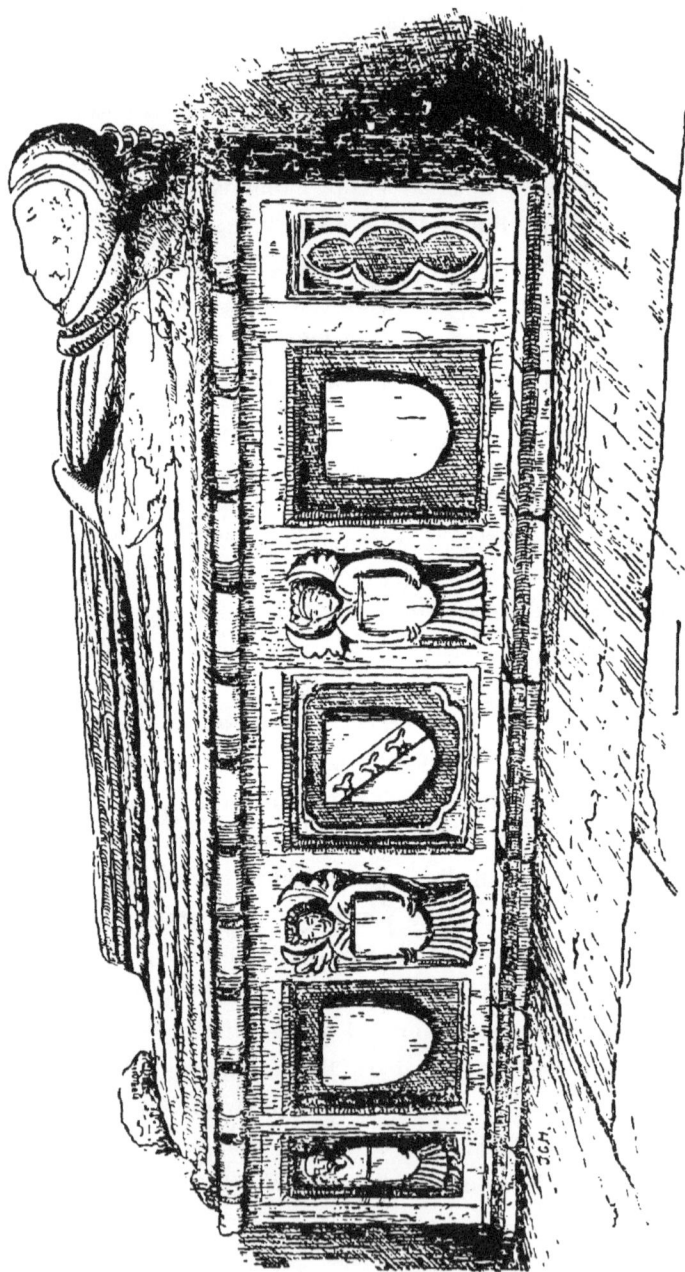

TOMB OF JUDGE PORTINGTON, IN ST. MICHAEL'S, EASTRINGTON.

March, in the 32nd year of his age, Ano dni 1696." There are also in this chapel several monuments of the family of Bell, also of Portington. On one of them is the following inscription :

" In memory of Henry Bell, of Portington Grange, Esq., who died July 3rd, 1839, aged 71 years. He was the eldest son of Henry Bell, Esq., of Portington Grange, by Mary, his second wife. His character combined integrity of principle and soundness of judgment, with amiability of temper, and his sincere piety and highly cultivated mind qualified him to sustain among the Wesleyan Methodists in his own locality, the duties of a Christian Minister, with zeal perspicuity and effect, enhanced by the uniform consistency of his life."

The Portington Chapel also contains three fine brackets, two of them enriched with dog-toothed ornaments. The Aysthorpe Chapel has a piscina and aumbrey. The font is octagonal.

The tower contains three fine toned bells, on which are these inscriptions : –

1st Bell.—Populum voco Deum Laudate. 1718.
2nd ,, Soli Deo Gloria pax Homnibus. 1663.
3rd ,. Sum Rosa pulsata mundi maria vocato.

The latter is a pre-Reformation bell.

PARISH REGISTERS.

The registers commence in 1563, and are almost perfect. There are some curious entries, especially the list of Anabaptists, buried in their own closes and orchards, collected by the vicar at that time, and preserved with the other registers. We extract the following from the list :—

" A Register of Dissenters who dyed and were buried in closes or orchards, 1695.

Mary Barker, of Gilberdike, widow, buried in a close, Jany. 12th, Anno Domini, 1697.

Envlle Coterill, of Gilberdike, buried in a close. Decr. ye 21. An affidavit made.

Daniel Raspin, of Gilberdyke, buried Jany. ye 13th, 1699.

Samuel Raspin, of Sandholme, buried and affidavit made 20th Jany., 1699.

Simon, son of Robert Gyliot, of Hive, buried May ye 8th, 1700, and affidavit made.

1702. Mary, wife of William Ramsay, of Gilberdyk, buried June ye 29. Buried in owne close.

John, son of Noah Ellashore, buried in orchard, Jany. ye 5th, 1702.

Ann, daur. of Willm. Carline, of Sandholme, Feby., 23rd. Buried in owne close. An affidavit made, 27th.

One, son of John Turner, of Gilberdike, buried in owne close.

1704.—One, son of Francis Holt, of Hive, buried in a close, June ye 7th, and called Richard, as he saith.

One, son of Willam. Jacks, of Ousney, buried in owne close, called Thomas, as he saith.

1705.—Mary, wife of John Byas, of Gilberdike, buried in owne close, April ye 18th. 1705.

A REGISTER OF YE ANABAPTIST BIRTHS.

Hanna, daur. of Cornelius Smithson, born Jan. 27th, 1714.

Hannah, dau. of Robert Gilliot, born 31st, August 1715.

Willm., ye son of George Twidal, born Mar. 25th 1715.

Elyzth, ye dau of Rich. Hole, of Hive, was born May 20th, 1715.

Thomas, son of Richd. Hornsey, born Oct., 20, 1723,

Elyzth. Smithson, daughter of Cornelius Smithson, of . . . . born Aug. 18, 1727."

CHARITIES.

"The free school, founded by Joseph Hewley, by will, dated 14th March, 1726, for the poor children within the parish, to be taught reading, writing, and the Church Catechism. Endowment, 12a., 1r., 39p. of land, let at the time of the report for £28 per annum.

John Atkinson's Charity, by will dated 8th November, 1678, rent charge of £8 per annum, to the deserving poor, in sums from 1s. to 5s. each person.

Burton's Gift, rent of one acre of land to poor persons, in sums from 2s. to 6s., each person.

Waterson's Gift, rent-charge of £1 per annum, to poor persons who attend church at the four great festivals." *

ANCIENT COATS OF ARMS, &c.

Glover gives the following list of coats of arms and monuments in the Church at his Visitation in 1584:

"These 3 graven in Stone without the Churche :

XIII. "On a bend 3 birds."

XIV. ——" 3 bars, an annulet for difference."

XV. "A bend flory."

On a Toombe Stone :—

XVI. "5 fusils in fesse."

XVII. "—— 3 bars, an annulet for difference, Aske, impailing on a pale argent a luce's head erased couped ——Gascoinge."

About the Toombe of Judge Portington, These 4 :—

XVIII. "—— 3 birds ——."

XIX. "——on a bend 3 birds."

XX. "—— 5 fusils in fesse, a label of five points ——."

XXI. "A bend between 6 martlets."

XXII. "An escochen gules, on a bend argent 3 Cornish choughs ppr. Crest :—over a helm mantled purpure, on torce argent and gules, a goat's head couped argent.

Hic jacet Thomas de Portington, armiger, et Agnes uxor eius qui obiit Dni MCCCCXXVII."

XXIII. "Upon a Toombe stone no arms, but the goat's head lying under his head.

Orate pro animabus Nicholai de Portington Militis, qui istam Capellam fieri fecit. No date."

XXIV.—"'Graven in Wood upon a Pewe.' Quarterly 1 and 4, a chevorn between 3 hind's heads, ——2 and 3 a chevorn between 3 mullets ——" Abbot of Bellasis."

These six in a glass Windowe in the Church aforesaid :—

XXV. "Or 3 bars azure."

XXVI. "Or 3 bars azure with an annulet for difference."

XXVII. "Quarterly 1 and 4 or a lion rampant azure, 2 and 3 gules 3 lucies hauriant argent."

* Charity Commissioners' 11th Report, p. 734.

M

XXXVIII.   " Or a lion rampant azure a label of three points gu."
XXIX.   " Azure 5 fusils in fesse argent."
XXX.   " Or on a chief gules 3 plates."

Arms.—Gules on a Bend Argent 3 Cornish Choughs Beaked and numbered of the first.

Pedigree of Portington of Portington, and Sawcliffe County Lincoln.

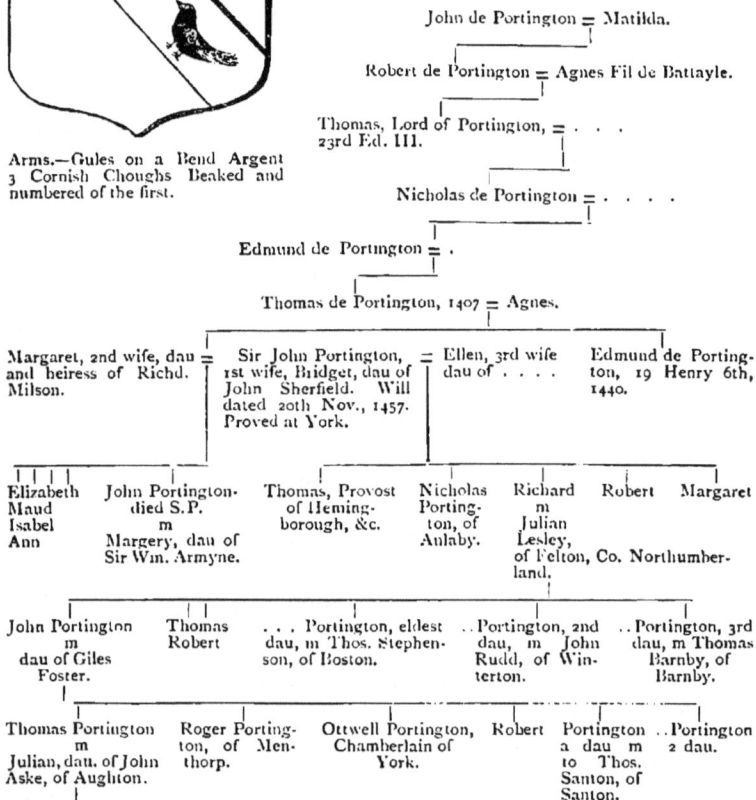

John de Portington = Matilda.

Robert de Portington = Agnes Fil de Battayle.

Thomas, Lord of Portington, = . . . 23rd Ed. III.

Nicholas de Portington = ...

Edmund de Portington = .

Thomas de Portington, 1407 = Agnes.

Margaret, 2nd wife, dau and heiress of Richd. Milson. = Sir John Portington, 1st wife, Bridget, dau of John Sherfield. Will dated 20th Nov., 1457. Proved at York. = Ellen, 3rd wife dau of . . . .   Edmund de Portington, 19 Henry 6th, 1440.

Elizabeth Maud Isabel Ann   John Portington-died S.P. m Margery, dau of Sir Wm. Armyne.   Thomas, Provost of Hemingborough, &c.   Nicholas Portington, of Anlaby.   Richard m Julian Lesley, of Felton, Co. Northumberland.   Robert   Margaret

John Portington m dau of Giles Foster.   Thomas Robert   . . . Portington, eldest dau, m Thos. Stephenson, of Boston.   . . Portington, 2nd dau, m John Rudd, of Winterton.   . . Portington, 3rd dau, m Thomas Barnby, of Barnby.

Thomas Portington m Julian, dau. of John Aske, of Aughton.   Roger Portington, of Menthorp.   Ottwell Portington, Chamberlain of York.   Robert   Portington a dau m to Thos. Santon, of Santon.   . . Portington 2 dau.

Continued next page.

Continued from previous page.

Henry Portington, of Portington and Sawcliffe, Co., Lincoln. m Matilda, dau of Sir Robt. Tyrwhitt.	Thos. Portington. of Easthorpe m Alice, dau of Johnson, wid. of Leonard Carter.	Anthony George Richard	Julian Anne Margaret Elizabeth	daus	.. Portington, m to Girlington.

Robert Portington.

John Portington m Anne, dau of John Langton.	George m Cassandra dau of Peck.	Thomas Richard Robert	Elizabeth Portington m to Truesdale, secondly to Robert Leedes, of Laceby, Co. Lin.	Anthony Portington of Winteringham, Co. Lincoln.	Julian Portington m to Alex. Nevill, of South Leverton, Co. Notts.

Edward　　Katherine.　　Mary.

Michael Portington, of Portington, living in 1612.　m Ann, dau. of Edward Beaumont.	Thomas Portington m Elizth. Skipwith, dau of Sir W. Skipwith of Ormesby, Kt.	George Edward Roger Ralph John	Joan, m first to Michael Wharton, and secondly to Ralph Rokeby; buried 14 June, 1608.	Rose Julian Elizabeth Francis Katherine

Michael Portington m Dorothy, dau. of Geo. Wentworth.	Joan Anne	Henry Portington, living in 1612. m	John	Ann, wife of John Skypwith, of Ormesby.	Elzth. Frances	Ursula Portington, m to Alexander Vavasour, of Spaldington.

Mary, m Wm. Grier, d 1673.	Elizabeth, m Wm. Blyth.	Dorothy Portington, m Wm. Bosville	Michael Portington of Portington m Barbara, dau. of Gervase Nevill, from whom descend the Nevills of Skeldbroke.	John Henry Grace Anne Dorothy Jane

THE PORTINGTON FAMILY.

The seat of this ancient County Family was situated at the hamlet of Portington, about a mile from Eastrington, where they were located for a period of four hundred years. The moat which surrounded the mansion may yet be seen, but no portion of the original building now remains.

Sir John Portington, the 7th mentioned in the above pedigree, and whose effigy is given in the engraving, was appointed a King's Serjeant on the 17th April, 1440 ; Justice of Assize in Yorkshire, in 1441 ; Judge of the Common Pleas, in 1444 ; and of the King's Bench, 1452. He was executor of Ralph Cromwell, Lord Treasurer of England, who died January, 1455. He died 1456.

Thomas Portington, M.A., his son, by his third wife, Ellen, was Provost of Hemingborough, 1457-71 ; Canon, 1447; Treasurer of York, 1477-85 ; mentioned in the will of Archbishop Booth, dated 28th September, 1479 ; admitted of Corpus Christi, 1482 ; and Rector of Goodmanham, which he resigned in 1480. He died in 1485, a Clerk in the King's Exchequer. Will dated 12th September, 1491.

GILBERDIKE.

Gilberdike is a township and large village, partly in Eastrington parish, on the high road from North Cave to Howden, being six miles from the latter place.

The township is generally alluded to in old records as "Dyk," from the ditch called Haunsar-damme.

In 1191, there was a fine between Philip, Bishop of Durham, and John, of Crigleston, his tenant, concerning amongst other lands, "120 acres juxta terram Mareschalli, between the fosse of Gilbert Haunsard, and the fosse of Grenaie."

In 1 Hen. IV. (1399), "a commission was issued to Laurence de Allerthorpe, one of the Barons of the Exchequer, Sir Thomas Metham, Will. Gascoigne, Robert Thyrwhyt and others, for the view and repair of the banks, ditches, &c. betwixt the town of Pokelingtone and the Rivers of Humbre and Derwent, before whom the Jurors presented that the watercourse called Blacktoft damme, otherwise Haunsardamme, which reacheth from Foulnay to the river of Ouse, was then obstructed and ought to be repaired by Richard Haunsard, and the town of Blaktoft for their lands in Blaktoft; and that the same ought to be XVI feet in breadth and VIII feet in depth. Whereupon the shireeve had command, &c. And they farther presented that the said Richard Haunsard ought to repair the same chanel from Haunsardamme to Foulnay unto the south end of Gylberdyke, and therefore that he was amerced."

There are in the village, places of worship for the Wesleyans and Primitive Methodists.

The burial-ground, formerly used by the Society of Friends, is now occupied by Mr. William Terry.

BLACKTOFT.

LACKTOFT is a township, parish, and village on the bank of the River Ouse, near its junction with the rivers Trent and Humber.

The church was re-built in 1841, and has chancel, nave, small vestry, organ-gallery, porch, tower, and three bells. The living is a vicarage in the gift of the Dean and Chapter of Durham. The tithes belong to the Ecclesiastical Commissioners.

The registers date from the year 1702.

The Wesleyan Methodists have a chapel with Sunday school attached.

C. W. Empson, Esq. is Lord of the Manor, and chief landowner.

In the year 1551, King Edward VI., for the sum of £277 2s. 8d., granted unto Walter Jobson, of Kingston-upon-Hull, Merchant, and his heirs and assigns, for ever, all his rectory and the Church of Brantingham, together with the chapels of Blacktoft and Ellerker, formerly belonging to the dissolved Monastery of Durham ; and in 1561, a fine is recorded "between Wilfrid Brand and George Fissher, Plaintiffs, and Walter Jobson, senr., Deforciant, relating to a Messuage with lands in Blacktoft, Ellerker, Brantingham, als. Brantinehm and Wakefeld, the rectory of Brantingham, and the free chapells of Blacktoft and Ellerker ; and a messuage, &c. in Kyngeston-upon-Hull, which, after a term of 40 years, remain to Walter Jobson, the son of Walter Jobson, senr." *

SCALBY.

Scalby is a township in the parish of Blacktoft.   Leland in his *Itinerary*, says :—" From North Cave to Scalby a three miles, al by low Marsch and medow ground, leving the Arme of Humbre on the lift Hond yn sighte."

Scalby was formerly a place of some importance, as is evident from the frequent references to it in old records.

Cheapsides, formerly an extra-parochial place on the common of Bishopsoil, has lately been included in the township of Scalby, by an Order of the County Council.

THORNTON HOUSE.

Thornton Manor House Farm in this township, the property of Mr. G. E. Weddall, formerly belonged to Thornton Abbey, in Lincolnshire.   The Thornton Estate, in Faxfleet and Scalby, passed into the hands of the Crown at the dissolution of the monasteries

A fine of the year 1557, between Peter Carewe, Knight, and Walter Haddon, plaintiffs, and Thomas Hennage and Ann, his

* Feet of Fines, 3 Eliz.

wife, deforciants, included forty messuages, with lands in Blacktoft, Scalby, and Newton. The Feet of Fines for 1574, records an information by Queen Elizabeth as plaintiff, against Thomas Hennage, Esq., and Ann, his wife, deforciants, concerning "the manor of Fauxflete, alias Thornton-houses and fifty messuages, with lands in Fauxflete, Thornton, Scalbye, and Blacketofte."

In 1760, Hugh Montgomery was the owner of the estate, which, in 1777 was sold by Sir Geo. Montgomery Metham, M.P.

STADDLETHORPE.

Staddlethorpe is a hamlet within the parish, and has a Station on the Hull and Selby Railway.

FAXFLEET.

AXFLEET a township and village, nine miles east from Howden, formerly part of the Parish of South Cave, but severed from it some years ago.

The Knight Templars at one time held the manor, and had a preceptory here. These preceptories were manors or estates, where erecting churches for the service of God and convenient houses, the Knight Templars placed some of their fraternity, under the government of one of those more eminent Templars, who had been, by the Grand Master, created "Preceptores Templi," to take care of the lands and rents in the neighbourhood, and so were only cells to the principal house at London.

The decree abolishing the Order of Knight Templars in England was promulgated by Archbishop Greenfield, from Cawood, on the 14th of August, 1312. Previous to the promulgation, their estates had been taken into the possession of the Crown, and custodians appointed to them. Adam de Hoperton was the first custodian of Temple Newsam ; he was appointed immediately after the seizure of the Templars' goods, and his term of office expired on the 1st of December, 1311, when he placed his charge in the care of Sir Alexander de Cave and Robert Amecotes. In 1323, the King appointed Humphrey de Waleden and Richard de Ikene, seneschals of the castles and towns of Tykhill and Scarborough, and keepers of the Park of Heywra and the Manors of Faxflete, Carleton, Hachelsey, Temple Hurst, Barley, Sandall, and Temple Newsam, with their respective appurtenances, in the County of York. These manors all belonged to the Templars, and such an arrangement seems to indicate that, when it was made, none of them had fallen into the possession of the Hospitallers, though they certainly held them in the following year (1324), when Thos. de Deyville * was appointed custodian. †

In the 1st year of Edward III. (1327), this manor (with all its members in North Cave, South Cave, Hotham, Cliffe, Yverthorpe, and Sancton), which formerly belonged to the Templars, had reverted to the King, and in the same year we find the manor was held by John de Mowbray, who had been Sheriff of Yorkshire, in 1316.

"In the 12th of Edward III., Ralph de Nevill, taking into consideration

The Deyvilles were an old family, the Lordship of Adlingfleet having been given by William the Conqueror to one of his followers, "John de Avill." In 1277, the Bishop of Durham gave Whitemoor Farm, at Hemingborough, to "Emeric d'Eyville." There the Deyvilles built a house, and were people of consequence, being connected in various ways with the Bishops of Durham. John Deyville, the third of that name, in an old pedigree given by Dodsworth, was a very great person indeed. He was one of the Barons who joined Simon de Montfort in his rebellion. The family was intimately connected with South Cave and district for two or three hundred years.

† *Yorkshire Archæological and Topographical Journal,* part XXXIII., p. 98.

the King's want of money for the public service of the Realm, lent him all his wools in his Manor of Faxfleet, Com Ebor, upon promise to have restitution when the Receivers of Yorkshire should have so much come to their hands. The above Ralph de Nevill, died on the 5th of August, 41st Edward III., and, among other possessions, he died siezed of the Manors of South Cave and Faxfleet." *

" In 1385, Petrus Vaux (or Vaus) de South Cave held in South Cave one messuage, five tofts, ten bovates of land ut de Manor of Faxfleet.

In 1391, the widow of John Strivelyn held the manor (in all its extent in South Cave) and one water mill, with divers lands in North Cave and Cliff.

In 3rd Henry V. (1416) the manor with its members in Southam, North Cave, Santon, and Hotham, belonged to the Le Scrope family."

Francis, Earl of Cumberland, was Lord of the Manor at a Court held 20th October, 1610, and, on reference to the Court Rolls, we find the following were the Lords of the Manor at the respective dates :—

John, Earl of Bridgwater, 1643.
Sir Thomas Tyte, 1666.
Sir William Holcroft, 1667 to 1672.
Sir John Cutler, 1674 and 1688.
Edmund Lloyd, 1693 and 1708.
Edward Marshall, 1715 and 1742.
Mrs. Elizabeth Marshall, 1743 and 1748.
William Dixon, 1751.
Robert Spofforth and John Scholfield, joint Lords, 1787 to 1800.
Miss Sarah Jowett, 1837.
Mr. George Baron, 1852.

The present Lord of the Manor is James Atkinson Jowett, Esq.

Dugdale, in his " History of Imbanking and Draining " (published in 1772), on pp. 115 to 137, has some most interesting

* Dugdale's *Baronage*, Vol. I., p. 294.

references to Faxfleet and the neighbourood, from which we extract the following :—

"In 4 Edward II, a commission was issued to William de Huke, Gerard
Salveyn, and John de Metham, for the view and repair of the banks, ditches, and
sewers betwixt Faxflete and Cawode ; and in 17 Edward II, Alexander de
Cave, Thomas Houke, Peter de Saltmersh, Robert d'Ancotes, Will de Lincolne,
and Geffrey de Edenham had a commission to view and repair all the banks
betwixt Suth Cave and Barneby, near Hoveden, then broken in divers places ;
as also for the water-courses and ditches of Belebywyk, Fulnath, Ragolf Dyke,
Lange Dyke, Skelflete, Hingbriksik, Blaktoft damme, Thornton's damme,
Temple damme, Miklestek, Hebewisgote, Crakput, Mulnedam of Broukflet,
Frisdike, and Hoddeflete, all which were diverted out of their right courses ; by
which diversions and obstructions, and the want of repairing those banks, the
low grounds betwixt Thornetone, Muleburne, Cathwayt, Suth Cave, Yverthorpe,
North Cave and Barneby, near Hoveden, were overflowed : and in case that
they who had thus diverted and obstructed these water-courses, were not able to
repair them again, then to distrain all such to give assistance therein, as by such
reducing them to their former chanels and deobstruction of those stops, should
receive benefit and safeguard."

"In 30 Edward III, a commission was issued to John de Moubray, Illard de
Usflet, John de Walton, and John de Feriby, for the repair of the banks, &c. upon
Humbre, betwixt Faxflet and Paulesflet ; and in 1 Henry IV., the Jurors presented
that the watercourse, called Thornton damme, which extended itself from Lang-
dyke, to the River of Ouse, was obstructed, so that the adjacent grounds were
thereby drowned ; and that the same ought to be repaired by the Abbot of Thorntone for Thorntone house ; and also that Thorntone damme and . . . . damme
ought to be XVI feet in breadth, and VIII feet in depth. The Shireeve therefore had command to summon the said Abbot, &c. And they also presented
that the said Abbot was obliged to repair, cleanse, and maintain the watercourse
from Langedyke unto the town of Skalby, and thence to the River of Ouse, as it
was before alledged : wherefore he was amerced, and command given to the
Shireeve to distress him by all his lands. And they, moreover, presented that
the watercourse, called Temple damme, which lately belonged to the Master of
the Temple in England, was obstructed, so that the lands adjacent were thereby drowned ; which watercourse ought to be repaired by Sir Stephen le Scrope,
of Masham, Knight (Lord of the Manor of Faxflete), from Milkilsyke, with the
ditches in Helwysgote and Crakeputte, to the water of Humbre, wherefore the
Shireeve had command to summon the said Sir Stephen, who, appearing by

Thomas de Waldeby, his Attorney, said that he could not deny but that he ought to repair the said watercourse called Temple damme, from Carbrygge unto the River of Humbre, but said that he ought not to repair the same from Mikilsyke, with its ditches in Hewysgote, and Crakepitte, to the said bridge called the Carbrigge, any otherwise than a commoner in Wallyngfen, and desired that it might be enquired of by the country, &c. And the said Jurors presented that a certain watercourse, called Pardyke, descending from Haunsardamme, eastwards to Templedamme, and thence betwixt Scalby and Scalby grene, unto Templedamme, ought to be repaired by the town of Blaktoft, from Haunsardamme to Thorntondamme, and thence to the Templedamme, by the Abbot of Thorneton, and the town of Scalby. And that the said watercourse was obstructed towards Scalby by Henry de Kelme, and others, who threw earth into it by the command of Sir Stephan le Scrope, of Masham, knight, Wherefore the shireeve was required to summon the said Sir Stephan and Henry, to answer, &c. Who accordingly appeared, and said, that there then was, and had been time out of mind, a certain road-way, from the town and manor of Faxflete, unto the same place, where, by the above specified presentment, the said obstruction was supposed to be, and thence to Hovedene, and divers other places. And they said, that the same Henry and others, by the appointment of the said Sir Stephan, did cast earth and sand there, for the amendment of that way : without that, that there was any ancient watercourse descending as abovesaid, into Templedamme, as it was presented ; and desired that the country might enquire thereof. And the said jurors also said, that there was not any common or ancient watercourse descending from Thorntondamme, aforesaid, unto Templedamme, as had been alledged ; wherefore the said Sir Stephan and Henry were discharged."

CHAPEL.

The Wesleyans have a chapel in the village, with a Sunday School attached.

BROMFLEET.

ROMFLEET is a township and village at the junction of the Market Weighton Canal and River Humber, and until 1861, formed part of the parish of South Cave.

It was the seat of a famous family of that name who formerly resided there. About the year 1200, Lord Eustace Bromfleet founded at North Ferriby, the Priory of the Knight Templars, or Knights of St. John of Jerusalem. Members of the family were afterwards Barons of the Realm, summoned by special writ by the name of Broomfleet de Vesci. Henry Broomfleet, in the third year of the Reign of Edward IV., procured the Prior and Convent of the Knights Hospitallers at Ferriby, by special instrument under their public seals, upon search of their evidences to declare him patron, forasmuch as his ancestors had been their founders. This Henry Broomfleet died about the 18th year of the Reign of Edward IV. (1479), possessed of " Brantingham, Ellercber, Faxfleet, Weeton, Estrop, Burreby, Wighton, Loundsburrow, North Cave, Cliff, Fangfoss, Holm, Brompton, Gaitsforth, Wymington, and lands and tenements in Hull, London, Bedfordshire, Buckinghamshire, and Sussex," which he directed should be all sold, and disposed of in chantries, masses and dirges for his soul. " He left besides a large estate which his heiress carried by her marriage to the Cliffords, then Earls of Cumberland."

In 1691, a grant was made by the Crown to Sir Thomas Chichley, "of 906 acres of derelict lands, lying in and adjoining to ye towns of South Cave, Eleeker, &c., in ye County of Yorke, for 99 years at £50 per ann. Rent from Lady [day], 1692. This is in consideration of a Release to ye Crown, of a debt due to Sir Henry Chichley, Lieutenant-Governor of Virginia, in ye Raign of King Charles ye II." *

By Articles of Agreement, dated 24th June 1693, "between Sir Thomas Chichley, on the one part, and John Bacchus, of Cottingham, gentleman ; Robert Gunby, of North Newbald, gentleman ; Christopher Tadman, of Beverley, gent. ; William Hardwick, of the same town, gent ; Thomas Lister and William Cannaby, both of Bromflete, yeomen, on the other part," it is recited that several lands in Bromfleet, commonly called Bromfleet New Sands, otherwise Bromfleet New Groves, were lands derelict by the sea, and as such were reputed to belong to the King and Queen, in right of their crown, who had granted them to the said Sir Thomas Chichley by certain "Letters Pattents" and he having been

* Return of Royal Grants made to the House of Commons in 1701.

disturbed in his possession by Bacchus and others, it had been agreed that the latter should give up their claim to the premises on his releasing them from all actions for trespass.*

LORDS OF THE MANOR.

The Courts of the Manor were held in the year, 1723, in the name of George Davies and Thomas Roebuck, gentlemen.

The same in 1726.

In 1731 "for Georgii Davies gent. : and Mary Roebuck, viz : Benjamin Ferrand, and Rivi Wilton, ar. fiduliar John Roebuck, gent."

In 1734-40-42-43-44, for George Davies and John Roebuck.

From 1723 until 1753, Jonathan Midgley was Steward.

In 1751, John Roebuck, Esq., and George Davies, gent., are still Lords of the Manor.

In 1753, the Court was held for Jn. Roebuck, Esq., George Davies, Clerk, and others.

In 1754, the same.

In 1764, Jn. Roebuck, Esq. and Jonathan Midgley, gent.

In 1767, Jon. Midgley and Henry Woolhouse Disney Roebuck.

In 1772 and 1777 the same.

In 1783, Mary Midgley, Spinster, Henry Woolhouse Disney Roebuck, are Lady and Lord of the manor.

Mr. Barnard and Mr. Jalland are the present Lords of the Manor.

FISHERY.

It may be of some interest to mention here, that when towards the close of last century Mr. Boldero Barnard purchased Mr. Henry W.D. Roebuck's half of the Manorial Rights in Broomfleet,

* From the Original Deed.

he also acquired that gentleman's Fishery there, for which, with the "Fish House," &c., he paid £500, so that the fishery must have been at that time of some importance. Now, however, owing to changes in the currents of the river, it may almost be said to have ceased to exist, while the fish-house itself seems to have entirely disappeared. For some years past large deposits of mud and sand have been formed at and near Bromfleet, so that the channel of the Humber is gradually receding, and it is said that the highest tide now only covers mud where the water was formerly more than twenty feet deep.

THE CHURCH.

There was formerly a chantry here, but it was destroyed during the Civil War. The stone altar was standing in a field until about the middle of last century, when "Squire Roebuck" had it cut up to make coping stones for a house which he was then building.

From its remote position, and the absence, until within the last thirty years, of any other means of communication with the mother church at South Cave, than a mere track across the fields, the inhabitants of Bromfleet had not only great difficulty in attending church themselves, but also in the decent disposal of their dead. Frequently during the winter months it was necessary to employ twelve horses to pull a waggon conveying a coffin to South Cave Churchyard, and it was impossible for children to attend the Parish Schools. It had for many years been the anxious wish of the late Mr. and Mrs. Barnard to remedy, so far as lay in their power, this state of things, and in 1859, Mrs. Barnard (Mr. Barnard being then dead) bought a desirable site in the centre of the village from Mr. Jalland (who kindly gave part of the purchase money as a subscription to the church), and commissioned the well-

N

known architect, Mr. John Pearson. F.S A., to prepare plans for the erection of a church, vicarage, and school. The buildings were carried out according to his designs, and the church and church-yard were consecrated by Dr. Longley, Archbishop of York, October 31st, 1861, in the presence of a large congregation.

Bromfleet, with Faxfleet and some outlying portions of South Cave, were then formed into a separate parish, the late Mrs. Barnard and the present Mr. Barnard joining in endowing the living with the rectorial tithes of the two townships, which, together with a donation from the Ecclesiastical Commissioners, form the endowment. Mr. Barnard is the patron of the living.

CHAPELS.

There are also chapels in the village for the Wesleyans and Primitive Methodists.

ROWLEY.

OWLEY is a parish on the Wolds, about eight miles north-west from Hull, and lies midway between South Cave and Cottingham. It comprises the hamlets of Bentley, Hunsley, Riplingham, Risby, Rowley, and Little Weeton, the latter village having a station on the Hull and Barnsley Railway.

The church and the rectory are pleasantly situated in a park about half a mile south-west from the Little Weeton Railway Station.

The entire parish contains 6,423 acres, with 500 inhabitants.

Mrs. Sykes is Lady of the Manor, and W. H. Harrison-Broadley, Esq., and Captain Ferguson-Fawsitt are the principal landowners.

The living is in the gift of Mrs. Robert Hildyard, and has been held since 1852 by the Rev. Henry Charles Thoroton Hildyard, B.A., of Merton College, Oxford.

In the Inquisitions Post Mortem we find frequent references to Riplingham and Risby, but, apart from the advowson of the church, we do not meet with any mention of Rowley.

The Manor of Risby belonged at the Conquest to the Saxon Gamel, who, evidently before the Domesday Survey, sold it to Archbishop Eldred. The soke of this land was formerly connected with the Manor of Welton, but Archbishop Thomas obtained King William's Writ, by which he granted the undisturbed possession of that soke, to St. John of Beverley.

Riplingham was part of the possessions of Editha, Queen of Edward the Confessor. She was the daughter of Earl Goodwin, and was married to Edward in 1044, and died in 1074. At the time of the Survey, Riplingham was a berewick of the Manor of Ferriby, and was given by the Conqueror to Ralph de Mortimer.

We learn from Torre that the church of Rowley was part of the possessions of the ancient family of Stuteville, and from them descended to the Wakes, and it is probable they also acquired a considerable portion of the land.

From an inquisition taken 10th of Edward I., it appears that Baldwinus de Wake, died seized of the Advowson of the Church at Rowley, and in the 1st of Edward II., Alexander de Cave had free warren in Riplingham. In 6th of Richard II., Petrus de Malo Lacu held a fee in Riplingham by Knight's service, and in the 20th of the same King's reign Thomas de Holland, Duke of Kent, held lands in Riplingham, with the Church of Rowley. In the 10th of Henry IV., the same lands were held by Edward Holland, Duke of Kent, and in 38th Henry VI., Richard Aske, Esq., held lands in Weeton and Riplingham.

Risby was for several generations the seat of the Ellerkers, a family that played an important part in the history of their country,

and of this county in particular. During the Reigns of Henry
VIII., and Elizabeth, they filled important positions in the service
of their country, both by land and sea. Numerous references to
the family are found in the state papers of those reigns. From the
following letter, written by Surrey to Wolsey, dated 14th August,
1523, it is evident that the gentry of those times did not always
dwell together in peace and amity.

"I have been four days at York with the Justices, hearing infinite com-
plaints of the poor people, which could not have been fully redressed in a whole
month. Found the greatest dissension here among the gentlemen—who would
have fought together if they had met. By advice of the Judges sent for all the
parties and got them to promise to continue friends. These factions were Sir
Robert Constable and friends, against young Sir Ralph Ellerker and John
Constable, of Holderness; Sir Richard Tempest against young Henry Saville,
Wolsey's servant, Sir Ralph Ellerker, the elder, against Edward Gower.

Eight thieves were executed at the same time."

The site of the mansion of this family may yet be traced in
the park at Risby, now the property of Arthur Wilson, Esq.,
J.P. The building was destroyed by fire, and re-built and
shared a similar fate a second time more than a hundred years
ago. No part of the building remains, but the terraces of the
south front are still visible. In the grounds is a large fish
pond, on the banks of which is a ruin of a brick building with ten
sides and tall pointed windows.

Burton, in his *Ecclesiastical History of Yorkshire*, thus refers
to this parish :—

"RIPLINGHAM.—Robert de Camavil gave to Fountains Abbey the
whole Town with the men dwelling therein, with all their families.

Adam, the Shoemaker (sutor), de Riplingham, gave two oxgangs of land to
the Priory of Huthum, which was confirmed by William and Nicholas, his sons.

Hugh de Riplingham gave half a carucate of land which Derna, his
mother, had in marriage; and Peter de Faxfleet quit claimed this grant.

This land was let to Adam, son of Robert de Driffield, for 10s. per
annum."

"RISBY.—Walter de Faucanberg confirmed a grant of two oxgangs of land here, made by Walter de Kabrune, to Roche Abbey.

Ralph, son of Ralph de Babthorpe, when his brother Martin took the habit, and became a Canon at Drax, gave to that Priory an Annual rent of 4s. 4d., payable out of his land in Risby, and afterwards gave 10s. per annum out of ten oxgangs of land in the same place."

THE CHURCH.

The church is dedicated to St. Peter, and consists of nave, chancel, north and south aisles, a south chapel, and south porch with a low tower at the west end. It was restored and re-fitted in 1852. In the chancel is an ancient piscina; and the font, which is one of the finest in the district, is of the early English period. The aisles are separated from the nave on each side by three arches resting on circular columns. The windows are chiefly of the square-headed type of the Tudor period. The alterations in the building have been considerable, but sufficient remains to attest its early English foundation. The dimensions are :—Nave, 41 ft. long by 34 ft., wide, including the aisles ; chancel, 34 ft. by 15 ft. In the tower is a bell, a pre-Reformation one, with this inscription in fine Gothic characters : —

"Ave Gracia Plena Dominus.."

The church contains several monuments, from which we have copied the following inscriptions.

In the floor of the chancel :—

"Here lyeth the body of Mrs. Catherine Chamberline, the wife of Mr. Leonard Chamberline, of Hull, brought from thence, and here interred, the 13th day of January, 1697, aged 53 years.

Here also lyeth interred the body of Leonard Chamberline, late of Kingston-upon-Hull, Woollen Draper, who departed this life the 22nd of September, Ao. Dni. 1716, ætat Suæ, 74."

On a blue marble slab :—

"Here lyeth the body of Richard Tate, of Hunsley, died March 5th, 1732, aged 65."

Near this, is part of a slab which has formerly had a fine brass effigy, with an inscription round the edge of the stone and armorial bearings.

On another slab :—

"Here lyeth the body of Mrs. Elizabeth Hildyard, relict of the Rev. Mr. Christpr. Hildyard, late Rector of Rowley, who departed this life the 8th day of October, 1741, aged 75."

On a stone adjoining : —

"Here lyeth the body of Mary Fawsitt, of Latham, wife to Mr. Hugh Fawsitt, died Feby. 23rd, 1732, aged 70."

"Near this place is interred the body of Hugh Fawsitt, Esq., of Hunsley, son of the above Hugh and Mary Fawsitt, he departed this life the 19th day of June, 1752, aged 47.

Within the altar rails :—

"Here lyeth the body of the Revd. Mr. Christpr. Hildyard, A.M., Chaplain to ye late Rt. Honble. Henry Earl de Loraine, Rector of Claxby, in Lincolnshire, and of Rowley, who dyed Sept. 21st., 1734, aged 64. Who was a kind husband, a tender parent, a learned and orthodox divine."

"Here lyeth the body of Mrs. Esther Hildyard, relict of Christopher Hildyard, of Winestead, Esq., who departed this life November the 12th, Anno dom. 1716, in the 70th year of her age."

"Here lays the body of Mr. Willm. Hildyard, A.M., Rector of Rowley, who departed this life the 8th of November 1715.

Here are also interred the remains of Nancy Hildyard, his wife, who died March 12th, 1764, in the 72 year of her age."

"Here lyeth the body of John Ellerker, of Risby, Esq., who died in the year 1655. He married Dorothy, the daughter and heiress of Launcelot Roper, of Hull, Esq., by whom he had issue John Nathaniel, who died at 14 years old, and Dorothy.

Here also lieth the remains of his said wife, Dorothy, who married to her 2nd husband, Tho. Cracroft, Dr. of Divinity. She made an Exemplary wife to both her husbands, was very charitable and truly religious ; she died 3rd Feb., 1703, ætate 76."

On the south wall of the chancel :—

A tablet to the late Reverend Levett Edward Thoroton, 23 years rector of Rowley.

On the wall of the south aisle :—

"Sacred to the memory of Henry Cumbrey, Esq., Captain in the Royal South Lincoln Militia, whose body lyeth near this place, and who departed this life, Nov. 23, 1794, Etat 66. "

On the same wall a fine marble tablet, as follows : –

"Sacred to the memory of Raspin Norrison, of Willerby, Esq., who died on the 17th of Decr., 1756, aged 63 years. Of Ann, his wife, who died the 20th Septr., 1735, aged 37 years. Of Jane, his second wife, who died the 3rd. of Novr., 1744, aged 65 years. Of John Raspin, the son of Ann, and of Ann the second daughter of the said Raspin and Ann Norrison, who all died young. also of Watson Norrison. Esq., the son of the above mentioned Raspin and Ann Norrison, who died the 5th of Aug., 1754, aged 22 years. ' Non perduntur sed prœgrediuntur.' "

In the Ellerker Chapel, a series of white marble tablets, with the following inscriptions :—

"To perpetuate the memory of this ancient family, this Mausoleum was built by Ellerker Bradshaw, of Risby, Esq.

Near this place lyeth the Remains of Sir Ralph Ellerker, of Risby, whose Grandfather, John Ellerker, of Ellerker, married the daughter and heiress of William Risby, of Risby, Esq., Anno 1401. The said Sir Ralph Ellerker, with his sons Ralph, William, and Robert, for their gallant behaviour at Flodden field, were there made Knights. He died Jany. 4th, 1540.

Sir Ralph, the eldest son, attended King Henry the 8th into France, at his own expence. He commanded the siege of Bolloyn, where he took the Dauphin of France's Standard, and was made Marshall Governor of the said town, and lies buried in St. Mary's Church, in Bolloyn.

Henry ye 8th, for his gallant behaviour, gave the device of the said Dauphin's standard to him, and his posterity. He married the daughter of Thomas Arding, of Kettlethorpe, Esq."

"Here lyeth the body of Sir Ralph Ellerker, of Risby Knight, High Sheriff of the County of York, he died the last of August, 1509. He married Catherine the daughter of Sir John Constable, of Burton Constable, and they had issue, Edward Ellerker, who lies in this place, who married Elizabeth, daughter of Sir Robert Constable, of Everingham, who had issue Ralph, Robert, William, John, Eleanor, Frances, Ann, and Margaret."

"Here lyeth the body of Sir Ralph Ellerker, of Risby, who was knighted by King James, at his entrance into York, April ye 17th, 1603. He married Ann, the daughter of Thomas Dalton, of Nuttles, Esq., and had issue Ralph, James, Edward, Henry, Robert, and John."

" Here lieth the body of Ralph Ellerker, Esq., who married Eleanor, the daughter of Thomas Metham, Esq., as also the body of James Ellerker, his Brother, who married Frances, the daughter of Allan Percy, Esq., and had issue John, who lies buried at the altar."

" Here lies the body of John Ellerker, of Risby, Esq., who married Elizabeth, the daughter of Charles Cracroft, of Louth, Esq., and had no issue. He died ye 4th day of October, 1616."

" Here lies the body of Sir James Bradshaw, of Bromborough, in the County of Chester, Kt., he married Dorothy, sole heiress of this ancient family, by whom he had issue Dorothy, Elizabeth, Frances, Susannah, Isabella, Ellerker, another son (twin) born dead, Isabella, Lucy, James, and Ursula. The said Elizabeth, Susannah, Isabella, Frances, and the son born dead, lie buried in the church in Castle Gate, York."

" Here also lies the body of Dorothy Bradshaw, and of James. In her each grace of the sex was fully blown, and man-like virtues in his bud were shewn.

Here also lies the body of Lucy Bradshaw, who died 18th July, 1712, aged 28."

" Ursula Bradshaw died Septr. 18th, 1731, at Chester, where she lies buried by her desire in St. Peter's Church, in the 43 year of her age."

" Here lieth the body of Dame Dorothy, the wife of Sir James Bradshaw, Kt., who was sole heiress to the ancient family of Ellerker, of Risby, she died the 15th Feby., 1724, aged 75. She was an indulgent mother, a loving wife, a great example of piety, virtue, and universal charity."

" Here also lieth the body of Rebecca, the second daughter of Ellerker Bradshaw, of Risby, Esq., by Rebecca, 2nd daughter of Sir Edward Northing, Kt., she died at London, April ye 8th, 1731, aged 8 years. She was a child of great qualifications, by which she was admired by all, and died by all lamented."

" Here lieth the body of Ellerker Bradshaw, Esq., of Risby, Son and heir of Sir Jas. Bradshaw, Kt., by Dame Dorothy, his wife, sole heiress of the Ellerker family of Risby. He married Rebecca, the 2nd daughter of Sir Edward Northing, Kt., Attorney General, by her he had issue two daughters, Lucy and Rebecca. In the two first Parliaments of his present Majesty, George, the 2nd, he was successively returned by the Burgesses of Beverley, one of their Representatives. He was born the 1st of Decr., 1680, and died the 28th of June, 1742, aged 62."

" Also in the Churchyard lieth interred (Pursuant to his own desire) Roger Mainwaring, Esq., who deceased at London, March the 7th, 1760, aged 71. He was descended of the very ancient family of the Mainwarings, of the County of Chester, and was of that branch, which still continues seated at Carmingham, in that county, by Elizabeth, his wife, daughter and co-heir, of Joseph Eaton, of London, Esq., he had issue Eaton, Roger, 2nd son, who is yet living unmarried, seated at Frostenden, Com. Suffolk, George, 3rd son, who entered the army and died in the campaign in Germany, at Sturm, 9th of Aug., 1761, aged 35 and unmarried, Elizabeth, their only daughter died an infant."

" Here also lieth the body of Eaton Mainwaring Ellerker, of Risby, Esq., son and heir of Roger Mainwaring Ellerker, which Eaton being related to Ellerker Bradshaw, Esq , before mentioned, was left by him heir to all his estates, to take the name and arms of Ellerker, which accordingly he did by Act of Parliament. He married Barbara, daughter of Edward Dixon, of Belford, Com. Northumberland, Esq., by whom he had issue Alice, who died young, Elizabeth, Roger, Abraham, who likewise died young, Charlotte, Arabella, and Harriet. He deceased at Risby, July 9th, 1771, aged 49."

" Here also lieth the body of Roger Mainwaring Ellerker, Esq., son and heir of Eaton Mainwaring Ellerker, and Barbara, his wife, before mentioned, who died at Bristol Wells, Nov. 17th, 1775, being then in the 23rd of his age, and unmarried.   By his decease his four surviving sisters succeeded to his inheritance."

" Elizabeth Mainwaring Ellerker is living yet, unmarried."

" Charlotte, who, Decr. 21st., 1777, was married to George Townshend, Lord de Ferrares, Bourchier Loraine, Basset and Campton, son and heir apparent of George Viscount Townshend, of which there is issue."

" Arabella, who, Decr. 23rd.. 1776, was married to the Hon. Thomas Onslow, son and heir apparent of George, Lord Onslow, of Crawly, of which marriage there is issue ; and Harriet, who is living and unmarried."

" These monumental tablets were completed by Barbara, the disconsolate relict of Eaton Mainwaring Ellerker, Esq., and her said four daughters."

" May this memorial, sacred to the virtues that constitute female excellence, perpetuate the memory of Barbara Mainwaring Eaton, widow of the late Eaton Mainwaring Ellerker, Esq., who lies interred at her own request near the place of her late residence, at Petersham. in the Co. of Surrey. She departed this life, June the 5th, 1804, leaving two surviving daughters, Harriet and Elizabeth to mourn their loss."

" Harriet Mainwaring Eaton Ellerker, youngest sister and co-heir of Roger Mainwaring Eaton Ellerker, died 23rd Sept., 1842, aged 82. Interred at Petersham."

TORRE'S LIST OF THE RECTORS.

Temp Instit.	Vicarii Eccle.	Patroni.
15th Jan., 1228	Rich. Fitz. Robert	Stuteville
17th Sep., 1299	Pet. de Weverthorp	
1304	Hugo Duket	Guardian of Thomas Wake
1309	Johe de Hotham	Ed. II. as Guardian
10th Jan., 1317	Egidus de Sledmere	Archbishop of York
12th June. 1348	Henry de Greystoke	Edward III.
20th Dec., 1368	Johe Calne	Henry IV.
10th Aug., 1400	Johe Walkington	
24th Jan., 1408	Johe Burnham	
11th Nov., 1419	Will. Grensoke	Attorn. of Earl of Salisbury
5th Oct., 1437	Johe Wyter	
21st Mar., 1469	Oliv. Almonde	
1469	Stephen Close	
18th June, 1471	Robt. Thomlyson	Duke of Clarence
20th Dec., 1472	Thos. Ottlay	
1st Mar. 1476	Will. Crief	
28th Feb., 1488	Xtopher Radclyft	Henry VIII.
	Bernado Holden	Countess of Salisbury
18th Jan., 1530	Ric. Sherwode, M.A.	
2nd Dec., 1540	Henry Browne	Henry VIII.
4th Aug., 1583	Jacob Gayton. M.A.	Dame Hastings
24th Nov., 1584	Jac. Gayton. M.A.	
2nd April, 1593	Hen. Picarde	H. Barrington, arm.
21st Feb., 1620	Ezekiel Rogers	
6th June, 1638	Thomas White	
9th July, 1667	Fras. Brooksbye, S.T.B.	

LIST CONTINUED SINCE TORRE.

Temp Instit.	Vicarii Eccle.	Patroni.
15th Aug., 1690	Thos. Walters	
24th Sep., 1704	Willm. Hildyard	
19th June, 1715	Christopher Hildyard	
9th Oct., 1734	Thos. Wakefield, M.A.	
25th Jan., 1787	Robt. Croft	
12th July, 1831	Ed. Thoroton, B.A.	
16th Jan., 1852	H. Chas. Thoroton Hildyard, B.A.	

TESTAMENTARY BURIALS.

A.D. 28th July, 1469.—Johe Wyter, Rector, to be buried in the Quire.

June, A.D. 1489.—Willm. Crieff, Rector, to be buried in the Quire, of All Saints, in the City of York, before the image of St. Francis, on the great altar.

June 11th, A.D. 1562.—Ralph Ellerker, of Risby, Knt., to be buried in the Quire at Rowley, where his ancestors do lye.

28th March, A.D. 1587.—Ed. Ellerker, of Risby, gent., to be buried in the Chancel, with his wife, in the sepulchre of his ancestors.

ST. PETER'S CHURCH, ROWLEY.

26th Sept., A.D., 1657.—Wm. Gee, of Bently, to be buried in the Church, near his Wife.

" 3rd April, A.D., 1622.—Henry Pickarde, of Rowley, Clerk, to be buried as near his wife as may be.

REV. EZEKIEL ROGERS.

If the contention of the late Mr. C. S. Todd ('Town Clerk of

Hull) be correct, the famous Battle of Brunanburg was fought on the plains near Little Weeton. The parish may be unable to claim this uncertain distinction, but its fame will be carried down to posterity, as the seedling from which the Town of Rowley, in the County of Essex, in the State of Massachusetts, in America, took its rise. In the year 1638, the Rev. Ezekiel Rogers, the then Vicar of Rowley, with about twenty families of his hearers, " most of them of good estate," emigrated to America and founded what is now the town of Rowley.* The following are the names of some of the emigrants who accompanied Mr. Rogers, namely Spofford, Jewett, Nelson, Brocklebank, Boynton, Mighill, Chaplin, Palmer, Burbank, Dickinson, Hopkinson, Stickney, Tenney, Jackson, and Bridges. The leader of this band of emigrants, and practically the founder of Rowley in America, was born in 1590, and was the son of the Rev. Richard Rogers, of Weathersfield, in Essex. Having finished his education at Cambridge, he became Chaplain to Sir Francis Barrington, in his native county, and after six years spent profitably and usefully in this family, Sir Francis bestowed upon Mr. Rogers the benefice of Rowley, in Yorkshire. After labouring here for seventeen years, and, being unwilling to conform, he was suspended, as he himself tells the tale, " for refusing to read that accursed Book that allowed sports on God's Holy Sabbath, or Lord's Day, and by it and other sad signs of the times, was driven with many of my hearers into New England."

Under Archbishop Matthews, it would seem that Mr. Rogers was left undisturbed, but Matthews having been succeeded by Laud, Mr. Rogers was suspended, and having determined to seek that freedom in foreign lands which he could not enjoy here, he ultimately sailed with his party from Hull, and arrived in New England in the

* Gage's *History of Rowley in America.*

Autumn of 1638. Mr. Rogers being under a promise to many persons of quality in England who depended on him to choose a fit place for them, consulted with the Ministers of Massachusetts as to the best position for a settlement, and, acting on their advice, he and his party concluded to take a place between Ipswich and Newbury, and these towns having offered some farms on this tract, Mr. Rogers' company purchased them at the price of £800, the settlement being first called Rogers' Plantation, but the name was soon changed to Rowley. Though Mr. Rogers only took over with him twenty families, by the time he settled in Rowley he had increased his company to about sixty families. Mr. Rogers continued his services as minister for many years, and died January 23rd, 1660-1, after a lingering illness. By his will, after bequeathing legacies to his relatives and servants, and his books to Harvard College, he gave the rest of his estate (as also the property left to his wife for life) "to the church and town of Rowley, to enable them the better to maintain two teaching elders in the church, for ever." His will was filed in the probate office at Ipswich the following March, the inventory of real and personal estate amounting to £1535 19s. 9d. In the year 1805, a monument was erected to his memory bearing the following inscription :—"Sacred to the Memory of the Rev. Ezekiel Rogers, first minister of the gospel in Rowley, who emigrated from Britain to this place with his church and flock, A.D., 1638. He finished his labours and life January 23rd, 1660, in his seventieth year. He was a man of eminent piety, zeal, and abilities. His strains of oratory were delightful. Regeneration and union to Jesus Christ by faith, were the points on which he principally insisted ; he so remarkably described the feelings, exercises, motives, and characters of his hearers, that they were ready to exclaim ' Who hath told him all this !' With the youth he took great pains, and was a tree of knowledge, laden with fruit which children could reach. He bequeathed a part of his lands to the town of Rowley, for the support of the Gospel, which generous benefaction, we (in the first parish) enjoy to the present day ; and here gratefully commemorate, by raising this monument to his memory."

The town of Rowley, in America, has now a population of about 1,300 inhabitants, and is described in a recent letter received from the Chairman of the Town's Selectmen, as a "lively little town."

Ellckar of Risby.*

Christa Concebitor Radulpho Ellerker de Rysby milito per Christoferum Barker, arg alias Garter principatem Regem Armoram p literas Patentes datus Londini, 20th Martij Ao. Dni 1545, 37 Hen. 8.

John Ellerkar, Serjeant = Elizabeth, dau of Sir
at law.   John Hotham, Knt.

John Ellerker, of Rysbye, 1468,   William
7 Ed. 4th   Robert
        m   Thomas
Isabel, dau of Robt. De la More
7 Ed. 4th

John Elleker   Thomas   Cesilie
   m
Elizabeth, dau. of
Sir Ralph Eure.

Sir Ralph Ellerker = ... dau of Sir Thos. Gower.   Henry   Margery
                                                  Elizabeth.

Sir Ralph Ellerker = Joan dau of John Arden   William   Elizabeth
                                          Thomas   Ann
                                          James   Margarie
                                          Robert
                                          Roger

Sir Ralph Ellerker, of Rysbe,   William   Jane   Ursula, m to Sir John Sal-
       m   Anne   ven of Newbeggin.
Catherine, dau of Sir John Con-   Margaret
stable, of Burton Constable.

Continued next page.

* From MS. copy of Glover's Visitation (1584), deposited in the Library, Holy Trinity Church, Hull.

Continued from previous page.

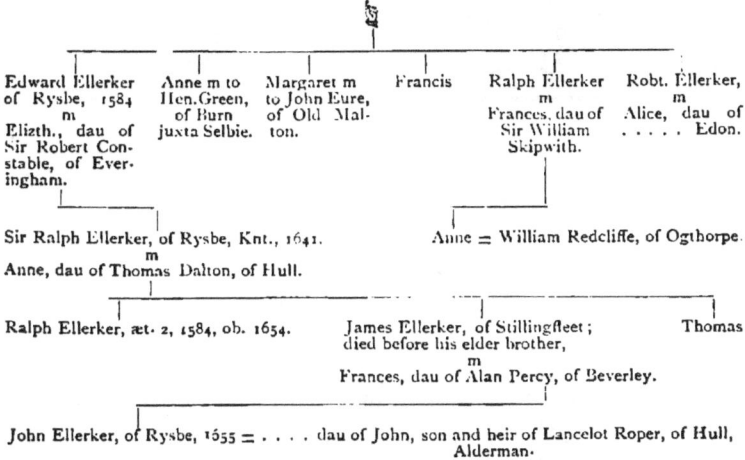

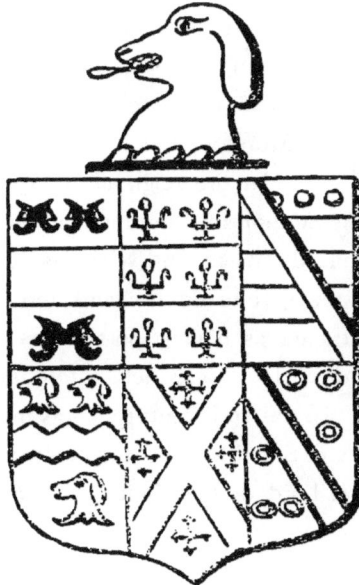

Edward Ellerker
of Rysbe, 1584
m
Elizth., dau of
Sir Robert Con-
stable, of Ever-
ingham.

Anne m to
Hen.Green,
of Burn
juxta Selbie.

Margaret m
to John Eure,
of Old Mal-
ton.

Francis

Ralph Ellerker
m
Frances. dau of
Sir William
Skipwith.

Robt. Ellerker,
m
Alice, dau of
. . . . . Edon.

Sir Ralph Ellerker, of Rysbe, Knt., 1641.
m
Anne, dau of Thomas Dalton, of Hull.

Anne = William Redcliffe, of Ogthorpe.

Ralph Ellerker, æt. 2, 1584, ob. 1654.

James Ellerker, of Stillingfleet;
died before his elder brother,
m
Frances, dau of Alan Percy, of Beverley.

Thomas

John Ellerker, of Rysbe, 1655 = ... dau of John, son and heir of Lancelot Roper, of Hull,
Alderman.

ARMS OF ELLERKER OF ELLERKER.

BRANTINGHAM.

I N Brantingham, the Bishop of Durham had four carucates and six oxgangs of land in full cultivation at the time of Domesday Survey, and the remainder, which belonged to Norman, the son of Ulphus, was given by the Conqueror to Roger of Poictou, the Earl of Moreton, and Robert Malet.

In the reign of Henry III., Roger Merley was Lord of the Manor of Brantingham, and in the 10th of Edward I., Baldwinus de Wake, and Nicholas de Cave held lands here. In the next reign, John de Holland and Walterus de Faucenburgh are mentioned as having possessions here. At a later period, Thos. Bromflete de Vescey held a toft and twenty acres of land in the parish. In the 16th century it was in the possession of a family of the name of Smethley. At the present time Christopher Sykes, Esq., M.P., is Lord of the Manor and principal landowner.

The village is at the foot of the Wolds, and has a population of 269.

THE CHURCH.

The church, dedicated to All Saints, stands in a picturesque valley at the north-east end of the village, and consists of a nave, chancel, north and south transepts, south porch, and a

ALL SAINTS CHURCH, BRANTINGHAM.

tower at the west end. In 1872, it was re-built (with the exception of the tower), chiefly through the liberality of Christopher Sykes, Esq. The church is of early English foundation, and that style has, to some extent, been carried out in the re-building. The dimensions are : nave, 40ft. by 20ft. 6in. ; chancel, 30ft. by 15ft. The east window is of three lights, and is a memorial window, the subject being the crucifixion. "In affectionate memory of Mary Elizabeth Sykes, died March 23rd, 1875."

The window of the north transept is by Taylor, of London, and has this inscription, "D. D. D., and in loving memory of Anne Westmorland, died Mar. 29th, 1875." On the north side of the nave is a window of three lights, by Clayton and Bell, subject: "The Presentation in the Temple," with an inscription, "To the Glory of God, and in loving memory of William Busfeild, M.A., 30 years Rector of Keighley, died 12th April, 1878, aged 76, and Sarah, his wife, died 21st Decr., 1885, aged 80. This window is erected by their daughter, Harriet Busfeild."

The west window of the tower is also a memorial window, subject: "Christ and the Centurion." "To the memory of Richard Fleetwood Shawe, Born on the 2nd of Aug., 1804; died on the 5th of Septr., 1872."

In the tower is a mural tablet to the memory of members of the Simpson family of Brantingham Grange; another to the memory of the Rev. William Richardson, Vicar of Brantingham 42 years, who died May the 27th 1742, aged 75.

On the east wall of the south transept is a mural brass to one Anthony Smethley, with his arms and this inscription, "Hic Iacet Anthonius Smetheley, armiger, quondam Dnus de Brantingham. Qui obit secndo die Janvarii Ano Dni 1578." Arms: "A Bend three Lozenges between two unicorns' heads erased." Crest: "Unicorn's head erased."

In the tower are three bells, two of which are pre-Reformation ones, the inscriptions are the following:—

1. Soli Deo Gloria, 1634.
2. Ora. Pro. Nobis Sancti Omnes.
3. Ora Pro. Nobis Sancti Georgi.

The font is a circular basin, around which are pillars enriched with dog-tooth ornaments ; it is probably coeval with the foundation of the church.

A board in the vestry has the following inscription :—" Miss Maria Simpson, Brantingham Grange, by her last will and testament, dated January 17th, 1840, gave the sum of £200 upon trust that her Trustee or Trustees do and shall pay the dividend, interest, and annual income thereof to the Vicar and Churchwardens, for the time being, of the Parish of Brantingham, to be by them annually expended in the purchase of blankets and other needful or useful clothing, to be distributed amongst such poor persons of or residing in the same Parish, in seasons of scarcity, as the said Vicar and Churchwardens shall think fit or determine."

From the Torre Manuscript we learn that " The Church of Brantingham, in Howdenshire, was part of the ancient possessions of the Cathedral Church of Durham, and in temp Hen. II., was reconed among the other Churches of St. Cuthbert's patrimony, which is in the diocese of York, concerning which that memorable agreement was made between the Archbishop of York and the Bishop of Durham, about Ecclesiastical rights."

"On the 4th of August, A.D. 1458, this Parish Church of Brantingham (Ebor diocese) was appropriated to the Prior and Convent of Durham, in aid of the yearly sustentation of eight monks of the said monastery and of eight scholars in the Durham College, in the University of Oxford., saving always a certain portion of money, viz., the sum of twenty marks for the yearly maintenance of the ppetual vicar therein, to be instituted at the presentation of the said prior and convent for ever, and payable to them by the said vicar. Also, the vicar for the time being, shall have and hold for ever the west part of the rectory of the said church, and the

mediety of the orchard toward the west, and shall pay all the pro-
curations due and customary, and the prior and convent aforesaid
and their successors, shall repair the chancel of the church and pay
the demise granted to the King and the annual pension which
is due to the Collegiate Church of St. John of Beverley, besides
an annual pension of 6s. 3d. annually due to the Cathedral Church
of Durham. Moreover, the Archbishop of York, on the 4th
of May, 1439, ordained that the said prior and convent shall pay
yearly, out of the fruits of this church, to the Dean and Chapter
of the Cathedral Church of York, 3s. 4d., on the Feast of St.
Michael the Archangel, for ever, and also cause to be distributed
3s. 4d. among the poor of the parish church on the Feast of Our
Lady's Annunciation. On the 7th Martii, 4th Edward 6th, King
Edward, for the sum of £277 2s. 8d , granted unto Walter Jobson,
of Kingston-upon-Hull, merchant, and his heirs and assigns for
ever, all his Rectory and Church of Brantingham, together with the
Chapels of Blacktoft and Ellcker, County Ebor, lately belonging
to the dissolved Monastery of Durham, and the advowson and right
of patronage of the vicarage of the Church of Brantingham, &c.
To hold of the King and his successors as of his Manor of Kingston-upon-Hull, by fealty, and for free socage, only not in capite.
Reserving besides the £3 6s. 8d. due to the Vicar of Brantingham for the time being, yearly issuing out of the said church and
chapels, and beside the allowance to be paid to Durham College ;
also the 3s. 4d. yearly to the Dean and Chapter of York, and the
3s. 4d. to be paid to the poor of Brantingham."

THE LIVING.

The living is a vicarage, yearly value £318, with residence, in the gift of the Dean and Chapter of Durham, and held by the Rev. Thomas Westmorland, M.A., of Sydney Sussex College, Cambridge.

A CLOSE CATALOGUE OF THE RECTORS.

Temp Instit.	Vicarii Eccle.	Patroni.	Vacat.
12th Nov., 1238	Henry de Melsamby	Prior and Convent	....
13th Dec., 1279	Tho. de Birland...............	of Durham.	....
	Ed. de Hawkesgarth.........	....	Res.
1314	Waltr. de Wetwang	....	Mort.
1347	Ric. de Tanfield.............	....	Resig.
1347	Ric. de Tweel	....	Res.
May, 1348	Thos. de Nevill	....	....
	Lawr. Allerthorp	....	Mort.
July, 1406	Thos. Tylton	....	Mort.
Mar., 1420	Robt. de Hage	....	Resig.
Feb. 1444	Robt. Beaumont	....	....

CATALOGUE OF THE VICARS.

Temp Instit.	Vicarii Eccle.	Patroni.	Vacat.
Septr., 1459	W Benson, M.A.	Prior and Convent	Mort.
28th Oct., 1479	Hugo Wren	of Durham.	Res.
12th Jan., 1485	Johes. Curwen	....	Resig.
19th July, 1486	Galfrid Wren, A.B.		....
20th Aug., 1496	Robt. Claxton, A.B.........	. ...	Mort.
12th Nov., 1521	Johes West.................	....	Res.
9th April, 1523	Thos. Jenyson		
17th Nov., 1542	Phil. Preston	Rad. Sellars	....
7th Oct., 1557	Will Gibson	....	....
	Edward Richardson	....	....
24th Oct., 1578	Robt. David	....	....
11th Sept., 1622	Geo. Hall	....	....
19th May, 1625	Geo. Gibson	....	....

CONTINUATION SINCE TORRE'S LIST.

Temp Inst.	Vicarii Eccle.	Patroni.	Vacat.
2nd Mar., 1699	William Richardson, M.A.		
2nd Oct., 1742	Matthew Whitaker, B.A.		
5th Aug., 1755	Thos. Bowman, B.A.		
17th Dec., 1768	James Foster, B.A.		
14th April, 1793	Thos. Davison		
3rd Oct., 1794	Robt. Fenwick, M.A.		
31st July, 1808	Joshua Stopford, M.A.		
8th Feb., 1818	John Carr, M.A.		
19th Jan., 1834	Saml. Mayelston, M.A.		
2nd Oct., 1843	Geo. Fyler Townsend, M.A.		
18th Dec., 1857	Thos. Westmorland, M.A.		

TESTAMENTARY BURIALS.

" 1st May, 1575.—Anthony Smetheley of Brantingham, in Co. Ebor, Esq., made his will, proved 7th March, 1577, whereby he gave his soul to God Alm., and his body to be buried near his father and mother, and willed that a great stone be set in the inside of the said church, near his grave, and theron be engraved his name and arms, and the day and year of his death.

27th January, A.D., 1562.—Thos. Ellerker, of Ellerker, in the psh. of Brantingham, made his will, proved 20th April, 1563, giving his soul to God Alm., and his body to be buried in the Psh. Church of Brantingham.

25th March, A.D. 1565.— —— Bunnage, of Brantingham, husband-man, made his will, proved, giving his soul to God Alm., his maker and Redeemer, and his body to be buried in the church.

28th Aug., A.D. 1582.—Gabriel Couper, of Ellerker, yeoman, will proved 20th, Oct., 1582, to be buried in the Church, near his wife.

5th July, A.D. 1584.—Elizabeth Wakefield, of Brantingham, spinster, to be buried in the church.

1st May, A.D. 1348.—Ralph Tweel, Rector of this Church of Branting-ham, made his will, proved 26th May, 1348. giving his soul to Alm. God, and his body to be buried in the Psh. Church of Thurlston. On 28th Sept. A.D. 1346, he was instituted to the prebend of Skelton, in the Church of Hoveden."

BRANTINGHAM-THORPE.

Brantingham-Thorpe formerly belonged to the late Mr. R. F.

Shawe, but was purchased some years ago by Mr. C. Sykes, M.P., who has almost entirely re-built the mansion, and otherwise greatly improved the estate. The house has, on several occasions since Mr. Sykes' purchase, been honoured by visits from members of the Royal Family. It is now the residence of J. E. Wade, Esq., J.P.

ELLERKER.

In the parish is the village and township of Ellerker (with a population of 299), which at an early period was in the possession of a family of the same name, for, in 1080, we find that a "William Ellerker, of Ellerker, Esq., Lord of Howdenshire, married Marrian, daughter and heiress of John D'avill, Lord of Adlingfleet."

In A.D. 1101, "John Ellerker, son of William, by the above Marrian D'avill, built the chapel of Ellerker (near South Cave, in the East Riding of Yorkshire, about eight miles from Adlingfleet and within one mile north of the Humber), and covered it with lead, which was enjoyned his father to have performed by King William Rufus, and gave the bells, and in A.D. 1241, John Ellerker, his great-grandson, repaired the chancel of Ellerker." *

This family was one of the most important of our local families, and many of its members filled offices of great trust and responsibility, nationally as well as locally, but want of space forbids our doing more than inserting a notice of Sir Ralph Ellerker referred to by Froude in his History, who gives the following interesting account of the manner in which Sir Ralph came into prominence during the Pilgrimage of Grace.

"The law vacation (in the year 1536) was drawing to its close, and younger brothers in county families who then, as now, were members of the

* Stovin's *MS. History of Hatfield Level Drainage.*

inns of court, were returning from their holidays to London. The season had
been of unusual beauty. The summer had lingered into the autumn, and during
the latter half of September, young Sir Ralph Ellerkar, of Ellerkar Hall, in
'Yorkyswold,' had been entertaining a party of friends for cub-hunting. Among
his guests were his three cousins, John, Robert, and Christopher Aske. John,
the eldest, the owner of the old family property of Aughton-on-the Derwent,
a quiet, unobtrusive gentleman, with two sons, students at the Temple. Robert,
of whom, till he now emerges into light, we discover only that he was a
barrister in good practice at Westminster; and Christopher, the possessor of
an estate in Marshland, in the West Riding. The Askes were highly connected, being cousins of the Earl of Cumberland, whose eldest son, Lord
Clifford, had recently married a daughter of the Duke of Suffolk, and niece,
therefore, of the King. The hunting party broke up on the 3rd of October, and
Robert, if his own account of himself is true, left Ellerker, with no other in-
tention than of going direct to London to his business. His route lay across
the Humber at Welton, and, when in the ferry he heard from the boatmen that
the commons were up in Lincolnshire he wished to return, but the state of
the tide would not allow him. He then endeavoured to make his way by bye-
roads and bridle-paths to the house of a brother-in-law at Sawcliffe; but he
was met somewhere near Appleby by a party of rebels. They demanded who
he was, and on his replying, they offered him the popular oath. It is hard to
believe that he was altogether taken by surprise; a man of so remarkable
powers, as he afterwards exhibited, could not have been wholly ignorant of
the condition of the country, and if his loyalty had been previously sound he
would not have thrown himself into the rising with such deliberate energy. The
people by whom he was 'taken,' as he designated what had befallen him,
became his body-guard to Sawcliffe. He must have been well-known in the
district. His brother's property lay but a few miles distant across the Trent,
and as soon as the news spread that he was among the rebels his name was
made a rallying cry. The command of the district was assigned to him from
the Humber to Kirton, and for the next few days he remained endeavouring to
organise the movement into some kind of form; but he was doubtful of the
prospects of the rebellion, and doubtful of his own conduct. The commons of
the West Riding beginning to stir, he crossed into Marshland; he passed the
Ouse into Howdenshire, going from village to village, and giving orders that
no bells should be rung, no beacons should be lighted, except on the receipt of
a special message from himself. *

The excitement of the times was contagious, and spread

* Froude's *History of England*, Vol. III., p 121.

through every town within our immediate neighbourhood, as well as throughout the northern counties. At the end of October, a council of the insurgents was held at Pomfret, and by this time "The powers of all the great families, except the Cliffords, the Dacres, and the Musgraves, had come into the confederacy. Six peers, or eldest sons of peers, were willingly or unwillingly with Aske at Pomfret. Lord Westmoreland was represented by Lord Neville. Lord Latimer was present in person, and with him Lord Darcy, Lord Lumley, Lord Scrope, and Lord Conyers. Besides these were the Constables of Flamborough, the Tempests, from Durham; the Bowses, the Everses, the Fairfaxes, the Strangwayses, young Ellerkar, of Ellerkar, the Danbys, St. Johns, Bulmers, Mallorys, Lascelleses, Nortons, Moncktons, Gowers, Ingoldsbys: we scarcely miss a single name famous in Border story. Such a gathering had not been seen in England since the grandfathers of these same men fought on Towton Moor."

The Chapel of Ease.

The chapel was restored in 1842, at an expense of £800, by subscription and a small parish rate. It is a stone building, and consists of chancel, nave, porch, and bell turret, with vestry on the north side of the chancel.

Glover, in his Visitation mentions the chapel, and the following is a copy of his reference to it. He states there were at that time (1584) three bells, but it is not clear from his account what inscription was on each.

"In the Church of Ellerker, upon three belles in the steeple :—
First bell : 'May Fortune', 1577.
Second Bell, about this bell :—
40. —— 3 fleurs-de-lis.
41. An eagle slantant or.

42. ——3 talbots heads erased.
A child in swaddling clothes.
Sanctæ Jhesu Mariæ Orate Pro Nobis.
43. Third bell —— , three bells."

PRIMITIVE METHODIST CHAPEL.

The Primitive Methodists have a small chapel which formerly belonged to the " Wesleyan Reformers."

ELLERKER HALL.

Ellerker Hall, occupied by Mr. Forster, was formerly the residence of the late Alderman Brownlow, of Hull, who lies interred in the churchyard.

Pedigree of Ellerker of Ellerker.

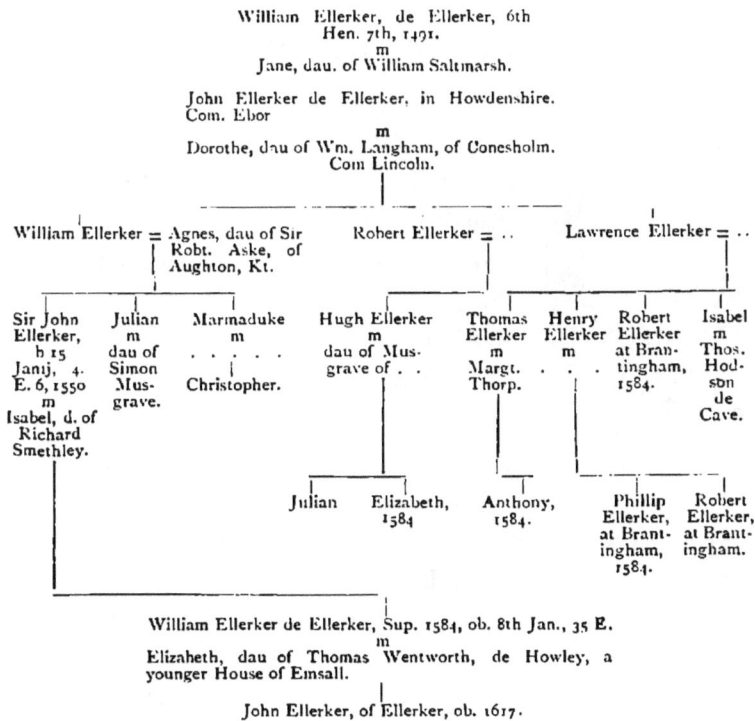

William Ellerker, de Ellerker, 6th
Hen. 7th, 1491.
m
Jane, dau. of William Saltmarsh.

John Ellerker de Ellerker, in Howdenshire.
Com. Ebor
m
Dorothe, dau of Wm. Langham, of Conesholm.
Com Lincoln.

William Ellerker = Agnes, dau of Sir
      Robt. Aske, of
      Aughton, Kt.

Robert Ellerker = ..

Lawrence Ellerker = ..

Sir John
Ellerker,
b 15
Janij, 4.
E. 6, 1550
m
Isabel, d. of
Richard
Smethley.

Julian
m
dau of
Simon
Mus-
grave.

Marmaduke
m
. . . . .
Christopher.

Hugh Ellerker
m
dau of Mus-
grave of . .

Thomas
Ellerker
m
Margt.
Thorp.

Henry
Ellerker
m

Robert
Ellerker
at Bran-
tingham,
1584.

Isabel
m
Thos.
Hodson
de
Cave.

Julian Elizabeth,
     1584

Anthony,
1584.

Phillip
Ellerker,
at Brant-
ingham,
1584.

Robert
Ellerker,
at Brant-
ingham.

William Ellerker de Ellerker, Sup. 1584, ob. 8th Jan., 35 E.
m
Elizabeth, dau of Thomas Wentworth, de Howley, a
younger House of Emsall.

John Ellerker, of Ellerker, ob. 1617.

ELLOUGHTON.

LLOUGHTON is a parish comprising the three townships of Elloughton, Brough, and Wauldby. The population of the entire parish is 966, namely, Elloughton, 503; Brough, 410; and Wauldby 53. W. H. Harrison-Broadley, Esq., J.P., is Lord of the Manor, and principal landowner.

DOMESDAY.

In Domesday Survey, Elloughton is referred to as follows :—
" In Elgendon and Walbi (Elloughton and Wauldby) there are seventeen carucates of arable land to be taxed where there may be 9 plough-teams. Archbishop Eldred held this for one manor, now Archbishop Thomas, and Godwin of him has there one caruca and 36 villains, and three bordars having eleven plough-teams. A Knight has 2 carucates of this land, and one plough-team there. There is a Priest and a Church there. There is meadow land five

quarentens long, and a quarenten broad, the whole manor is two leagues long and one league broad. In the time of King Edward the value was seven pounds, now it is one hundred shillings."

TORRE'S ACCOUNT.

From Torre's Manuscript we gather the following particulars respecting the parish, with a list of the vicars and an account of the testamentary burials : —

"The Manor of Elloughton is parcel of an ancient possession of the Archbishop of York, who held therein 10 carucates of land in demesne. Which said Manor was taxed at £20 18s. 6d.

"The Prebend of Wetwang is Rector of the Living of Elloughton, which is endowed with four oxgangs of land ; the Prebend, as rector, having also 2 tenants, all the tythe of corn thereof, and all maner of jurisdiction whereof to be rented at 16 marks per annum. The vicarage had an augmentation of £20 per annum settled on it, 24th May, 44th Elizabeth, out of the fruits of the Prebend of Wetwang."

A CLOSE CATALOGUE OF THE VICARS.

Temp Instit.	Vicarii Eccle.	Patroni.	Vacat.
1st Feb., 1349	Richd. de Wetwang	Prebend of	Mort.
11th Aug., 1355	Will Reynald de Stormworth	Wetwang.	....
19th May, 1380	John Humfrey	....	Res. pro vic Roxby
25th Oct., 1391	John Wyberd...................	... .	Lincolnshire.
	John Braytoft................	....	Mort.
2nd May, 1418	Willm. Fisher	....	Res.
11th Dec., 1436	Thos. Young	....	Mort.
19th June, 1439	Wm. Welton alias Fisher...	....	Res.
19th Jan., 1450	Wm. Ingram	....	Res.
22nd Ap., 1458	Ric. Rumbley	....	Mort.
12th Dec., 1459	Will Bossall	... .	Res.
Dec. 1475	Ric Walker	....	Mort.
23rd Dec., 1479	John Spencer................	....	Mort.
26th Jan., 1519	Rich Laikoke................	....	Mort.
19th Jan., 1528	Thomas Waylte...............	....	Res.

A Close Catalogue of the Vicars.—*Continued.*

Temp Instit.	Vicarii Eccle.	Patroni.	Vacat.
29th June, 1529	Johe Bykerton	Prebend of	Mort.
2nd June, 1531	Rad. Wilkinson...	Wetwang.	....
26th Nov., 1582	Rad. Coulson..........	....	Mort.
	Fol Bethame	....	....
29th May, 1592	Rad Barlow	....	....
25th May, 1613	Will Surfleet	....	....
	Jeremiah Collyer	....	....
7th Aug., 1622	Jac Bynkes.............	....	....
24th Aug., 1623	Valentine Mason	....	Mort.
19th Nov., 1639	Chas. Forge	.... •.......	....
1661	Tho. Tope	....	....
1665	Robt. Croupton.............	....	....
1670	Ric Peters	....	....
1672	Lien Walterill	....	....

Continuation List since Torre's.

Temp Instit.	Vicarii Eccle.	Patroni.	Vacat.
1678	John Lambert	....	....
1702	Peter Hickington	.........,..	....
1754	John Robinson	....	....
1783	Joseph Sommers	....	....
1798	Wm. John Wilkinson	....	....
1804	Nicholas Bourne	....	....
1825	John Overton.............	....	....
1842	Thomas Williams	....	....
1876	W. M. Bennett, M.A.	....	....

Testamentary Burials.

" 1st May, A.D. 1539.—William Simsone, of Elloughton, made his will, proved, whereby he gave his soul to God Almighty, St. Mary, and All Saints, and his body to be buried in the Pshe Ch., of Elloughton.

5th Nov., A.D. 1449.—William Fisher, Vicar of the Pshe Church of Elington, made his will, proved 5th Jany., 1450, whereby he gave his soul (ut Supra) and his body to be buried in the Quire of this Church of Elington.

20th Decr., A.D. 1519.—John Spenser, Vicar of Elloughton, made his will, proved 19th Jany., 1520, giving his soul (ut supra), and his body to be buried in the Quire of the Pshe Church, of Elloughton.

3rd Jany., A.D. 1523.—Richard Laikoke, Vicar of Elloughton, made his will, proved 13th June, 1528, giving his soul (ut Supra) and his body to be buried before his stall, in the High Quire of Our Blessed Lady, in the Pshe Church of Elloughton, and 20 shillings to the buylding of Elloughton Church Steple.

16th Mar., 1536.—William Waldbie, of Waldbye, gent., made his will, proved 17th June, 1536, giving his soul (ut Supra), and his body to be buried in the Church of Elloughton, in the south aisle, afore the image of our Blessed Lady.

12th Aug., A.D. 154·.—Phillip Waldbie, of Swanland, gent., made his will, proved 14th Feby., 1542, giving his soul to God Almighty, His Creator and Redeemer, and his body to be buried in the Parish Ch of Elloughton, in the Ladies' Quire."

THE CHURCH.

The church is dedicated to St. Mary, and consists of a nave, chancel, north and south transepts, and a tower at the west end. It was partly re-built in the year 1845. The dimensions are : nave, 33ft. 9in. long, by 23ft. 6in. wide ; the chancel, 34ft. 9in. long, by 14ft. wide.

Most of the stone work at the south door is very old, it has a pointed arch, and is very similar to that of St. Cross, Hampshire (see Rickman's *Architecture*), except that at Elloughton the dog-tooth work not only extends from the apex of the arch to the top of the circular shafts, but a single row of perpendicular dog-toothing runs between the two shafts on either side of the door. Three of these shafts are modern, and made of perishing sandstone, but the other is true early English or late Norman work. They stand "free," and have two rounds at the base of each, with a deepened hollow between, which holds water. This is an example of the only moulding used in English work which will hold water.

There are several memorial windows of stained glass. In the

P

south transept, two lancets to the memory of Thos. Williams, M.A.,
34 years vicar of the parish, who died Aug. 1st, 1876, the gift of
his sister.   In the north transept, two lancets in memory of
Catherine Thompson, who died on Ash Wednesday, 1876, the gift
of her husband.   In the tower, a window in memory of Captain
George Hall, placed there by his daughter, Mrs. Neale.   The
church is evidently of early English style, nearly all the win-

ST. MARY'S CHURCH, ELLOUGHTON.

dows being of the lancet pattern.   The tower is of two stages, embattled with pinnacles at the angles, and a window of two lights in
each face of the belfry stage.   The tower contains three bells with
the following inscriptions : —

    1. James Harrison, founder, 1790.
    2. Warner & Sons, Crescent Foundry, London, 1856.
    3. Will Ringrose, Churchwarden, 1790.

In the churchyard there are tombstones bearing the following inscriptions :—

"Joseph Scaife, born 24th April, 1803 ; died 15th June, 1881."

"Matthew Scaife, born 29th April, 1809 ; died 7th June, 1886."

"Robert Prescott, who died Feby. 16th, 1876, aged 77 years."

"Captain George Hull, who died 29th August, 1855, aged 83 years."

"Thomas William Palmer, J.P., of Brough, born 31st March, 1800 ; died 28th Feb., 1881. Twice Mayor, and for 40 years Justice of the Peace for Kingston-upon-Hull."

"John Everatt, died July 26th, 1860, aged 52. Mary, relict of the above, died Aug. 23rd, 1885, aged 75."

"James Williamson, died Nov. 20th, 1877, aged 66 years."

"Robert Day, of Brough, died July 29th, 1864, aged 80 years."

"Peter Nicholson, died 21st May, 1879, aged 52 years."

"William Carlill, died August 24th, 1875, aged 85."

The Living is a vicarage, yearly value, £300, in the gift of the Archbishop of York, and held by the Rev. William Millard Bennett, M.A., of St. John's College, Cambridge.

The registers commence in the year 1653, and amongst the earlier entries are those of baptisms, marriages, and burials of members of a branch of the Portington Family.

ANCIENT MONUMENTS. &C., IN THE CHURCH.

Glover, in his visitation, gives the following arms which were at that time (1584) in this church :—

I.   "Argent a lion rampant azure, crowned or."   East end.

II.   "Argent, diapore, on a chief sable, 2 mullets of six points or very ould."

III.   "Or 2 bars and chief 3 Torteax."

IV.   "Gules on a patonce or."

V.   "Azure, a cross patonce argent."

VI.   "Gules, 3 water boughets argent."

VII.   "Argent, 3 asses heads cuyped gules."

VIII.   "Azure fretty argent."

IX.   "This one Escochen standeth on a grave stone, argent on a bend

——cottised　3 escallops——impaling azure, a lion rampant azure between 6 cross crosslets or."

　　X.　" Gules, a fess between 6 cross crossletts or."

　　XI.　" Argent 3 popinjays vert, beaked."

　　XII.　" Gules a lion rampant between 12 Billets or."

　　XIII.　" Argent 3 martletts gules."

　　XIV.　" ——broken a tortiure engrailed sable."

　　XV.　" ——a lion rampant —— crowned or."

　　XVI.　" ——a lion rampant."

　　XVII.　" Argent on a chief sable 2 mullets of 6 points or."

　　XVIII.　" Gules a lion rampant argent within a ‑‑ — engrailed on th last.' '

　　XIX.　" Or a lion rampant gules."

CHARITIES.

The Rev. William Mason, " Presbyter in the Church of England, and in the City of York," by his will, dated 11th April, 1705, left £120 " to purchase a dwelling-house for the use of the Vicar of the Parish of Elloughton, and of his successors for ever, for their better discharge of their Ministry in that Church, and to encourage their residence according to Law." " Item :—My Will is that till a fit Vicarage House can be bought and settled as above written, that the said money go at interest, to be half-yearly paid to the present Churchwardens and Overseers of the poor, or major part of them, towards hiring of such fit house for the vicar to reside in, and in case he refuses such constant residence, then I will the said interest be distributed among the poor of Elloughton, till my will above written be fulfilled by him or his successor, that this, my last will be not defeated."

There were 602 acres of church land in this parish, the reversionary interest in which was sold by the Ecclesiastical Commissioners in the year 1849, for £9,500, the computed value of the fee simple of the land being £20,000 at the time of sale.

THE REV. BARNABAS SHAW.

Barnabas Shaw, a pioneer missionary to South Africa, was born at Elloughton, on the 12th of April, 1788. Mr. Shaw's parents, who were married in 1777, at Elloughton, had six children, of whom four died in infancy and lie interred in Elloughton churchyard, beside their parents and grandparents. The two survivors were James and Barnabas. The latter joined the Wesleyan Methodist Society in his youth, and was afterwards called into the regular ministry of that body. In the year 1813 he devoted himself to missionary work in foreign lands, and, according to an entry in his journal, this resolution was made on "Mill Hill, at Elloughton," a place to which he often retired for meditation. After undergoing a course of special preparation for the work, and having in the meantime been married to Miss Jane Butler, of Bridlington Quay, he sailed for South Africa, in December, 1815. Probably no missionary ever landed in South Africa under such unfavourable circumstances, but he bore all with patience, and persevered through difficulties which would have appalled most men. When Livingstone arrived in South Africa, in 1840, Barnabas Shaw had been there for a quarter of a century, doing a truly noble work, and he may fairly be said to have been the father of Wesleyan Missions in South Africa. Mr. Shaw came over to England in 1827, and the following extract from his journal refers to the visit which he paid to his aged parents on the eve of his return to the land of his adoption :

"January, 24th, 1829. I went to Elloughton, the place of my nativity, to take leave of my aged parents. On my arrival here, a year and a half ago (after an absence of nearly twelve years), how peculiar were my feelings ! The cottage in which I first breathed the vital air still stood at the bottom of the garden ; the little spots of ground where I used to plant my flowers were adorned with the beauties of spring ; and my dear, aged mother had led the blooming roses above the tops of the windows. The adjacent hills where I used to sit and play my flute, while tending the lambs of the flock, were clothed in living green ; the fields I had frequently ploughed were waving with corn ; and the beautiful Humber was rolling its mighty stream at the foot of the hills. The morning larks were ascending on high, the doves were cooing in their lofty habitations, and on the Sabbath (sweet day of rest !) I again heard " the sound of the church-going bell." What a contrast to the dreary deserts through which I had been travelling ! My father is yet alive, and his head is adorned with locks of silver. Both he and my mother have passed the bounds of three score years and ten, and are gradually sinking into the grave. How shall I leave them ! My engagements with the committee, the erection of our chapel at the Cape, and some other circumstances call me to go ; but, after all, it is hard work. Some of the strongest bonds of affection must be torn asunder. The aged pair frequently kissed their grandchildren as they prattled round them, having no hope of again seeing them in this vale of tears. The shades of evening came on. The vehicle which was to bear us away approached. We prayed and parted. Farewell, my aged parents ! May the God of Abraham, and of Isaac, and of Jacob be your God, the strength of your hearts, and your portion for ever."*

Mr. Shaw continued his useful labours in South Africa, and died at his residence in Mowbray, near Cape Town, on the 21st of June, 1857, in the 70th year of his age, and 47th of his ministry.

CHAPELS.

In the centre of the village, at the corner of the four ways, is a neat Congregational Church, with accommodation for 250 persons. The foundation stone was laid on July 6th, 1876, by Evan Fraser, Esq., F.R.C.S., of Hull, and was formally opened for public worship, June 28th, 1877. It occupies the site of an older structure, originally built as a school-house, and supplied with a teacher, through the effort and liberality of Mr. Carlill, the then owner and occupier of Elloughton-Garth, but was fitted up for public worship and opened for this purpose on Good Friday, April 8th, 1814. An

* *Wesleyan Methodist Magazine* for 1830, p 21.

interesting memorial, of much liberality and interest on the part of the Carlill family exists in the form of two valuable silver cups, still used in the Communion Services of the church, bearing an inscription, "Presented by Miss M. Carlill, 1821." In the earlier building, service was conducted by the minister of the South Cave congregation, aided by lay-helpers. After the opening of the present building, the Elloughton Congregational Church was formed on a basis of its own. The present minister is the Rev. James Smith, M.A., formerly Tutor in Classics, and in Greek New Testament Exegesis and Literature, in the Old Independent College, at Rotherham.

Connected with the church, and used for members of the Congregation, is a small burial ground, formerly belonging to the Society of Friends. A list, containing the names of more than fifty persons who have been interred there at intervals, from A.D. 1685 to A.D. 1765, shews that a considerable number of the members of that society must have lived in the district. We extract the following from the list :—

    1686. Eleanor, wife of John Randall, Elloughton.
    1694. William Stather, Ellerker.
    1702. Robt. Stephenson, Ferriby.
    1715. John Craythorne, Brantingham.
    1716. William Hunsman, Brough.
    1720. John Baines, South Cave.
    1721. Elizth Watkin, Elloughton.
    1723. Mary, wife of Robt. Evasse, South Cave.
    1727. Rebecca, daughter of Ambrose Stickney, Risby.
    1734. Joannah, wife of John Hutchinson, Newbald.
    1742. William, son of Timothy Harper, Welton.

The Primitive Methodists have a neat chapel in the village, with schoolroom attached.

An Odd Fellows' Hall was built in the year 1871, connected with the Manchester Unity.

A modern-built house, opposite the Vicarage, is the residence of Alderman J. T. Woodhouse, Mayor of Hull in 1890-91.

In the year 1887, when digging in a gravel pit on the Mill Hill, at Elloughton, the workmen came across a mammoth's tusk, which was found to measure eight feet in length, and eighteen inches round the thickest part. Unfortunately the tusk was broken in pieces in attempting to remove it from its bed. The men afterwards found another tusk measuring over five feet in length, and, special means being adopted, it was got out entire, and was forwarded to the museum at Scarborough. During the last few years five skeletons have been found in the pit. Two of these skeletons were lying together, and near to one of them was a jar or urn.

There is an old square stone in the churchyard, which may have formed the base of the ancient village cross.

BROUGH.

Brough is a pleasant village on the bank of the Humber, ten miles west from Hull, and has a station on the Hull and Selby Railway. By some it is thought to have been the Roman Station of Petuaria, mentioned by Ptolemy. It is highly probable that on this spot the Romans first planted their standard when they took possession of the north bank of the Humber. The Roman Road (Ermine Street) from Lincoln to York, had a ferry from Winteringham to Brough, and traces of this road have been discovered here; in fact, the whole neighbourhood abounds with distinct evidence of the Roman occupation. Large numbers of Roman coins have been found from time to time, indeed, on digging in any part of the gardens at Brough, portions of Roman pottery, &c., are readily met with.

Brough House, the residence of T. W. Palmer, Esq., J.P., stands on what is called "Castle Hill," which doubtless formed a portion of the site of the old Roman camp.

A regular ferry was formerly maintained across the Humber at Brough, and about the year 1840, a steam packet was brought into use in connection with it. From a deed, dated in 1794, it appears that the Ferry and all its rights were at that time sold by James Wood, of Brough, mariner, to John Barker, of Howden, gentleman, for £465.

BROUGH HOUSE.

About half a mile from the village, on the high road to South Cave, at the extremity of an avenue of fine ornamental trees, may be seen an imposing obelisk bearing the following inscription :—

"To Brigadier General Thomas Palmer, Col. 72nd Regt. Bengal N. I., who, after 51 years of arduous and eventful service, died at Mussoorie whilst in Command of the Cawnpore Division, 15th April, 1854, aged 68 years. This Obelisk was erected in 1873 as a tribute to his memory, by his cousin, Thomas William Palmer, J.P., of Brough, East Yorkshire, who died 28th February, 1881, aged 81."

"Dick Turpin," the notorious highwayman, is said to have resided in an old house, near the Castle Hill, and he was arrested in the village prior to his last trial at York.

Mr. Richard Everatt, of Brough, has a cannon ball in his possession, being one of many which have been found here at different times, and it is probable that there may at some time have been a naval engagement on the Humber.

Mr. W. H. Harrison-Broadley, J.P., and Mr. T. W. Palmer, J.P., are the principal land-owners.

The Wesleyan Methodists have a neat little chapel near the Railway Station.

WAULDBY.

Wauldby is on the Wold Hills about two miles east from Elloughton.

The Chapel of Ease, which occupies the site of an ancient chapel, was erected in the year 1835, at a cost of about £1000, by Mrs. Ann Raikes, Lady of the Manor, and is held in connection with the Living of Elloughton. In the old chapel there was a mural tablet in memory of "John Parkinson, Lord of Wauldby," who died in 1676, and in the floor there was a slab inscribed to one of the Burton family, and dated in 1784. In the churchyard there are few gravestones, the oldest of which records the death, in 1692, of Matthew Meagar, merchant, of Wakefield. Another in memory of Arabella, wife of William Walker, of Kingston-upon-Hull, surgeon, and daughter of William Barry, of Wauldby, Esq., and relict of the late Mr. Richard Zouch, of Wakefield, merchant, who died in 1789. Other stones are to the memory of members of the Barry family.

WELTON.

HE Parish of Welton forms the easternmost extremity of the Manor of Howden, of which it is part, and comprises the townships of Welton and Melton, the former having a population of 659, and the latter 171.

DOMESDAY.

In Domesday Book, we find the following reference to Welton:—

"Land of the Bishop of Durham. In Welleton (Welton) eighteen carucates, with these Berewicks, Alrecher (Ellercar), eight carucates; Walcheton (Walkington), nine carucates: Hundeslege (Hunsley), two carucates and a half: Lugufled (Yorkefleet), one carucate and a half: there are to be taxed thirty-nine carucates, and there may be twenty ploughs   Morcar held this for one manor. The Bishop of Durham now has in the demesne six ploughs, and thirty-three villanes : and three bordars having nine ploughs, and ten sokemen with six ploughs ; and three mills pay eighteen shillings. Meadow one mile long and four quarentens broad. Coppice wood, four quarentens long and three broad. The whole manor two miles long and half a mile broad. Value in King Edward's time twenty pounds, at present thirteen pounds."

TORRE'S ACCOUNT.

" The Church of Welton was parcel of the possessions of the Prior and Convent of Durham, of whose patronage it was a long time till it came into the hands of the Nevills of Raby.

" 27th Septr., A.D. 1439, appropriation of the Parish Church of Welton and its universal rights and members to Richd. Burton and John Barneby, Chaplains of the ppetual chantry founded at a certain altar in the Cathedral Church of Lincoln, before which the Lady Katherine, late Duchess of Lancaster, lyes interred, to have and to hold to them and their successors Chaplains and their ppetual use for ever. Reserving to the vicar in this church to be ordained a competent portion for his sustenance, viz., Who hath hereby to him ordained the mansion house of the rectory of the Church, together with ye glebe and all the tythe and emoluments whatsover to the same Church pertaining, which said vicar to whom the perquisites of the Autumnal fruits do appertain, shall pay to the said Richard and John and their successors Chaplains celebrating in the Church at Lincoln for ever, the Annual pension of £13 6s. 8d. at the feast of Easter and All Saints. Furthermore willing that the said Chaplains shall present a fit chaplain to this vicarage within a month after the vacation thereof, and the said vicar, when instituted, shall also pay these Annual pensions :—

	s.	d.
To the Archbishop of York, and his successrs.	13	4
To the Dean and Chapter of York	6	8
To ye Prior and Convent of Durham	13	4

at the feast of St. Michael, out of the fruits of this Church at Welton, which appropriation was confirmed by John, Archbishop, on ye 25th Novr., 1424, and by the Dean and Chapter of York." *

* Torre's *Peculiars*, p 1227.

CATALOGUE OF THE RECTORS OF WELTON.

Temp Instit.	Vicarii Eccle.	Patroni.	Vacat.
12	Hugo de Evesham...	Prior and Convent of	Resig.
1272	R. Burnell	Durham.	....
1280	Richd. de Hertlepole	....	....
1307	Wm. de Pykering............	....	....
1312	Rad. de Anlagby	....	....
1316	Rog. de Heslarton	....	....
1317	Ric de Baldock	....	....
1322	Thos. De Symingthorpe ...	....	Resig.
1328	Thos. de Nova Kaya	....	Mort.
1349	Henry de Gareyangs	....	....
	Adam de Dowell	....	....
1383	Johe de Scardeburgh	John de Nevill de Roby	....
	Thos. Sandewyke	....	Mort.
1416	Nich Dixon	.. ..	Resig.
1417	Wm. Fallan	....	Resig.
1417	Robt. Dibbon	Prior & Convt. of Durham	Resig.
1421	Richd. Kellons	Rad Camin	....
1430	Thos. Hebbeden	Johe Camin	....
1435	Rob. Knayton.	....	....

A CATALOGUE OF THE VICARS.

Temp Instit.	Vicarii Eccle.	Patroni.	Vacat.
1439	Joh Kayingham	Capelena et Alan Elyth.	....
	Robt. Clark	....	Resig.
1479	Thos. Lawson	....	Mort.
1494	Hugo Clyderhouse	....	Mort.
1528	Joh Alynson	....	....
1610	Geo. Procter	Rex.	Mort.
1617	Johes Norton	Rex.	....
1660	Robt. Jobson	Rex.	Mort.
1670	John Dove	Rex. ....

VICARS SINCE TORRE'S LIST.

Temp Instit.	Vicarii Eccle.	Patroni.	Vacat.
1682	Richard Brawell		....
1691	Stephen Thompson	....	....
1740	Peter Simon	....	....
1779	Dr. William Welfit	....	....
1795	N. Simon	....	....
1800	William Champney	....	....
1845	Thomas B. Paget M.A......	....	....

CONTINUATION OF TORRE'S ACCOUNT.

MELTON CHANTRY.

"There was within this parish and Church of Welton, the Chapel of St. James of Melton, wherein this Chantry was thus formed, viz., 1st Feby, A.D. 1354. Ordination, William de Feriby, Canon of the Cathedral Church of York, and one of the executors of the testament of William de Melton, by the King's consent, and of John, Archbishop of York, gave and granted, and in pure alms perpetually assigned unto God, St. Peter and St. James ye less, and to 3 Chaplains and their successors, viz., the one celebrating at the Altar of St. Innocents, in the Cathedral of York. And the other 2 daily celebrating in this Chapel of St. James, of Melton, and to their successors for ever, 20 M: arising out of his lands in Hotham, N. Cave, Feriby, Swanland and Elvey (viz.), to each of these 2 Chaplins 100s., to be paid them annually on the feast of St. Martyn and Pentecost by equal portions. Who are to celebrate herein for the souls of Edward of Canarvon, late King of England, and of William de Melton, sometime Archb. of York, and for the souls of their predecessors and successors, (viz.), One of them shall daily celebrate the mass, ad Requiem for their said souls, and the other the mass de die de Trinitate, or to other souls as they shall be devoutly disposed, so that every day one mass shall be celebrated in the said Chapel de Regio for their souls, unless it be on the grand festivals, when both the Masses shall be celebrated. Also every one of these Chaplains shall say daily for their souls a placebo dirge in consideration of the dead.

CATALOGUE OF THE 1st CHAPLAINS THEREOF.

Temp Inst.	Vicarii Eccle.	Patroni.	Vacat.
1354...	Richard Edwards	William de Feriby...	Res.

CATALOGUE OF THE 1st CHAPLAINS THEREOF.—*Continued.*

Temp Inst.	Vicarii Eccle.	Patroni.	Vacat.
1371...	Alan Lawrence		
	Will Chaffer		Resig.
1397...	John de Halington		Res.
1397...	Wm. Keyworth		Mort.
1406...	Johe Kelsey	Robt. Tyrwhitt	Res.
1414...	Wm. de Clyton		
1424...	Thos. Rudde	John Tyrwhitt	Resig.
1428...	Rich. Yonge	Ric Pyckering	
	Adam Person		Resig.
1440...	Wm. Barneby		
	Wm. Bernom		
1444...	Johe Rudd		Res.
1455...	Johe Bryan	Johe Whitcote	Mort.
	Robt. Gilling		
1478...	Thos. Chapman	El Whitcote	Res.
1478...	Wm. Synk		
	John Whitcote		Res.
1507...	Will Brockelbank		Res.
1509...	Robt. Evers		
1521...	Robt. Stone	Robt. Whitcote	Res.
1529...	Robt. Michell	Thos. Whitcote	Res.

CATALOGUE OF 2nd CHAPLAINS THEREOF.

Temp Inst.	Vicarii Eccle.	Patroni.	Vacat.
1354...	Nich de Feriby	Will de Feriby	
	John Hillet de Elsey		
	Alan de Kelham		Res.
1382...	Thos. de Castleford		
1389...	Wm. de Balkholme		
1406...	Phil Burton	Robt. Tyrwhitt	Mort.
1436...	Will Wilson	R. Pykering	
1440...	Will Smyth		
	Will Clayton		Mort.
1446...	Johe Dale		

CATALOGUE OF 2nd CHAPLAINS. *Continued.*

Temp Instit.	Vicarii Eccle.	Patroni.	Vacat.
	John Clerk	Johe Whitcote	....
1458...	Richd. Cohem	....	....
1458...	Johe Fitling	....	Res.
1462...	Ric Taylor	....	Res.
1464...	Pet Lowther	....	Mort.
1516...	Wm. Apelby	....	Mort.
1521 ...	Johe Rodes..	... .	Mort.
1521...	Johe Bently..................	....	Mort.
1523...	F. Talboys..................	....	Mort.
1528...	Wm. Johnson..................	....	Res.
1546..	Wm. Tatler	Assigns of H. Whitcote	....

TESTAMENTARY BURIALS.

" 27th Aug. A.D. 1564.—William Brockelbank, of Welton, Husbandman, to be buried in the Church of Welton. near unto his Father and Mother.

26th Dec. A.D. 1562.—Peter Michell, Clerk, to be buried in the Church.

16th Sep. A.D. 1582.—John Carlill. of Melton, Husbandman, to be buried in the Church.

1st April, A.D. 1586.—Jennett Newmarch, of Welton, Widow, to be buried in the Church.

13th Jan., A.D. 1587.—Thomas Lyon, of Welton, to be buried in the Church.

17th Aug., A.D. 1588.—Robert Baion, of Welton, to be buried in the Church. near his wife.

1st. Sept , A.D. 1589.—Peter Lyson, of Melton, Husbandman, to be buried in the Church.

27th Feb., A.D. 1591.—Robt. Carlill, of Melton, to be buried in the Church at Welton.

28th Dec., A.D. 1590.—John Moore, of Welton, yeoman, Body to be buried in the South Isle of the Parish Church where he used to sit.

30th July, A.D. 1591.—William Langley, Body to be bnried in the Church.

17th Sep. A.D. 1592.—Agnes Moore, of Welton, widow, to be buried in the Church.

" 26th July, A.D. 1592.—Robert Hunt, of Melton, to be Buried in the Church.

22nd Feb., A.D. 1594.—Ellen Gunson, of Welton, made her Will, proved 12th May, 1595, giving her soul to Alm. God, her Saviour and Redeemer, and her body to be buried in ye psh. Church of Welton."

THE CHURCH.

The church, dedicated to St. Helen, is a cruciform building in the early English style, and consists of chancel, nave, aisles, north and south transepts, and a square tower with four bells. It was completely restored in 1863 under the supervision of Sir G. Scott,

ST. HELEN'S CHURCH, WELTON.

at the expense of the late Miss Sophia Broadley, of Welton House.

The earliest mention of this church occurs in a document in the reign of William the Conqueror, by which Welton was confirmed to the See of Durham; but in all probability the church had its origin in Saxon times.

The handsome east window was the gift of the Rev. T. B. Paget. The memorial window in the chancel was erected there

Q

by Mrs. Galland, to her husband's memory. The window in the south transept, and another in the north aisle, were the gifts of members of the Broadley family, in memory of the late Miss Sophia Broadley. In the south aisle is a stained window with the following inscription :—

"To the Glory of God and in memory of Thomas Thompson, F.S.A., Born at Eastdale, 12th March, A.D. 1791, died at Spring Ville, 19th April, A.D. 1871 ; these windows were designed and presented to this Church by his widow, Jane Thompson, who died 8th March, 1879, not surviving to see their completion."

In the north aisle is an effigy of a Knight Templar much defaced.

MONUMENTAL INSCRIPTIONS IN THE CHURCH.

At the east end of the nave is a brass with a female figure in a kneeling position, bearing the following inscription :—

"✠ To the memory of Sophia Broadley, of Welton, who restored and enlarged this Church, A.D. MDCCCLXIII."

At the west end of the south aisle is a monument

"In memory of Andrew Fitzgerald Reynolds, of Melton, who died on the 23rd day of July, 1856 ; also of a son and daughter."

In the same aisle is another monument, erected by subscription among the parishioners :—

"In memory of two private soldiers, natives of Welton, William Ruston, aged XXVII. years ; Thomas Henry Clayton, aged XXIII. years, who died in the Crimean Campaign, A.D. MDCCCLIV."

At the west end of the nave is a mural monument

"To the memory of James Shaw Williamson, of Melton Hill, son of Joseph Williamson, Esq., who departed this life Feb. 25th, 1819, aged 35 years."

"In a vault near this place are deposited the remains of Charles Whittaker, of Melton Hill, Esq., who departed this life in the humble hope of a blessed resurrection, Jan. 6th, 1850, in the 70th year of his age. He was Deputy Lieutenant for the East Riding of the County of York, and eminently connected for many years with the town and trade of Hull ; and in private life he was highly esteemed and respected by a large circle of relatives and friends."

"In the same vault rest the remains of Rachel Whittaker, the Widow of the said Charles Whittaker, who departed this life Jany. 3rd, 1874, aged 82 years."

In the north chapel are the following tablets :—

"Near this place lie the Bodies of James Shaw, Esq., and Dinah, his wife, ——, 1769."

"Here also lieth the body of Ann Williamson, who died 8th Jany., 1792, aged 63."

"To the memory of Joseph Williamson, of Melton Hill, who died 28th Feb., 1785, aged 54 years."

"To the memory of Thos. Williamson, Esq., of this place, Obit. Julii, VII., MDCCCIX, Aetis LXXIV."

There are also two tablets to members of the Richardson family.

In the south aisle a tablet—

"In memory of John Wilson, Esq., of Melton Hill, who departed this life the 6th day of Jany., 1822, aged 56 years ; also of Ann, his widow, daughter of Caius Thompson, of Hull, merchant, who died May 5th, 1855, aged 86 years."

In the vestry are memorials to the Hammond and Rokeby families, with a long latin inscription to Alexander Rokeby who died in 1667.

Also to the memory of—

"Robert Mason, Gent., Collector of the Customs, and twice Mayor of Kingston-upon-Hull, who was buryed before this pillar, the 5th of May, 1718, in the 86th year of his age, who was indefatigable in assisting the injured and helpless on all occasions, and a common arbitrator, peace-maker, and constant Benefactor, for which he was beloved, and his loss lamented by all. Also Elizabeth, his widow, Buryed the 26th Feb. following, in the 87th year of her age, they having been happy together in a married state above 60 years."

In the churchyard is the well-known tombstone to Jeremiah Simpson, with its quaint inscription. The original stone is now used as a footstone, as the letters were becoming obliterated. After the restoration of the church, in 1863, E. S. Wilson, Esq., by permission of the Vestry put down a new stone, on which the inscription was copied, as follows :—

> " Here lieth he, ould Jeremy,
> Who hath eight times maried been,
> But now in his ould age
> He lies in his cage
> Under the gras so green.

Which Jeremiah Simpson, departed this life in the 84 year of his age, in the year of Our Lord, 1719."

THE BELLS.

The four bells bear the following inscriptions :—

(1). " Exaltabo te Deus. Barrow. 1764."
(2). " C. and G. Mears, founders, London, 1848."
(3). " Sancta Simon et Juda Apostoli Dei Orate Pro Nobis."
(4). " Nos cum prole pia benedicat virgo Maria."

THE LIVING.

The present incumbent is the Rev. T. B. Paget, M.A., Canon of York, who was appointed by the Crown in the year 1845. The patronage was subsequently transferred from the Crown to the late Miss Broadley in exchange for the living of Ecton, in Northamptonshire.

TERRIER.

A terrier, dated in 1809, after describing the vicarage-house and giving particulars of the glebe, &c., has the following :—

" There are, belonging to this vicarage, certain houses and lands called and known by the name of Priesthold, for which the Vicar receives yearly outrents and fines at every change, and he the said Vicar keeps a Court at pleasure. Easter Offerings due to the Vicar for every communicant he receives two pence. The Vicar likewise receives a mortuary of ten shillings at the death of every male householder who dies worth thirty pounds and upwards, and for every householder under that sum, three shillings and fourpence."

CHARITIES.

" The White Bread Charity Land. Robert Mason, by surrender, dated 16th November, 1694, appointed the sum of £1 14s. 8d. out of divers lands in Welton to be expended in the purchase of White Bread for the poor of Welton ; and James Shaw, Esqre., by his surrender, bearing date 17th April, 1764, and Will dated 13th December, 1764, gave all his interest in the surplus of the rents and profits of the same lands for the following purposes ; two guineas per annum to the Schoolmaster for teaching six poor children to read and write, and the residue of the rents is applied in occasional assistance to the poor in house-rent, coals, and medical relief, and sometimes in money weekly —the Commissioners censured the directions of the Deed, as to the sums laid out in bread, and expected that the Charity would henceforth be administered with more care and attention.

" The Bull Ings and poor land, 5a. 1r. 23p. of land let at the time of the report for £9 10s. per annum, granted by award dated 1st May, 1752, and under an Act, passed 24th Geo. II., the Commissioners awarded to Robert Best and John Dilock, the then Constables, and other inhabitants of Welton, 3a. or. 22p. of ings land for the buying and keeping a bull for the use of the inhabitants, and 2a. 1r. 1p. of land for the poor ; the rents are divided in the proportion of two thirds to Welton and one third in the township of Melton, to poor persons by the Overseers, respectively ; that to Welton being confined to poor persons not receiving collection. The Commissioners reported that from 1813 to the time of the report the rents had been included in one and the same account for the benefit as presumed of Welton township only, and they intimated that the rents ought to be divided and applied as they used to be in 1787, and that the application in Melton should be according to established custom.

Randall's and Askam's gifts, £20 and £5 ; the interest £1 5s. od., was formerly paid by a William Nelson, and applied for the benefit of the poor of Welton, but about 1811 the money was paid in and supposed to be applied to parochial purposes, no interest being now received therefrom.

Walter Stickney's benefaction, by will dated 21st Oct., 1791 : interest of £5 5s. od. for bread for the most needy poor which is distributed in loaves of three pennyworth each at the Church on every Trinity Sunday at the discretion of the Minister and Churchwardens." *

CHAPELS.

The Wesleyans and Primitive Methodists have Chapels in the village.

* Charity Commissioners' 10th Report, p 663.

WELTON DALE.

At a short distance from the village is Welton Dale, a place of great resort by the inhabitants of Hull and neighbourhood. After passing the cottage at the entrance to the Dale, there is a wood on the left, and a hill to the right. From the latter, extensive and delightful views may be obtained of the Humber and the adjacent country. In the Dale is

THE MAUSOLEUM.

This building was erected as the last resting place of members of the Raikes family. It is a circular building, very chaste, of the Doric order, surmounted by a dome. The whole is of stone sixty-seven feet in circumference and thirty-eight feet high. A mural marble tablet in the building has the following inscription :—

"Within this Mausoleum are deposited the mortal remains of Robert Raikes, Esq., of Welton House, who departed this life on the 20th day of August, 1837, aged 72 years."

Other members of the family are also interred there.

NORTH FERRIBY.

N Domesday we find the following references to North Ferriby :—

"Lands of the Earl of Morton.

In Ferebi (Ferriby) Siward had half a carucate to be taxed, and there may be one plough. In these Nigel has three villanes having half a plough.

Land of Ralph de Mortimer.

Manor. In Ferebi (Ferriby) Eddina has ten carucates of land to be taxed. There is land to five ploughs. Ralph has now there fourteen villanes with three ploughs. There is a Church and a priest. Value in King Edward's time one hundred shillings, now sixty shillings." *

At North Ferriby there was formerly a priory of the Knight Templars, or Knights of St. John of Jerusalem, founded about the

* Bawdwen's Translation, p 184.

year 1200 by Lord Eustace Broomfleet. In the reign of Edward
IV., Sir William Taylboys, Knt., was Lord of Ferriby, but forfeiting
it to the King for rebellion, it was granted to Bourchier, Lord
Cromwell. One of the Earls of Cumberland endowed the
Monastery with £95 11s. 8d. per annum, but it was dissolved
in the time of Henry VIII., the revenues being then valued at
£60 1s. 2d. The site of the priory was said to have had a
hundred different owners between its dissolution in 1536 and the
year 1696, and "all those were commonly ruined or reduced to
beggary who had anything to do with it." * In an old account of
St. Mary's Church, Hull, mention is made of the Knight Templars
of Ferriby obtaining a license for divine service there in behalf of
their parishioners, and there is a memorandum "that the Low
Church of Kingston-upon-Hull was impropriate unto the monastery
of Ferriby, the ministers thereof being called curates." In the
twenty-seventh Henry VI. "the convent of the house and church
of the blessed Virgin Mary of North Ferriby, of the order of the
Temple at Jerusalem, granted liberty to lay leaden pipes from
Anlaby to North Ferriby, to convey fresh water." Nothing at
the present time remains of this once venerable monastery.

A free-school was founded here by L. Lillington, Esq., and
endowed by him with ten pounds per annum, "for the instruction
of twelve children in reading writing and accompts."

The handsome house built of red brick, formerly the residence of the Etherington family, is now the property of Mrs.
Turner, the Lady of the Manor.

TORRE'S ACCOUNT.

"The Church at Ferriby was a rectory anciently belonging to the Lord
Veseys till the Advowson thereof was given by William de Vesey to the new

* Hadley's *History of Hull*, p 850.

founded priory of the Knight Templars of North Ferriby, and on the Ides of March, 1332, was, by William, Archbishop of York, appropriated to that religious house, who, for indemnity of his Cathedral Church thereby, and in sign and subjection of it thereunto reserved out of the profits and fruits thereof to himself and successors Archbishops, the Annual pension of 40s., and on 2nd none of May, 1332, he ordained that a perpetual vicar should be in this Church of North Ferriby, presentible by the prior and brethren of the order of Knight Templars thereof, and should personally reside in the Church, having government of the parishioners and exercise the cure of Souls, and so cause the Church to be laudably served in divine offices, in which respect he shall have for the portion of his vicarage and sustentation 20 marks sterling, payd him quarterly per annum by the said prior and brethren out of the fruits and profits of the Church ; also, he shall have for his habitation the third part of the area of the mansion of the rectory, the said prior and brethren bearing all burdens ordinary and extraordinary of the Church, so as the vicar shall be tyed to none of them, only that he shall serve the Church by himself or a sufficient substitute, and at his cost to find one Chaplain to celebrate thrice a week in the chapel at Swanland, and shall find and sustain that Chantry as the rector of the Church of North Ferriby was herebefore accustomed to do, and on 16th May, 1348, licence was granted to the prior and Convent of Ferriby."

LIST OF THE RECTORS.

Temp Instit.	Vicarii Eccle.	Patroni.
12th April, 1272	Ricardus de Vescy....................	Dame Agnes de Vescy
8th Jan., 1281	Wm. de Monceux	
2nd Sep., 1282	Tho. de Romenara	
12th June, 1294	Wm. de Bollington	Wm. de Vescy.
17th Aug., 1315	Wm. de Moynge	Prior and Brethren of N. Ferriby.
23rd July, 1322	Wm. de la Mare	
23rd Dec., 1328	Walt. de Bedewynd	
13th June, 1330	Wm. de Ferriby.......................	

LIST OF THE VICARS.

Temp Instit.	Vicarii Eccle.	Patroni.
10th July, 1343	Robt. de Fenningley...................................	
10th Oct., 1348	Wm. de Givendale	
10th Oct., 1349	Johe de Kilbom	

LIST OF THE VICARS.—*Continued.*

Temp Instit.	Vicarii Eccle.	Patroni.
20th Mar., 1371	Pet de Newton Canon	....
	Pet de Crayke	
20th Jan., 1377	Wm de Anlagnby Canon	
10th Dec., 1389	Robt. White	
14th April, 1412	Johe de Martin	
1st Jan., 1434	Richd. Hessyl	
	Tho. Barton	
19th April, 1458	Peter Frothyngham	....
3rd Jan., 1479	Johe Baynton	
24th Feb., 1481	Johe Yorke...........	...
	Rich Hothome	
22nd Nov., 1506	Johe Holme	...
	Johe Bawdewyne	
20th June, 1532	Johe Burgh	
3rd July, 1540	Robt. Langryg	Hen. VIII.
24th Dec., 1569	Joh Morgan	Elizth. Regina
3rd June, 1573	Egidus Baynes	....
2nd Aug., 1589	Geo. Thompson, B.A.	
29th April, 1608	Tho. North............................	F. Haldenby
5th Oct., 1611	Tho. Browne	
9th Sep., 1629	Johe Nelson	
11th June, 1635	Jas. Roberts	

CONTINUATION SINCE TORRE'S LIST.

Temp Instit.	Vicarii Eccle.	Patroni.
1702	Henry Tiplin	....
1731	William Huntington	.....
1766	Joseph Milner	....
1800	Josiah Rodwell	
1801	John Scott	... .
1846	Thomas Dykes	....
1847	Charles Newby Wawne	....
1880	Thomas Maylin Theed, LL. B. ...	....

TESTAMENTARY BURIALS.

"27th March, A.D., 1342.—Nicholas Swanland, Son of John, to be buried in the Churchyard of North Ferriby, and bequeaths his best animal for his mortuary.

22nd Nov., A.D., 1452.—Thos. Haldenby, of Swanland, in the psh. of North Ferriby, to be buried in the Church of All Saints.

3rd. Jan., A.D. 1458.—Nicholas Kirkman, of Swanland, (a true Catholic, believing as the Church believes) to be buried in the Church.

16th June, A.D. 1591.—Giles Baynes, Vicar, to be buried in the Church."[*]

THE CHURCH.

The church, dedicated to All Saints, is at the southern end of the village, and is surrounded by lofty trees. It is a beautiful structure, consisting of a nave, with aisles, a chancel, north and south porches, and a west tower surmounted by an octagonal spire. It stands on the site of the old church, and was entirely re-built in 1849. The interior is neat, the nave and aisles are separated by arcades of four pointed arches. The east window, and the windows of the south aisle are filled with stained glass. There is an elegant modern font, the gift of the late Edward Smith, Esq. ; it is octagonal, the stem being surrounded by eight polished granite columns, and round the rim is an appropriate verse of scripture. The body of the church is seated with open pine seats. The dimensions of the nave are 50ft. long by 43ft. wide, including the aisles ; and of the chancel, 28ft. by 16ft.

The tower contains a ring of five bells, one of which is a pre-reformation bell, with an inscription in fine Gothic letters. It probably dates from the commencement of the 15th century. The inscriptions on the bells are as follows :—

1. " O Lord, in thee have I trusted and have not been confounded.
        —Mears, founders, London, 1848."
2. " G. Mears and Co., Founders, London, 1864."

* Torre's MSS., p 1001.

3. "IHESVS BE OVR SPEDE 1601 RC, OL."
4. "IHE. Ave Maria Gracia plena."

ALL SAINTS CHURCH, NORTH FERRIBY, BEFORE ITS RESTORATION IN 1849.

5   "Deo Gloria in SVPREMIS, 1726.
        Chr. Watson, Peter Burrill, Churchwardens."

THE LIVING.

The living is a vicarage, in the patronage of Mrs. Turner, and in the incumbency of the Rev. T. M. Theed, LL.B., of St. John's College, Cambridge.

MONUMENTS, &c., IN THE CHURCH.

Within the altar-rails, in a recess on the north side, is a handsome marble monument to the memory of Brigadier Luke Lillington and his wife. It consists of an altar-tomb, surmounted by the kneeling effigies of a man in armour with a flowing wig, and a truncheon in his hand, and a lady in a loose robe—both life size. Beneath is the following inscription :—

" Here lieth Brigadier Luke Lillington, late of Battesford, in the County of Lincoln, who departed this life April the 6th, 1713, in the 60th year of his age ; and of Elizabeth, his wife, daughter of Robert Saunderson, late of Bommel, in the province of Gulderland, who died Oct. 18th, 1699, aged 58."

On the wall of the north aisle a large mural tablet,—

" This monument, erected to the memory of the Etherington family, who for many years resided in this village, and whose remains are deposited below. Henry Etherington, Esq., Merchant, twice Mayor of Kingston-upon-Hull, died 2nd of November, 1760, aged 67 years.

Jane, his wife, daughter of George Porter, Gent., died 15th April, 1739, aged 40 years.

Lady Maria Constantine Etherington, daughter of the late Sir Thos. Cave, Bart., of Stanford Hall, Leicestershire, and Wife of Sir Henry Etherington, Bart., son of the above, died 24th Feby., 1811, aged 66 years.

Sir Henry Etherington, Bart., who was twice Mayor of Hull, created a Baronet in 1773, Died without issue, August 16th 1819, aged 88 years. His Estates descended to his great-niece, the Rt. Hon. Mary Beauclerk, only daughter of the Duke of St. Albans, who was married in 1811 to the Rt. Hon. Viscount Deerhurst, eldest son of the Earl of Coventry.

Taught of God, we should view losses, sickness,

Pain and death, but as the several trying stages by which a good man like
    Joseph is conducted from a tent to a Court.

Sin his disorder, Christ his physician,

Pain his medicine, the Bible his support, the grave his rest, and death it self an angel expressly sent to release the worn-out labourer, or crown the faithful soldier."

On the wall of the south aisle :—

"Mr. Francis Pryme, of Hull, died the 7th July, 1769, aged 67. Rebecca, his wife, the 28th of May, 1750, aged 39. Frances, their daughter, the 31st Oct., 1746. Christopher Pryme, son of Francis Pryme, by Mary, his first wife, the 20th Oct., 1784, aged 46. Alice, his widow, died at Hull on the 16th of October, 1834, aged 86."

Under the tower :—

" Sacred to the memory of Jane, wife of Henry Watson, of North Ferriby, who departed this life June 26th, 1808, aged 48 years ; also the above named Henry Watson, who died April the 23rd, 1820, aged 61 years."

On the opposite wall :—

" To the Memory of Robert Galland, Attorney at Law, of Kingston-upon-Hull, who died 19th Sept., 1817, aged nearly 56."

A mural brass over the south door :—

" In memory of John Todd of Tranby Park, and Halnaby Hall, in the County of York, Esq., who deptd. this life 6th June, 1854, aged 65 years ; also of Jane, his wife, who died 19th Sep., 1866, aged 77 years."

Another in the south aisle :—

" In memory of Edward Smith, of Ferriby, born 16th of May, 1809, died 16th August, 1873. In memory of Hester Smith, Widow of the above, born 15th Oct., 1816, died 30th June, 1888."

ROMAN CATHOLICS.

By a return, under the hands of the Mayor and Aldermen of Kingston-upon-Hull, in 1604, it is certified that at North Ferriby there were :—

" John Thompsone, Anne Craven, laitelie kept in the house of Robert Dalton, Esquier, and departed from thence vpon Easter even last ; new Recusants. Anne Dalton, mother to the said Robert Dalton. Elizabeth, his wife. Thomas Dalton, his sonne. Robert Bacon, ye younger. Anne, his wife, and Margaret Crathorne. Recusants since Marche, 1603." *

* Rawlinson's MS. (B 452), Bodleian Library.

CHARITIES.

" Luke Lillington's charity; by will, dated 5th November, 1773, dividends on £333 6s. 8d., three per cent consols, for teaching ten poor children reading and writing.

Sir Henry Etherington's, Charity; by deed, dated, 14th February, 1781, rent charge of £11 1s. od. per annum, £10, part thereof, for teaching 10 poor children, boys and girls, reading, writing, and accounts, and the remaining £1 1s. od. to the minister for reading the deed every Whit Sunday, after the sermon.

Thomas Walker's dole; by will, dated 22nd November, 1596, rent charge of 20s. per annum to the poor of N. Ferriby and Swanland. Payment now refused, as the Churchwardens are unable to identify the property."*

CHAPEL.

The Primitive Methodist Chapel, erected in 1877, at a cost of £1000, will accommodate two hundred persons. The old chapel, built in 1828, is now used as the Odd Fellows' Hall.

SCHOOL.

The Turner Memorial School, was built in 1877, and is one of many gifts by Mrs. Turner, in memory of her late husband, Charles Turner, Esq., M.P. for Liverpool.

The population of the parish is 446.

SWANLAND.

Swanland is a township and village lying partly in the parish of North Ferriby, the remainder being in Kirk-Ella parish. The township covers an area of 4118 acres, with a population of 453.

The village is delightfully situated, about a mile to the north of Ferriby, and, from elevated positions in the township, magnificent views may be obtained of the whole course of the

* Charity Commissioners' 9th Report, p 814.

Humber down to Spurn, the Lincolnshire and Yorkshire coasts of that river, and of Holderness.

SWANLAND MANOR.

Swanland Manor is the residence of James Reckitt, Esq,, J.P., who is Lord of the Manor of Swanland.

SWANLAND MANOR.

It is situated in a small but beautifully wooded park. The house was built about half a century ago by the late Henry Watson, Esq., near the site of an older structure, and is a handsome specimen of pure Elizabethan architecture. The interior is decorated in the Jacobean style, the hall and drawing-room ceilings being fine specimens of this form of decoration.

The mansion contains the largest collection of modern pictures in the neighbourhood, amongst which are fine examples by the following artists :—

Virginia Water ...	*Turner, R..1.*
Tivoli	... *Do.*
Noon	*W. H. B. Davis, R..1.*
Ireland ...	*E. Long, R..1.*
Andalusian Horses ...	*R. Ansdell, R..1.*
Le Medicine malgre lui ...	*W. P. Frith, R..1.*
Sheep and Oxen	*T. S. Cooper, R..1.*
Falaise ...	*Birket Foster.*
Venetian Scenes	... *Do.*
Forest Solitudes ...	*Mc. Whirter, A.R..1.*
Cupid's Curse ...	... *Leslie, R..1.*
A Cooling Draught	*Harry Marks, R..1.*
Cornfield	*Vical Cole, R..1.*
Wee Auntie Jeanie...	*T Faed, R..1.*
The Lord hath given, &c.	*Frank Holl, R..1.*
Eastern Beauty	... ...*Carl Haghe*
Turkeys...	*Phil Morris, A.R .1.*
Dewy Morn	*B. W. Leader, A.R..1.*
Family Portraits	... ... *J. Sant, R..1.*
Charles I., and Courtiers before the Battle of Naseby : a large historical picture	... *Laslett J. Pott.*
Girl and Dogs	*Heywood Hardy, A.R..1.*

The pictures by Leader, Ansdell, and Laslett Pott, are supposed to be their masterpieces, and the work by Holl the picture that first brought him into notice.

There are also fine examples by Goodall, R.A., Carl Ritter, Pyne, T. M. Richardson, Prout, Louis Hadg, Herring, Perugini, James Hardy, Hayllar, Wm. Hunt, Brett, A.R.A F W. W. Topham, J. W. Topham, Mrs. Angel, G. Boughton, A.R.A., Armfield, Fred Tayler, Ed. Duncan, Josef Israels, H. Dawson, Edward Frere, Calderon, R.A., and many others.

INDEPENDENT CHAPEL.

In the centre of the village stands the Independent Chapel, erected in 1803, near the site of an earlier one, built in 1693. Little is known of the origin of the congregation, which is one of the oldest Independent Societies in the County. Tradition has it that for many years antecedent to the erection of a chapel, the worshippers had met in a ruined chantry, all trace of which is now lost, except a small mound covering part of the foundations, in a paddock at the west end of the village, and which possibly may be the only remaining portion of the chantry formerly connected with the monastery at Ferriby. The former chapel appears to have been larger than the present one, for in a record, dated in 1715, the congregation is reported as "consisting of 450, of whom 20 had votes for the County." At that period, the worshippers gathered from very distant places. The present chapel, altered and renovated in 1881, will accommodate 250 persons. The solid silver cups, used at the Communion services, form interesting historical links with the past. One of them bears the inscription—"The gift of Thos. Watson to ye Dissenting Congregation in Swanland, 1723." And the other was "the bequest of Jeremiah Turner, in 1789." During the entire history of the chapel, its pastor has been the sole minister resident in the village, the only other place of worship being a small Primitive Methodist Chapel, served by the Circuit Ministers from Hull. The present occupant of "The Parsonage" is the Rev. J. E. Whitehead, who undertook the pastorate in 1872.

For a long period of years the school-room attached to the

chapel was used for both Day-School and Sunday-School purposes. It is worthy of note that the Sunday School is the oldest in the East Riding. It was commenced early in 1798 (only nine years after Robert Raikes founded the first Sunday School in Gloucester) and was followed the same year by one at Beverley. The day school was established at a still earlier period, dating from the close of the 17th century.

In the year 1876, the present handsome school buildings were erected for the accommodation of both the day and Sunday schools. With their site and complete furnishings they were the gift of John Todd, Esq., J.P., of Swanland Hall.

CHARITIES.

"Nathaniel Woodmansey's gift ; by will dated 29th July, 1719, rent of 1a. 1r. of land. One half to the Presbyterian Minister of Swanland and the remainder to the Schoolmaster.

Jeremiah Turner's charity ; by will dated 14th July, 1789, dividends on £815 16s. 1d. navy five per cents, to the Minister of Swanland and his Clerk, to be chosen by the men communicants for that purpose, to officiate every Lord's day in the old Chapel at Swanland, the Minister to keep the testator's tomb and tombstone in North Ferriby Church yard in good repair. The dividends on £204 6s. 10d., part of the said £815 16s. 1d., to be paid to the Minister's Clerk, who should act as schoolmaster, for which he teaches twelve poor children between the ages of six and twelve years reading and writing. The children are appointed by the Minister." *

* Charity Commissioners' 9th Report, p 814.

HESSLE.

ESSLE is a township and parish on the bank of the Humber, four miles west from Hull. It is alluded to in Domesday Survey as follows :—" Land of Gislebert Tison. East Riding. Manor. In Hase (Hessle) Alwin and Chetel had seven carucates of land to be taxed. There is land to four ploughs. Gislebert has now there one plough and seventeen villanes, and two bordars with three ploughs. There is a Church and a Priest there. One mile long and half broad. Value in King Edward's time sixty shillings, now fifty shillings." *

Burton has the following reference to the Parish :

" Richard the Monk gave 12 acres of land here to Gisburne Priory. Allan, son of Oionisius de Hesell, gave pasture here for 9 score sheep with their young till one year old, which was confirmed by Robert, the Lord of Hessel.

* Bawdwen's Translation, p 191.

The church was given to the priory of Gisburne, but by whom or when does not appear, yet in A.D. 1202, Robert Duket, parson of this Church of Hasel, recognised himself to owe to Ronald, prior and convent of Gisburne, those 2½ Marks which they had paid to Pope Innocent the 3rd, for the charge of one year of this church, which was afterwards appropriated to the said Monastery, and a vicarage endowed, and on 19th of June, A.D., 1324 it was ordained that the prior and convent of Gisburne shall present one of their own canons to the vicarage when vacant, to which vicarage the Chapel of St. Trinity, of Hull, was annexed."*

In 1487, Robert Sisson, of Hessle, by his will gave two acres of land in the field of Hessle, to pay two shillings yearly for ever to the Priests and Guilds celebrating mass, and other twenty shillings yearly for a mass, and obsequies to be celebrated for the good of his own soul in the said church, upon the next Holy day for ever after the feast of the nativity of St. John the Baptist as expressed in two indentures made for that purpose.

"In 1525, William Hayton, of Hessle, by his will bequeathed to Robert Hayton and his heirs three acres of land, upon condition that he and they should for evermore cause a mass and dirge to be said in the same church, for the good and welfare of his soul.

In the year 1526, Thomas Michael, by his will, directed that the Church-wardens of the Church of Hessle should have for ever two shillings a year out of a parcel of land and meadow called Plumpton, containing about two acres, towards the perpetual upholding of the said church, and that other two shillings a year should be paid yearly out of the same to the vicar of the said church "to keep an obit for the good of his soul, upon the 6th day of April, or within the eight days following, and if he neglect the same, the Churchwardens are to enter upon the land, receive the two shillings, and cause it to be expended as above directed."

* Burton's *Monasticon*, p 346.

In 40 Edward III., William de la Pole died seized of the Manor of Hessle.

At this place lived Thomas le Moyne, whose descendants intermarried with the Ferribys of Ferriby, the Portingtons of Portington, the Anlabys of Anlaby, and the Legards of Anlaby.

The parish formerly extended as far as the Western bank of the River Hull, and included the Lordship of Myton, and the site of the present town of Kingston-upon-Hull, with the exception of a small portion which constituted the chapelry of St. Mary, then belonging to the Knight Templars at Ferriby. Hessle Church was consequently considered the Mother Church of the Holy Trinity at Hull, and this connection lasted for over 300 years. The separation was effected by an Act of Parliament in 1661.

An Act was passed in the 32nd of George III., for dividing, enclosing, draining, and improving the open fields, meadows, pastures, commons and waste grounds within the several townships or hamlets of Hessle, Anlaby, and Tranby.

The population is 2810.

Charles Percy Sykes, Esq., of Westella, is Lord of the Manor.

THE CHURCH.

The church, dedicated to All Saints, was restored in 1869, at a cost of £8000. It has a chancel, with chancel aisles, nave and aisles, tower, spire, two porches, and organ; the arcades of the nave and chancel, and the north and south doors, are of early English architecture; the windows of the south aisle, and the east and west windows are decorated, the remainder of the church being of the late perpendicular.

The register dates from the year 1561.

In the tower are four bells with these inscriptions :—

1. "God save the Church. 1756. Robert Lambert, Vicar.
   Chr. Pincham, Robt. Wetwang, Churchwardens."
2. "Deo Gloria pax Homnibus. 1684."
3. "Iesvs Be ovr Speed. 1611."
4. "All men that hear my movrnfvl sovnd
   Repent before yov lie in Grovnd.
   W.W. GO, Churchwardens, 1641."

The living is a vicarage, tithe rent-charge £30, gross yearly value £396, including 180 acres of glebe, with residence, in the gift of the Lord Chancellor, and has been held since 1884 by the Rev. Arthur Kaye, M.A, of Magdalen College, Oxford.

Monuments, &c., in the Church.

On the North wall of the chancel is a small brass which was found during the restoration of the church, bearing the following inscription :—

"Here under lieth dame an percy, Wife to syr henry percy, to him bair xvij. children which an departed the xix. day of december the year of our Lord mvxxi. on wobis soullis Jhu have mercy."

In the floor of the nave on a blue stone :—

" He whose remains now rest beneath this stone
In social grace and filial duty shone ;
Good was his judgment, his discernment clear,
Ardent his friendship and his soul sincere ;
Such was't thou, Pease, here peaceful rest thy dust
Till waked at the revival of the just.

Robert Pease, Esq., Banker, son of Joseph Pease, Esq., of Kingston-upon-Hull, Merchant, died 19th March, 1770, aged 52 years."

Within the altar rails, in a recess on a brass :—

" To the Glory of God and in memory of Joseph Robinson Pease of Hesslewood, who died May 27th, 1856, aged 76, this chancel window is dedicated by his family, Easter, 1870. "

In the Nave :—

"Within this vault are deposited the remains of Mary, the wife of James Keiro Watson, Banker, and daughter of Francis Hall, Merchant, in Hull, who died the 18th of April, 1806, aged 27 years.

Also Ann Hassel, obit 18th March, 1808, æ 33 years. Also the body of Caroline Swan, Obit 28th June, 1809, Et 27 years. Also Mary, wife of Francis Hall, Esq., and mother of the above, who died 26th Feby., 1824, aged 74 years. Also Isabella, wife of John Burstall, Esq., merchant, of Hull, and last surviving daughter of Francis and Mary Hall, who died 2nd Sept., 1824, aged 52 years. Also Francis Hall, Esq., who died January the 7th, 1831, aged 85 years. Also Francis Hall, only son of the above-named Francis and Mary Hall, who died Nov. 25th, 1843, aged 67 years. Also the remains of Mary, daughter of the above-named Caroline Swan, and wife of Thomas Bentley Locke, of Hessle Mount, Esq., who died 7th January, 1846, aged 43 years. Also under the floor of the vestry are deposited the remains of Francis Hall Hassell, Son of Samuel Talbot and Eunice Mary Gertrude Hassell."

On a mural monument in the south aisle :—

"In memory of John Barkworth, Esq., of Tranby House, who departed this life on the 19th of July 1815, aged 57 years, and of Elizabeth, his wife, who, on the 30th of December, 1838, was, during the enjoyment of domestic intercourse, suddenly snatched from the Bosom of her family at the age of 78. This monument was erected by their children as a token of filial regard to the departed worth of their affectionate and indulgent parents."

Under the tower is a brass with full length effigy, bearing this inscription :—

"To the Glory of God and in affectionate remembrance of Anthony Bannister, J.P., Alderman, twice Sheriff, and twice Mayor of Kingston-upon-Hull. Sixteen years Churchwarden of Hessle, who died 18th July, A.D., 1878, aged 61 years.

This Brass was subscribed for by 120 of his friends."

In the churchyard a tombstone to George Prissick, plumber and glazier, has the following lines :—

> "Adieu, my friend, my thread of life is spun,
> The diamond will not cut, the solder will not run,
> My body's turned to ashes, my grief and trouble's past,
> I've left no one to worldly care, and I shall rise at last."

TORRE'S LIST OF VICARS, &c.

Torre gives us the following list of the Vicars and testamentary burials.

Temp Instit.	Vicarii Eccle.	Patroni.
19th Sep., 1251	Nich de Brune	Prior and Convent of
24th Sep., 1274	John Aslakby	Gisburne.
6th Nov., 1301	Will de Pocklington	
5th Feb., 1322	Rad de Hoton vel Barber	
20th May, 1324	Johe de Stokton	
23rd Nov., 1326	Robt. de Marton	
17th Oct., 1345	Pet de Aslakby	
	Pet de Walton	
31st July, 1349	Thos. de Brainbriggs	
10th May, 1362	Joh de Hurtworth	
7th May, 1364	Ric Lestbury	
	Johe Stanygrove	
1391	Richd. Marke	
24th Oct., 1400	Johe de Barton	
27th June, 1416	Joh de Cyngwald	
3rd Feby., 1430	Thos. Bywell	
27th May, 1433	Thos. de Bewyk	
28th Dec., 1444	Thos. Delyngton	
22nd April, 1455	Johe Harewode	
25th Nov., 1467	Will Merington	
30th Sept., 1468	Joh Yelton	
4th Dec., 1492	Robt. Hedlam	
20th Oct., 1503	Jac. Cokrell	
16th July, 1519	Geo. Dent	
21st April, 1522	Thos. Logan	
25th Oct., 1558	Wm. Peres	
24th Sep., 1557	Thos. Fugill	Philip and Mary
	Melcharius Smyth	
8th Sep., 1591	Theopolis Smyth, M.A.	Elizabeth Reg.
1615	Richard Perrot	James R.
23rd Feb., 1661	Richd. Raiks	Chas. II.
8th March, 1670	Thos. Faxman	

Continuation Since Torre.

Temp. Instit.	Vicarii Eccle.	Patroni.
1689	Tim Raiks	
1st Nov., 1722	Will Garton, M.A.	
7th July, 1731	Robt. Lambert	
16th Nov., 1757	Thomas Browman............	
30th April, 1799	Ed. Garrod...............	
15th June, 1837	Hen. Newmarch, B.A..............	
25th Mar., 1884	Arthur Kaye, M.A.	

Testamentary Burials.

"28th Sept., 1458.—John Habilthorne, of Hesile, to be buried in the Church.

7th May, 1468.—John Harwood, Vicar, to be buried in the psh. Church of All Saints, Hesil, or in the quire of the Church or Chapel of St Trinity, of Hull.

24th Nov., 1540. —Edmund Boynton, of Hesil, to be buried in the Church.

17th Sept., 1538.—Thomas Logan, Vicar of Hesil and Hull, to be buried in the Quire of Essel.

28th Sept., A.D. 1458.—Margaret Haluthorne, Widow of John Halu-thorne, to be buried in the Church.

20th Aug., A.D., 1468.—William Merington, Vicar, dying intestate, Administration was granted to Thos. Durnton, prior of Gysburn.

3rd June, 1433.—Thos. Bywell, dying intestate, Administration was taken.

4th Aug., 1558.—Hugh Langdale, of Hessle, gentleman, to be buried in the Church." *

Charities.

"The Hospital and School.—These consist of a building containing four rooms, three of which are for the habitation of three poor persons, and the other for a school room. Built by the Rev. Joseph Wilson, and, by the will of Mr. Leonard Chamberlain, £1 each per annum is paid to the poor persons and £5 per annum to the schoolmaster for teaching ten poor children to read.

* Torre's MSS., p 1055.

John Garrat's Charity.—Rent of 2a. 3r. of land, let at the time of the report for £18 per annum distributed to the poor on St. Thomas's Day.

Robert Raikes' Gift.—£100 applied many years previous to the report in building a poor house—the sum of £5 per annum is paid out of the poor rates as the interest, and is added to and applied with the rents of the above-mentioned charity estate.

William Green's Charity.—By will, dated 25th March, 1812, dividends on £100 Navy 5 per cents. added to and applied as above.

The poor's allotment, rent of 11a. of land. Rent distributed on St. Thomas's day among the poor of Hessle and Anlaby, whether they receive parish relief or not.

Bread Charities.—John Marshall's gift, by will dated 3rd Jany., 1803, dividends on £160 10s. Navy five per cents, distributed in bread every Sunday.

Unknown Rent Charges.—£1 11s. per annum one issues out of Mr. Wm. Dealtrey's house, the other out of William Valace Esquire's Close, near pulcroft, distributed in bread on every Sunday." *

CHAPELS.

The Wesleyan Methodists have had a chapel in the village for many years, the present building having been erected in the year 1878 at a cost of £5000. It is in the Gothic style and will seat about 600 persons.

The Primitive Methodist Chapel was built in the year 1857, their former place of meeting being a room in Chapel yard.

The United Methodist Free Church was erected in the year 1863.

The Congregationalists formerly had a chapel in Eastgate, but the building was taken down about 50 years ago.

SCHOOL.

In 1716 Mr. Leonard Chamberlain left an endowment of £5 a year for the school, but it has considerably increased since that

* Charity Commissioners' 9th Report, p 818.

time. About thirty-three years ago a bazaar was held towards the alteration and enlargement of the school. Mr. John Clark was then the master, and on his retirement in 1876, Mr. Thomas Banks, the present schoolmaster was elected. The ratepayers elect the schoolmaster.

SHIPBUILDING.

Shipbuilding was formerly carried on at Hessle Cliff. In 1693 an 80-gun man-of-war was built here, and between 1747 and 1762 Mr. Hugh Blaydes, of Hull, built several men-of-war for the Government.

HESSLEWOOD.

Hesslewood is situated a mile to the west of the village of Hessle, in a finely timbered park, and commands beautiful woodland and river views. It is the seat of H. J. R. Pease. Esq., J.P., D.L.

The family of Pease have for upwards of three centuries been connected with the town of Hull. Amongst the early members of the family we find that John Pease became a burgher of Hull in 1582. George Pease, his brother, also took up his burghership, and was for many years the Master of the Wool House, a post granted only to the most responsible merchants of the town. His daughter, Anne, was the second wife of the Rev. Andrew Marvell, and the mother of Andrew Marvell, M.P.

The family have for generations been known for the great hospitality which they have always freely shewn in promoting the interests of the ancient Borough of Hull. Hesslewood during the

last century has frequently been the home of the most distinguished personages when visiting Hull or its neighbourhood.*

* For a further account of the Pease Family, see Wildridge's *Old and New Hull*, pp 155-158, 195-196.

ARMS :—Vert, a chevron between three stags trippant or, in the centre chief
point a bezant, on a chief per fesse gu and arg, an eagle displayed counter-changed.

CREST :—An eagle's head erased arg., holding in the beak or a pease-cod
vert.

MOTTO :—Confide recte agens.

Pedigree of Pease, of Hesslewood.

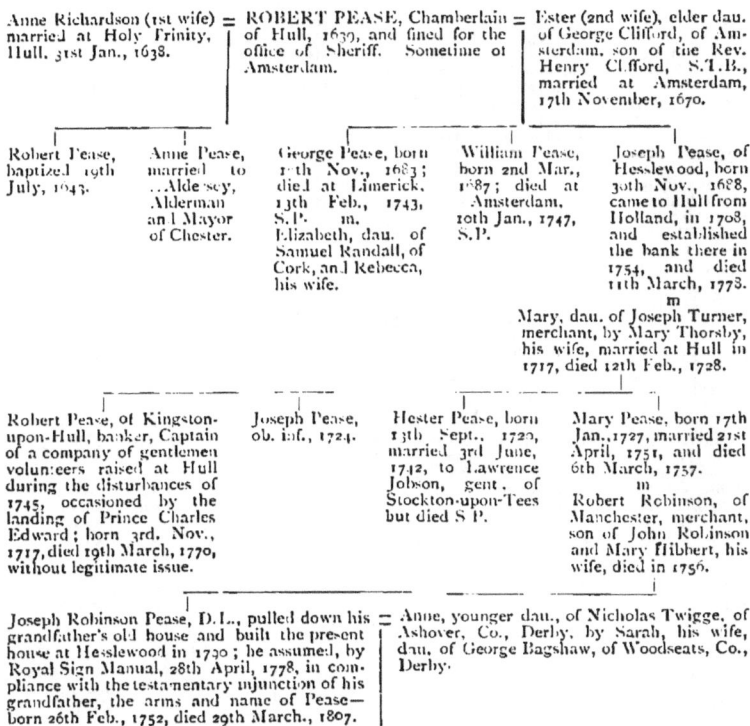

Anne Richardson (1st wife) = ROBERT PEASE, Chamberlain = Ester (2nd wife), elder dau.
married at Holy Trinity, | of Hull, 1639, and fined for the | of George Clifford, of Am-
Hull, 31st Jan., 1638. | office of Sheriff. Sometime of | sterdam, son of the Rev.
| Amsterdam. | Henry Clifford, S.T.B.,
| | married at Amsterdam,
| | 17th November, 1670.

Robert Pease, | Anne Pease, | George Pease, born | William Pease, | Joseph Pease, of
baptized 19th | married to | 11th Nov., 1683; | born 2nd Mar., | Hesslewood, born
July, 1643. | ...Aldersey, | died at Limerick, | 1687; died at | 30th Nov., 1688,
| Alderman | 13th Feb., 1743, | Amsterdam, | came to Hull from
| and Mayor | S.P. m. | 10th Jan., 1747, | Holland, in 1708,
| of Chester. | Elizabeth, dau. of | S.P. | and established
| | Samuel Randall, of | | the bank there in
| | Cork, and Rebecca, | | 1754, and died
| | his wife. | | 11th March, 1778.
| | | | m
| | | Mary, dau. of Joseph Turner,
| | | merchant, by Mary Thorsby,
| | | his wife, married at Hull in
| | | 1717, died 12th Feb., 1728.

Robert Pease, of Kingston- | Joseph Pease, | Hester Pease, born | Mary Pease, born 17th
upon-Hull, banker, Captain | ob. inf., 1724. | 13th Sept., 1720, | Jan., 1727, married 21st
of a company of gentlemen | | married 3rd June, | April, 1751, and died
volunteers raised at Hull | | 1742, to Lawrence | 6th March, 1757.
during the disturbances of | | Jobson, gent. of | m
1745, occasioned by the | | Stockton-upon-Tees | Robert Robinson, of
landing of Prince Charles | | but died S.P. | Manchester, merchant,
Edward; born 3rd Nov., | | | son of John Robinson
1717, died 19th March, 1770, | | | and Mary Flibbert, his
without legitimate issue. | | | wife, died in 1756.

Joseph Robinson Pease, D.L., pulled down his = Anne, younger dau., of Nicholas Twigge, of
grandfather's old house and built the present | Ashover, Co., Derby, by Sarah, his wife,
house at Hesslewood in 1790; he assumed, by | dau. of George Bagshaw, of Woodseats, Co.,
Royal Sign Manual, 28th April, 1778, in com- | Derby.
pliance with the testamentary injunction of his
grandfather, the arms and name of Pease—
born 26th Feb., 1752, died 29th March., 1807.

Continued next page.

Continued from previous page.

Joseph Robinson Pease, Esq., of Hesslewood House, Co., York J.P. & D.L., for the East Riding, born 21st Novr, 1789, died May, 27th, 1866. m Harriet, younger dau. of James Walker, Esq., of Sand Hutton, and sister to Sir James Walker, Bart, married 7th April, 1818.	Clifford Pease, born 24th Dec. 1793, died 27th Dec., 1873. m Sarah Paulden, 2nd dau. of the late Robert Cookson, Esq, of Elliory, Co Westmoreland married 25th June, 1846.	George Pease, M.A. in H.O., Vicar of Darlington, County York, born 30th June, 1796. m. Jane, 8th and youngest dau. of the late John Swinfen, Esq., of Swinfen, Co. Stafford, by Anne, his wife, sister of the late Sir Francis Ford, Bart.	Anne Pease, married 5th April, 1811, to Arthur Maister, Esq. of Winestead, Col. of the East York Militia, 25th Sep., J P. & D.L.	Mary died 4th July 1839. Sarah, died unmard. 1840.	Charlotte Pease, married 23rd May, 1823, to Captain Henry Browne Mason, R.N., of Aldenham Lodge, Co. Herts., and died 24th Feb., 1824.

Mary Anne Pease.

Clifford Robinson Pease, born 27th Dec., 1850.
Douglas Clifford Pease, born 29th, Aug., 1854.
Annie Sarah, married 14th Oct., 1868, to Richard Fegan, M.D.
Catherine Maria.

Joseph Walker Pease, Esq., of Hesslewood House, Co., York, J.P. & D.L., Lieut-Colonel, East York Rifle Vol., born 24th May 1820; M.P. for Hull, 1872. m Barbara Catherine, eldest dau. of the Rev. Henry Palmer. M.A., of Withcote Hall, Co. Leicester.	George Clifford Pease, M.A., Rector of Routh, Beverley, born 21st Nov., 1822, m 26th Sep., 1850, to Clarissa, youngest dau. of John Turner, Esq., of Gravetye Manor, Co. Sussex.	James Robinson Pease, M.A., born 28th Feb., 1824. m 28th Feb., 1854, Louisa Frances, dau. of the late John Barkworth, Esq., of Tranby House, nr. Hull.	Arthur Burton Pease, born 27th May, 1825, m. 14th May, 1857, Emma Caroline, youngest dau. of John Wilkinson, Esq., of Welton Grange, Co., York.	Harriet Pease, m. 29th June, 1842, to the Rev. John Richard Hill, M.A., Rector of Thornton, J.P. & D.L.	Emily Jane m. (1st) 11th June, 1857 to Henry, eldest son of Hewley Mortimer Baines, Esq., of Bell Hall, who died Feb., 1865, and (2ndly) 20th Feb., 1873 to the Rev. Norman Dumesnil Straton, M.A. Rector of Kirby Wharfe.

Arthur Godfrey Pease, born 29th Nov., 1861.

Leonard Joseph Pease, born 29th April, 1867.

a　　　　*b*　　　　*c*

Continued next page.

Continued from previous page.

☞

a   b   c

b	c
George Turner Pease, born 10th July, 1851, died 5th June, 1870.	James Cecil Robinson Pease, born 18th Sep, 1855, died 14th Nov., 1860.
Percival Henry Pease, born 4th August, 1857.	Harold Robinson Pease, born 7th Dec, 1859.
Arthur Clifford Pease, born 10th August, 1859.	Hugh Robinson Pease, born 23rd, February, 1862.
Joseph Frederick Pease, born 16th March, 1861.	Alice Louisa Pease.
James Ernest Pease, born 21st February, 1863.	Katherine Frances Pease.
Clara Harriet Pease.	Emma Cecilia Pease.
Fanny Maria Pease.	
Edith Catherine Pease.	

Henry Joseph Robinson Pease, eldest son, born 29th Dec., 1843 m 15th April, 1869, Dorothy Elizabeth, eldest dau. of John Boulderson Barkworth, Esq., of Raywell, Co. York.	Charles Clifford Pease born 7th Dec., 1845.	Francis Richard Pease, born 25th May, 1849. m Isabel Mary, dau. of William Cole Hamilton, Esq., of Beltrim, Co., Tyrone.	Edward Heyrick Pease, born 27th Dec., 1858, died 1883.	Barbara Mary Pease m 20th April, 1876, Rev. William Greville Hazlerigg, 4th son of Sir Arthur Gray Hazlerigg, Bart., of Nosely Hall, Co. Leicester, and has issue.	Eleanor Louisa Pease, m 22nd Jan., 1874, to Arthur Hancock Edwards, Esq., 4th son of Sir Henry Edwards, Bart, of Pye Nest, Co., York.	Charlotte Emily Pease, m 1870. Lt. Col. H. Willoughby Trevelyan, of Rothley Co. Northumberland, son of Major Gen. Trevelyan, C.B.
Joseph Robinson Pease, born Jan., 1873.	Dora Mary Robinson Pease.	Francis Claud Pease, born 7th Nov., 1886.			William Geoffrey Pease, born 8th Jan, 1888.	

KIRK-ELLA.

IRK-ELLA, anciently called Elvelay, is a neat village and parish, about five miles west from Hull. The Hull and Barnsley Railway passes through the parish and has a station here. The village is of considerable antiquity, and appears to have had a church at the time of the Domesday survey. Its Saxon owners Torchil and Siward, had two manors of four carucates, and Nigel had five villanes with one plough. Eddiue had ten carucates and land to live ploughs. Alwin, Chetel, and Canute had also twenty-three carucates.

Ralph de Mortimer, Gislebert de Tison, and Hugh, the son of Baldric, appear from the same record to have been its Norman possessors.

The present owners of the soil are Charles Percy Sykes, Esq.,

John Smyth Egginton, Esq., of Kirk-Ella, and Arthur Egginton Esq., of South-Ella.

The population is 354.

In Burton's *Monasticon* we find the following reference to this place.

"The Church and tythe of Kirk-Ella were given by Gilbert de Tyson, to the Abbey of St. Germain, of Selby, and confirmed thereto by a charter of Richard I. and continued a rectory while it remained in the hands of that Abbot and Convent, but on the 9th of March 2nd Ed. III. (1328), at the request of Thomas Wake, the founder, granted his license to the prior and convent of Haltemprice, to give 20 librates of land in Hessel to the Abbot and Convent of Selby, in exchange for the advowson of this Church, to appropriate the same to their priory; and in full Chapter at Selby, A.D. 1331 (5 Edward III.), John, Abbot of Selby, and the Chapter thereof, granted to Thos. Wake, of Lyddel, and his heirs the advowson of this Church and one messuage against the Ch.-yard.

At Cawood, on the 10th May, A.D. 1343, William la Zouch, Archbishop of York, after the decease of Robert de Spigurnell, then rector of the Church, appropriated the same to the prior and convent of Haltemprice, and to indemnify his Cathedral Church reserved to him and his successors Archbishops, out of the fruits of this Church the annual pension of ten marks, and to his dean and chapter five marks, payable at Pentecost and Martinmas by equal portions. On the 3rd of May, A.D. 1343, the said Archbishop ordained that there be in this Church a perpetual vicar presented thereto by the said prior and convent out of one of the Canons of the Monastery, who shall be in priest's orders, the portion of whose vicarage shall consist in one mansion against the church, for the vicar's habitation, built at first at the cost of the said religious, also he shall have all minute-tythes belonging to the church as of wool and lamb, and all oblations and mortuaries either within the said parish or within the chapel of Traneby within the same, the yearly value of which amounts to £8 5s. 4d.; also he shall have the tythes of ducks, pigs, pidgeons, to the value of 16s.; and the tythes of line and hemp, value 10s.; the tythes of mills, valued at 8s.; the tythes of wax and honey, valued at 1s. 6d.; the tythes of garths in Braythwate, valued at £2, all which values were so found by inquisition taken by the Archbishop's authority. Moreover, the prior and convent shall pay nothing for burials in their Monastery or oblations made therein, nor tythes for increase of their own cattle or gardens cultivated at their own cost within the parish, and as for all ordinary burdens incumbent on the church the vicar shall bear them, excepting the pensions due to the Archbishop and dean and chapter, and as for extraordinaries the vicar shall bear them according to his position. And on the 23rd of October, A.D. 1438, this new ordination was made, viz., that the vicar shall have the old mansion against the church-yard, wherein he and his predecessors used to dwell, and shall receive of the prior and convent of Haltemprice twenty marks per annum, quarterly, payable on the high altar of this church, and the vicar, at the rate of the said sum, shall contribute with the prior and convent in the charge of all extraordinary burthens of the church, and the priory and convent shall bear all other burthens, ordinary and extraordinary, and shall present one of their own canons to the vicarage in all future vacations thereof." *

At the dissolution the patronage was given to the Ellerkers, from whom it passed in 1686 to the Bradshaws, and in 1794 to the Sykes's family.

The church is valued in Pope Nicholas's taxation at £46 13s. 4d., and in the King's Books, the vicarage is valued at £13 2s. 8d. per annum.†

TORRE'S LIST OF RECTORS, &c.

Temp Instit.	Vicarii Eccle.	Patroni.
	John de Wresil	Abbot and Convent of Selby.
10th Dec., 1274	Will de St. Leonards	....
2nd Oct., 1292	Johe de Gateford	... .
9th Mar., 1302	Thos. Browne	....
4th May, 1328	Ric de Arymine..............	Dismissed
6th Aug., 1329	Robt. de Bridlington	....
11th Nov., 1338	Will de Twyna	....
21st Nov., 1338	Robt. de Spigurnell	....

LIST OF THE VICARS.

Temp. Instit.	Vicarii Eccle.	Patroni.
20th June, 1344	Stephen de Cottingham ...	Prior & Convent of Hautemprice
26th June, 1349	John de Gedney	....
16th May, 1353	Walter de Wharram Percy	....

* Burton's *Monasticon*, p 315.

† Lawton's *Collections*, p 352.

List of Vicars—*Continued.*

Temp Instit.	Vicarii Eccec.	Patroni.
17th Nov., 1367	Ric de Kyrkam	
19th July, 1411	Robert Halam	
6th Feb., 1429	Robert Tweng	
17th Nov., 1432	Johe Tweng	
27th Oct., 1433	Ric Worlaby	
24th Oct., 1436	Ric Roos	
2nd July, 1449	Robt. Normanton	
18th Sep., 1456	Johe Cawthorpe	
16th Dec., 1480	Johe Yorke	
18th June, 1484	Jho Wymberley	
26th Nov., 1506	Ric Tancom	
27th May, 1523	Willm. Gibson	
20th April, 1534	Ric Wagner	
4th Oct., 1554	Phil Preston	Rad Ellerker, to whom t was
16th July, 1566	Will Say	given by Hen. VIII.
31st June, 1582	Ham Hall	
6th April, 1583	Marm Kitchen	
21st May, 1587	Johe Sympson	
25th Aug., 1591	Carolus Denton	
8th, July, 1595	Seth Thompson	
20th Feb., 1598	Will Kery	
*	Ric Foster	
30th May, 1671	Hen. Plaxton, M.A.	
13th July, 1686	Hen. Jefferson	

Continuation since Torre's List.

Temp. Instit.	Vicarii Eccle.	Patroni.
1696	Henry Tiplin	
1722	William Huntington	
1783	William Wade	

* The registers date from 1558. Seth Thompson signs as vicar from 1558 to 1596. William Kery signs from 1598 to 1648, and was himself buried 2nd Sept., 1649. Ric Foster was buried 11th Dec., 1670.

CONTINUATION SINCE TORRE'S LIST.—*Continued.*

Temp Instit.	Vicarii Eccle.	Patroni.
1793	Nicholas Bourne	....
1804	W. J. Wilkinson	....
1842	Joseph Thompson............	....
1858	W. T. Vernon, M.A.	....
1878	James Foord, M.A.	....

TESTAMENTARY BURIALS.

"24th October, 1441.—Robert Legard, of Anlaby, to be buried in the ch. of St. Andrew, at Elveley.

4th January, 1444.—John Wike, of Willardby, to be buried in the Church.

7th November, 1460.—William Appulby, of Elveley, to be buried before the cross in the Church.

12th January, 1476.—The Anlaby clerk to be buried in the church at the foot of Sir John, late rector thereof, in a certain Isle on the south side which is called the chapel of St. Mary Virgin, under that marble stone where his ancestors lie interred.

2nd July, 1533.—Robt. Legard, of Anlaby, gent , to be buried in the church.

12th May, 1559.—Dame Jane Ellerker, of Hautemprize, to be buried in the church.

31st October, 1582.—William Lee, Clerk, to be buried in the Quire.

2nd July, 1591.—John Sympson, clerk, minister of the congregation of the parishoners of Kirk elley, to be buried in the chancel.

3rd October, 1595.—Charles Dainteth, minister of the word of God in Kirk elley, to be buried in the Quire, where the table in the said Quire now standeth.

3rd. February, 1602.—Nicholas Faukes, of Farnley in Holderness, to be buried in the ch. yard. near to his Father.

3rd February, 1679.—William Legard, of Anlaby, gent., to be buried in the Church." *

THE CHURCH.

The church is dedicated to St. Andrew, and consists of nave, north and south aisles, chancel, and a fine tower at the west end.

* Torre's MSS., p 1337.

It is of the early English and perpendicular periods, and was restored and partly re-built in 1860. The tower was restored in 1883, and the bells were hung at the same time.

From an inscription on the south side of the tower, it is probable that it was built or re-built by one John Berrys. The inscription is now difficult to decipher, but it appears to have been a solicitation to pray for the soul of Johannis Berrys. This John Berrys was buried 15th July, 1562.

ST. ANDREW'S CHURCH, KIRK-ELLA.

In the interior are many monuments, amongst which are the following :—

In the tower is a memorial :—

"To the honour and Glory of God, and in memory of Fanny Egginton, died 2nd February, 1877. These Bells were given to this Church by her son, Arthur Egginton."

Another to William Sparks, of Kingston-upon-Hull, who died 21st Sept., 1792.

"Near this monument rest, in hope of a joyful resurrection, the mortal remains of Josiah Corthine, of Anlaby, Esq., late Collector of the Customs of the port of Kingston-upon-Hull. He was born Sept. 3rd, 1717, and died Nov., 11th, 1783."

In the North aisle :—

"In a vault near the centre aisle of this church are deposited the remains of William Williamson, Esq., formerly an eminent Merchant in Hull, who died Feb. 5th, 1825, aged 88 years. Also of Jane, his wife, who peacefully, and in humble hope of a joyful resurrection, departed this life on the 19th of September, 1837, aged 88 years."

"Underneath are deposited the remains of Henry Legard, Esq., late of Beverley, he died the 23rd day of May, 1819, aged 79 years. In the early part of his life he served as an officer in the wars in Germany, and during the last fifty years honourably filled and conscientiously discharged the duties of the office of Register of the East Riding of this County."

"Here lieth interred the body of Sir Robert Legard, Kt., late of Anlaby, in the County of the town of Kingston-upon-Hull, who departed this life the 14th of Sept., 1721, aged 87 years. He was one of the trustees in chancery. He first married the daughter and heiress of William Phillips, of Staffordshire, gent., and afterwards the daughter of Sir James Stonehouse, of Amerden Hall, in the County of Essex, Bart. By the first he had a numerous issue, of whom, the eldest son, John Legard, in memory and honour of his father's extraordinary virtues, has, with grief, deservedly placed this monument."

On the north side of the chancel is a chapel in which are numerous memorials of the Sykes's family.

Within the altar rails there is a fine marble monument by Chantrey,

"To the memory of Joseph Sykes, Merchant, Alderman, and twice Mayor of the town of Kingston-upon-Hull, and Patron of this Church; also a Justice of the Peace and a Deputy Lieutenant for the East Riding of this County. He was born in the year, 1723, and died in the year 1805."

There is also a bust by Bacon, of Daniel Sykes, who was M.P., for Hull, from 1820 to 1830. He was Recorder for the Borough, and was returned Member for Beverley in the year 1830. He died at Raywell in 1832.

There are also several fine monumental windows to members of the Egginton family.

In the tower are six bells, by Taylor and Son, of London, which were hung in 1883.

THE LIVING.

The living is in the gift of the Rev. Richard Henry Foord, Rector of Foxholes, East Yorkshire, and is held by the Rev. James Foord, M.A., Brasenose College, Oxford.

CHARITIES.

"Francis Wright's Charity; by will dated 6th June, 1674. Rent of 8a. or. 37p. of land. 1s. 2d. a week distributed in bread every Sunday after the sermon amongst those that are in greatest need, and the remainder by the Minister and Churchwardens to the poor on Easter Sunday.

John Marshall's Charity; by will dated 3rd. January, 1803. Dividends on £180 16s. navy five per cents., distributed in bread to the poor on Sundays, with that of Wright's Charity, at the discretion of the Minister and Church-wardens." *

WILLERBY.

Willerby is a township partly in Kirk-Ella, North Ferriby, and Cottingham parishes, and has a population of 719.

The principal landowners are Sir Charles Legard, Bart., and Arthur Wilson, Esq.

In the village is a Primitive Methodist Chapel.

At an early period a considerable portion of this parish was given by its owners to various monastic institutions, referring to which, Burton, in his *Monasticon*, has the following :—" Here the heirs of Stuteville held three carucates and six oxgangs of the King

* Charity Commissioners' 9th Report, p 813.

in capite, and John de Melsa, two and a half carucates, whereof
the Templars held two in Frank-almoigne, and Richard de Roos
held two and a half oxgangs. Henry de Willardby, in A.D. 1152,
with the consent of Adelard and Henry, his sons, gave ten acres
and a half in this field, with pasture for three hundred sheep in the
pasture there which the abbot and Convent of Riveaux gave to the
Priory of Bredlington in A.D. 1175. Sir John de Meaux, of
Bewick, in A.D. 1361 (35 Edward III.), gave this manor and six
acres of land therein to the Prior of Haltemprice, on condition
that the said prior should pay to him £32, and keep three canons
regular to celebrate divine offices for the good of the souls of
Maud, his wife; Sir Godfrey de Meaux, his father; Lady Scolas-
tion, his mother, &c.; and Anthony de Spanneby, cousin and heir
of Sir John Meaux de Bewyke, in A.D. 1379 (2nd Richard II.),
confirmed the same. Thomas Wake, the founder, gave this town
with all his natives therein, with a pasture for eighty-eight oxen,
in a place called Wythes." *

TRANBY CROFT.

Tranby Croft, in the parish of Kirk-Ella, is the seat of Arthur
Wilson, Esq, J.P., D.L. The house is pleasantly situated in a
well-wooded park.

ANLABY.

Anlaby is a township chiefly in the parish of Kirk-Ella, and
extends also into the parishes of Hessle and North Ferriby.

The Church of St. Peter, a chapel of ease to Kirk-Ella, is a
Gothic brick building; it was built in 1864, and entirely re-built

† Burton's *Monasticon*, p 317.

in 1884, with the addition of north and south aisles, and has chancel paved with encaustic tiles, and nave, and is seated in the modern style ; the east and west windows are stained, and were the gifts of John Leaper, Esq., and Thomas Voase, Esq. The windows by Hardman, and that by Burlison & Gill, were added after the church was re-built. The reredos, chancel stalls, &c., were given at the same time by A. Wilson, Esq., and members of his family. The pulpit was the gift of W. S. Bailey, Esq. There is a small endowment of £78 per annum to the church.

There is a Wesleyan Chapel, and one in connection with the Primitive Methodists.

The population is 729.

Charles Percy Sykes, Esq., is Lord of the Manor and principal landowner.

This place was formerly the residence of the Anlaby family, from whom it passed to the Legards, and they, being united to the leading families of the locality by marriage, acquired great possessions in Anlaby, Hesslè, Wolfreton, Kirk-Ella, Swanland, Tranby, Welton, Weighton, Bently, Cottingham, Hull Bank, and Ruston in the County of York, and in several places in the County of Durham. One of the descendants of the family married into the family of Sir Edward Coke, Lord Chief Justice of England.

John Legard, a member of this family, in the 17th century, fought a duel with a Mr. Bolls at Louth, Lincolnshire, and was so unfortunate as to slay his opponent. From some records preserved at Melbourne Hall, Derbyshire, it appears that his father, Robert Legard, petitioned the King for the royal pardon. The petition goes on to say that :—

" John Legard, being at Louth, in the County of Lincoln, upon necessary business, one, Mr. Richard Bolls, came into his company ; a man altogether unknown to your petitioner's son, but hearing him called Bolls, the said John Legard asked what Bolls it was, saying that if it was Bolls of Ganton he owed him a debt of £40. Some of the company told him it was son of him of Ganton who was dead. Thereupon Legard told Mr. Bolls there was a debt of £40 owing by his father, to one Mr. Brampton, which Legard said was now due to him. Bolls replied that Brampton owed his father 100 marks, for which he had a statute and judgment upon it. Legard said he never heard of such a thing. Bolls said it was true, and that Brampton was a base fellow and a footman. Legard said if he was a footman, it was to a Queen, and that Brampton was a gent as well descended as himself for ought he knew. Bolls said he lied. Mr. Legard thereupon struck him. Mr. Bolls dared him to fight with him, and called him a coward and a schoolboy, Legard accepted to fight with him and presently went together into a pit a little way out of the town to fight ; nobody being with them, but one Jackson, an acquaintance and friend of Mr. Bolls', who followed after him with his sword. Legard fought in his riding coat with a little stick in his left hand. A smith, dwelling near the place, seeing them draw their swords, came to part them with a staff, but Jackson would not suffer him, but took the staff from him, and with it struck Legard's stick out of his hand as he was fighting. Legard hurt Mr. Bolls in the shoulder at the first encounter, and then they breathed ; and at a second pass Legard hurt him in the right arm, and then they breathed again. Legard took up his stick again intending to have left, but Jackson struck the stick out of his hand again with his sword as he was fighting. Notwithstanding, Legard hurt Mr. Bolls that time, likewise in the arm, all of them being slight wounds and in no ways dangerous. Legard, seeing Mr. Bolls hurt, moved to leave, saying they had done enough and that he hoped he had satisfied Mr. Bolls, but Mr. Bolls replied that he was a coward. Legard said no, he hoped he had satisfied him otherwise, but said Mr. Bolls was hurt, therefore he wished him to leave, which Mr. Bolls seemed to condescend unto. But Jackson said to Mr. Bolls, 'I pray thee, Dick, one bout more for my sake,' whereupon Mr. Bolls would needs fight again, and the place being strait where they fought, and compass'd with high hills, Legard went back till he had almost fallen on the hill, Mr. Bolls striking violently at him. It was Legard's unfortunate hap to hurt Mr. Bolls on the right side, whereupon, Mr. Bolls, being ready to fall, Legard said 'Woe is me, I have done too much' : and Mr. Bolls, about half an hour after, died ; but did before his death confess it was his own seeking, and that he followed of his own death. Whereupon the Coroner's inquest being taken the next day, upon sight of the body and examination of witnesses, found that your petitioner's said son had committed manslaughter in killing the said Mr. Bolls." *

* *Lincolnshire Notes and Queries* Vol. II., p 57.

Then follows "the humble suit of a sorrowful father," &c. The petition seems to have been granted, as John Legard lived to succeed his father, and married Jane, the daughter of Robert Hildyard, by whom he had a numerous family. The Anlaby line of the family, which was the oldest branch, died out towards the close of the eighteenth century, when Henry Legard, of Beverley, being unmarried, left his property at Anlaby to his distant cousin, Sir Thomas Legard, 7th Bart., of Ganton, whose family is now represented by Sir Charles Legard, 11th Bart., late M.P. for Scarborough.

The old hall, the ancestral home of the Legards, is now occupied by W. S. Palmer, Esq., it has been much modernised, but the old moat on the north side is distinctly traceable.

"The inhabitants of this and the surrounding villages, about the year 1400, were a source of great discomfort to the people of Hull in the matter of their water supply. Many conflicts and some fatal encounters took place, until the interference of the Pope of Rome was secured, who, making them great promises of spiritual good, their animosity ceased from thenceforth." *

* Hadley's *History of Hull*, p 57.

APPENDIX.

DOMESDAY BOOK.

The incomparable record of Domesday was begun by order of William the Conqueror in the year 1080, and completed in 1086. Commissioners were sent into every county, and juries empanelled in each hundred out of all orders of freemen, from Barons to the lowest farmers, to give in, upon oath, to the commissioners, by verdict or presentment, due information for the faithful and impartial execution of it. These inquisitions being taken, they were sent up to Winchester, and the substance of them was afterwards methodized and formed into the record we now call Domesday. It is comprised in two volumes, one a large folio and the other a quarto. The description is generally :—How many hides or carucates the land is gelded or taxed at. Whose it was in the time of King Edward. Who the present owner and the sub-tenants. What and how much arable land, pasture, meadow, and wood there is. How much in demesne—how much in tenancy, and what number of ploughs it will keep. What mills, salt pits, and fisheries. How many freemen, socmen, villanes, bordars, &c. What churches and priests. What land is waste, and what the land was let for in the time of King Edward ; and what the then present rent, &c.

Explanation of some of the Terms used in Domesday Book.

BORDARS.—(Bordarii), boors or husbandmen holding a little house with some land of husbandry bigger than a cottage. Cowell says the Bordarii were distinct from the Servi and Villini, and seem to be of a less servile condition, having a bord or cottage with a small parcel of land allowed them on condition that they should supply the Lord with poultry and eggs, and other small provisions for his board and entertainment,

SOKEMEN.—Some of the King's sokemen were very great, as were also some of the larger sort of other great men's, and had manors within the soke, which sort we now call Mesne Lords ; but the most general sort of sokemen were such as the Saxons called lesser thanes ; the Danes, young men, and we still call yeomen, being free of blood and fit for honourable service.

VILLANES.—So called because they lived chiefly in villages and were employed in the rustic works of the most sordid kind, belonging chiefly to the Lords of the Manors and annexed to the Manor or land, or else they were in gross or at large, that is, annexed to the person of the lord and transferable by deed from one owner to another. They could not leave their Lord without his permission, and their children were in the same state, being the property of the Lord of the Manor. They could acquire no property of their own either in land or goods.—*Sir Ed. Coke.*

CARUCATE. One hundred acres of land, six score to the hundred. — *Dr. Thornton.*

DEMESNE.—Demain or Domain signifies Patrimonium domini. Demain, according to common speech are the lord's chief manor places, with the lands thereunto belonging, which he and his ancestors have from time to time kept in their own manual occupation for the maintenance of themselves and their families ; and all the parts of a manor, except what is in the hands of freeholders, are said to be demains.

AN OXGANG.— *Una bovata terræ* was originally as much land as an ox-team could plough in a year. Eight oxgangs, of fifteen acres each, have been said to make a carucate, but the quantity of land in an oxgang varied from eight to twenty-four acres. Carucate terræ and bovata terræ are words compound, and may contain meadow, pasture, and wood necessary for such tillage. *

THE FEUDAL SYSTEM.

The feudal polity, which by degrees established itself over all the continent of Europe, seems not to have been received in this part of our island, at least not universally, and as a part of the national constitution, till the reign of William the Norman.

This introduction of the feudal tenures into England, by King William, does not seem to have been effected immediately after the Conquest, nor by the mere arbitrary will of the Conqueror ; but to have been gradually established by the Norman Barons and others, in such forfeited lands as they received from the Conqueror ; and upon the principle of self-security. In consequence of this change it became a fundamental maxim and necessary

* Coke on Littleton, Inst., 1, p 5.

T

principle (though in reality a mere fiction) of our English tenures, "that the King is the universal lord and original proprietor of all the lands in his kingdom ; and that no man doth or can possess any part of it, but what has mediately or immediately been derived as a gift from him, to be held upon feodal services." Almost all the real property of this kingdom was formerly, by the policy of our laws, supposed to be granted by and holden of some superior lord, in consideration of certain services to be rendered to the lord by the tenant or possessor of the property. The thing holden is therefore called a *tenement*, the possessors thereof, *tenants*, and the manner of their possession a *tenure*. All tenures being thus derived from the King, those who held immediately under him were called his tenants in *capite* or in chief. Where the service was free but uncertain, as military service with homage, that tenure was called *Knight-service*. A Knight was bound to serve the King on horseback, or maintain a soldier in war at his own cost. One who held land by Knight service was obliged to attend his lord in war for forty days in every year if called upon ; which attendance was his redditus or rent for the quantity of land which was called a Knight's fee. Where the service was not only free, but also certain, as by fealty only, or by rent and fealty, &c., that tenure was called *free socage*. These were the only free holdings ; the others were villenous or servile, the services being such as were fit only for peasants or persons of a servile rank ; as to plough the lord's land, to make his hedges, to carry out his dung, or other mean employment. Thus much for the species of tenure, under which almost all the free lands of the kingdom were holden till the restoration in 1660. *

* Blackstone's *Commentaries on the Laws of England*, Vol. II. pp 47-79.

FEET OF FINES.

The collection of fines now in the Public Record Office, and extending from the time of Henry II., to the year 1834, is a splendid example of a system of registration of assurances. It dates from a period when the only other common mode of transferring freehold lands was by charter of feoffment, which did not possess the great advantage which a fine had, of being a matter of record, and therefore always available as evidence, when a feoffment might be lost or destroyed. Fines therefore, were very generally used in former days as a means of transferring property, and from the many details which they give, both of genealogy and topography, and from the long period which they cover, they may well be said to be among the most valuable of all the public records.

Fines were abolished by Statute 3 and 4 William IV., c 74, from the 31st December, 1833, and more simple modes of assurance were substituted. They are, therefore, now not often met with in the investigation of the titles of freehold estates, and the study of this branch of the law of real property is gradually being abandoned to students of family history and topography.

A fine, then, is understood by conveyancers to be a means of transferring property through the agency of an action or suit at law, whether real or fictitious, between the demandant and tenant with the consent of the judges. To effect this purpose of transfer, the following plan was adopted : a suit was commenced concerning the lands intended to be conveyed, and when the writ was sued out, and the parties appeared in court, a composition of the suit was entered into, with the consent of the judges, whereby the lands in question were declared to be the right of one of the contending parties, and this agreement was enrolled among the records of the court.

The agreement entered into openly in the Court of Common Pleas, or before the Chief Justice of that Court, or Commissioners duly authorised for the purpose, was the substance of the fine, and it was usually an acknowledgment from the deforciants or those who kept the others out of possession, that the lands in question were the right of the demandants.

JAMES TORRE, THE HISTORIAN.

Mr. James Torre, an author from whose MS. writings we have made liberal extracts, was born at Haxey, in the Isle of Axholme, in 1650. He was the son of a Mr. Gregory Torre (who was buried there in 1660) by Anne, daughter and heiress of John Fane, of Epworth. James Torre sold his Lincolnshire property in 1669, and purchased Snydale Hall, near Normanton. In the Cathedral Library at York there are five folio volumes of Torre's Manuscripts relating to Yorkshire, which were given to the library by the executors of Archbishop Sharp. These folios contain a vast amount of valuable information respecting churches, livings, testamentary burials, &c. Torre also wrote a supplement to Sir William Dugdale's Baronage, carrying on the genealogical descents and historical remarks therein contained. He died in 1669, and was buried at Normanton.

SUBSCRIBERS.

His Grace, the Archbishop of York.

The Right Rev. the Bishop of Beverley.

The Right Rev. the Bishop of Hull.

The Right Rev. the Bishop in Jerusalem and the East.

The Lord Braye.

The Lord Herries.

Sir Albert K Rollit, LL.D., M P.

C. H. Wilson, Esq., M.P.

H. S. King, Esq., C.I.E., M.P.

F. B. Grotrian, Esq., M.P.

H J. Farmer-Atkinson, Esq., M.P.

C. G. S. Foljambe, Esq., M.P.

Alcock, Mr. C. ...	... South Cave
Ames, H. St. V. Esq. ...	Westbury-on-Trym
Anderson, Mr. Henry ...	South Cave
Andrews, Wm. Esq., F.R.H.S.	Hull
Appleton, Mr. John P. ...	.. ... ,,
Atkinson, Joseph, Esq., J.P.	Elloughton Rise
Atkinson, Mr. James	North Cave
Baitson, Mr. Henry	... Bromfleet
Ball, W. H. Esq....	Barton on-Humber

Bannister, Edwd., Esq.   Grimsby
Banks, Mr. ...   .   Hessle
Barff, Mr. R. H.   ...   . Huahine, South Sea Islands
Barnard, C. E. G., Esq., J.P.   South Cave Castle
Bartram, Mr. Alfred   ...   Little Weeton
Bennett, Rev. W. M.   Elloughton Vicarage
Black, Mr. A.   North Cave
Blakie, Mr. Alex.   ...   Brough
Blodgette, Geo. B., Esq.   Rowley, U.S.A.
Bohn, George, Esq.   ... ... Tranby Park
Bond, Fras., Esq. ... President of the Hull Philo. and Literary Institute
Bricknell, F. W., Esq.   ...   ... Hull
Briggs, H. H. Esq. ...   ,,
Brindle, Mr. ...   . Howden
Brown, Mr. Walter ...   (A. Brown & Sons, Hull)
Brown, Mrs. ...   . :. Hull
Bruce, Mr. John Eddy   ...   Settle
Bruce, Mr. Robert   South Cave
Buckton, G. F., Esq.   North Cave

Cameron, R. D., Esq., M.D.   ..   ... North Cave
Carlile, E. Esq.   ..   Holme Hall, near Huddersfield
Carlile, E. Esq. ...   Kingsbury, Richmond, Surrey
Cave, Col. T. Sturmy   ...   ... Yateley Lodge, Twickenham
Cave, Charles D., Esq.   Stoneleigh House, Clifton Park, Bristol
Cave, Lewis, Esq. ...   ... Manor House, Woodmanstone, Epsom
Charlesworth, Councillor James   ...   Hull
Chilman, J. W., Esq. ...   . ,,
Clapham, W. W., Esq.   Crumpsall House, Manchester
Clarke, Mr. Ingham   ...   ... Hessle
Clarke, G. H., Esq. ...   The Park, Hull
Clarkson, Mr. William   Newbald
Cleminshaw, Mrs. ...   ...   Hull
Conte, Mrs. ...   .   South Cave
Cook, John Travis, Esq., F.R.H.S.   Hull
Cook, Mr. G. R. ...   Hessle
Copeland, Mr. J. ...   ...   Hull
Coulson, Mr. William ...   ... Riplingham
Cousens, Mr. F. W. ...   Womersley. Pontefract

Cousens, Mr. Edwin ... South Cave
Cowell, W., Esq. ... Newbald
Crissey, Mr. T. ... ... Newton Heath
Crowhurst, Mr. J. E. South Cave

Darling, Mr. P. ... Newport
Darling, Mr. A. T. ... ... ,,
Davenport, John D., Esq. 13, Old Square, Lincoln's Inn, London, W.C.
Dawe, R. Hill, Esq., Town Clerk, Hull
Dawson, Mr. Isaac ... Hull
Dawson, Miss E. J. ... South Cave
Dennis, Mr. David ,,
Dennis, Mr. T. ... ... ,,
Denton, Rev. Canon, M.A. ... The Vicarage, Ashby-de-la-Zouch
Denton, Mr. T. ... ... North Cave
Des Forges, Mr. Samuel ... South Cave
Dibb, A. K., Esq., J.P. ... Kirk Ella
Dodge, Phineas, Esq. Rowley, U.S.A.
Dodge, Joseph D., Esq. ,,
Donkin, Mr. Robt. ... ... South Cave
Downs, Mr. Thomas ... Yass, New South Wales
Duffin, Miss E. ... ... South Cave
Dummer, Joseph N. Esq. Rowley, Mass., U.S.A.
Dyer, Rev. Walter ... Rochdale

Evans, Mr. George ... Hull
Everatt, Mr. Richard Brough

Farthing, Mr. R. ... South Cave
Ferguson, D. W., Esq., M.D. Wallingfen
Fewster, C. E., Esq. Hull
Fisher, Mr. John W. .. ... ,,
Foord, Rev. James, M.A. ... Kirk-Ella Vicarage
Foss, Joshua, N., Esq Rowley, America
Foster, Mr. M. .. Sancton
Fowler, Mr. ... North Cave
Fox, W. H., Esq. Bradwell Grove, Burford, Oxon
Frank. Mr. C. R. ... Sheffield

Gelder, Mr. W. A., (A.R.I.B.A.) ... Hull
Gelder, Mr. William North Cave
Gilfoy, Mr. W. ... Hull
Gillatt, Mr. Charles The Weir, Hessle
Glegge, Rev. Wm. ... Bromfleet Vicarage
Glew, Mr. T. A. ... ... Hull
Goodwill, Mr. Thomas South Cave
Gospel, Mr. Henry North Cliff
Graham, C. C., Esq. ... ... Hull
Gray, W., Esq. Drewton Manor
Gray, Mr. Robert ... Melton
Green, Mr. Robert Brantingham
Greenwood, Mr. C. Hull

Heseltine, G. W., Esq., ... Hull
Hildyard, Rev. H. C. T. ... Rowley Vicarage
Hill, Mr. J. S.... ... ... Hull
Hill, Mr. Francis ,,
Hindle, J., Esq. ... ... Bradford
Hine, H., Esq., M.R.C.S. South Cave
Holderness, T. Esq. ... Driffield
Hornsey, Mr. Robert... Low Hunsley
Horsley, Mr. John ... North Cave
Hull Police Library ... ...
Hull Subscription Library... ...
Hulse, Mr. J. ... Brough
Hunter, Mr. ... ... Hull
Hutchinson, Rev. H. T. ... Vicar of Sancton

Jackson, Thomas, Esq.. M.D.... ... ... Hull
Jackson, Councillor Wm., M.D. ... ,,
Jackson, Mr. Wm. Henry ... South Cave
James, Mr. Philip ... ... Brough
Jameson, W. B. Esq. South Cave and East Ella House
Jaques, Mr. T. G., ... Blacktoft
Jarratt, W. O., Esq. ... ... Hull
Jefferson, J. J. D., Esq. ... ... Thicket Priory
Johnson, Rev. George J. ... North Ferriby
Johnson, Mr. John ... Burn Park, Cottingham
Johnson, Mr. James... South Cave

Johnson, Mr. J. W.	Riplingham Grange
Judge, Capt. Chas.	... Hull
Kaye, Rev. Arthur	Hessle Vicarage
Key, Mr. Walter	South Cave
King, Mr. Charles	Little Weeton
Kirby, Mr. William ...	... Hull
Knapton, Miss A.	North Cave
Knowles, H. Esq.	Hull
Lacy, Mr. Chas. ...	Little Weeton
Lambert, Rev. J. Malet, LL.D.	... Hull
Langdale, Chas., Esq., J.P.	... Houghton Hall
Leak, Ald., John	... Hull
Leake, Mr. Thomas	South Cave
Leake, Mr. John	South Cliffe
Leeson, Miss ...	North Cave
Leighton, Mr. George	South Cave
Leighton, Mr. R. W.	... Hull
Leighton, Robert. Esq.	Goodmanham
Livingston, J. G. Esq.	Clifton, Bristol
Lloyd, Mr. G. M. ...	... Brough
Mc.Dougall, Rev. T. H.	... South Cave Vicarage
Mc. Alister, Rev. W. H.	... Alvinston, Ontario, Canada
Macfarlane, Mr. J. ...	... Brough
Mackintosh, Rev. W. Teesdale	Thirsk Vicarage
Macturk, G. G., Esq.	... South Cave
Macturk, Miss Jane	... ,,
Macturk, K. T.. Esq,	,,
Marshall, Mr. W. N.	Hull
Marshall, Mr. F. ...	Swanland
Massey, Councillor W. A.	... Brough
Medcalf, Miss Jane	Boston Spa
Middlebrook, Mr. R.	North Cave
Millington, J. T. Esq.	Liverpool
Mills, Mr. Joseph ...	... ... Hul
Mills, James, Esq.	Town Clerk, Beverley
Milner, T. G., Esq. ...	Hull

Mitchell, Mr. Wm.	Riplingham
Morrill, Henry, Esq., J.P.	... Hull
Morrison, Mr. T.	South Cave
Mortimer, Mr. J. R.	Driffield
Mossman, Mr. R.	Newbald
Moxon, Mr. Walter	Brough
Nelson, Mr. Richd.	Welton
Newton, Coun. G. B.	... Hull
Nickless, Mr. Edwd.	North Cave
Norman, Mr. W. S. ...	,,
Oliver, Mr. Edwd. ...	Faxfleet Grange
Ombler, Mr. Edwin ...	... Hull
Paget, Rev. Canon	Welton Vicarage
Palmer, Mr. W. S. ...	Old Hall, Anlaby
Palmer, T. W., Esq., J.P.	... Brough House
Park, Alderman, G. R.	... Hedon
Parkinson, Mr. H. S. ...	North Cave
Pearson, Mr. Charles	North Cave
Pearson, Mr. James	Everthorpe
Pearson, Mr. William	... Hull
Pearson, Mr. John	North Cave
Pearson, Miss. A.	... ,,
Pears, Mr. Robert	Market Weighton
Pease, F. R. Esq., J.P.	Hessle Wood
Pease, Arthur B., Esq. ...	Melton Hill,
Pickard, Mr. Anthony	Hessle
Pigott, Rev. W.	... Hull
Pinder, Mr. Daniel ...	South Cave
Prescott, Mr. Robert	Brough
Pudsey, Col. H. Fawcett	Hull
Reckitt, James, Esq., J.P.	Swanland Manor
Reynolds, Mr. Butler	... London
Rhodes, Mr. John	Little Weeton
Richardson, Mr. W.	South Cave
Richardson, Councillor	Hull
Robinson, Mr. W.	Welton

Robson, E., Esq., J.P.	Mayor of Hull
Rose, Rev. W. ...	Newport
Rose, Mr. W. ...	Wallingfen
Ross, Mr. Charles W.	.. Elloughton Lodge
Rudd, Mr. Charles ...	Greendale, New Zealand
Saltmarshe, Philip, Esq., J.P.	Saltmarshe
Scaife, Mr. G. B.	Elloughton
Scaife, Mr. Matthew	,,
Scales, Mr. G. W. ...	South Cave
Scotchburn, W. ,Esq.	Driffield
Scotchburn, Mrs. Alfred ...	,,
Scott, Mr. A. E. ...	North Cave
Scott, Councillor	Hull
Seaton, Alderman J.L.	,.
Seed, Mrs. A.	Halifax
Semper, Mr. Herbert	Hull
Sharp, Mr. Samuel	Manor House, South Newbald
Shaw, Mr. Edward ...	Elloughton
Shepherd, Mrs.	... North Ferriby
Sherburn, John, Esq., M.D. ...	Hull
Sipling, Councillor G. ...	... Brough
Smeddle, Rev. John M.A.	Blacktoft Vicarage
Smith, Col. Rowland	Red Hall, Lincoln
Smith, Clarence, Esq., J.P.	... ... Hull
Smith, H. Y., Esq. ...	The Grove, Hackney, London
Smith, T. R., Esq.	... Hull
Smith, T. J. Esq.	... Hull
Smith, Mr. George	South Cave
Smith, Rev. James, M.A.	Elloughton Mount
Smith, Mr. Alfred	... Sheffield
Smith, R. G., Esq.	Sewerby Fields
Snell, Mr. Matthew ...	... Wallingfen
Snow, Mr. T. R.	... Ellerker
Soady, Rev. S. J.	Newbald Vicarage
Stancer, Mr. George	Pocklington
Stather, Mr. W.	North Cave
Stewart, Mr. W.	Ellerker Grange
Stickney, Mr. Walter M. ... '	Danthorpe Hall

Stobbart, Mr. G.	Provence Farm
Stobbart, Mr. Thomas	... Ellerker
Storr, Mr. Charles	Elloughton
Storry, Mr. ...	Hull
Stuart, Alderman James, J.P.	... Hull
Suddaby, Mr. Arthur	South Cave
Suddaby, Mr. Jno.	... Hull
Sykes, Daniel, Esq.	... Kirk-Ella
Symons, Alderman John, M.R.I.A.	Hull
Taylor, Rev. R. V.; B.A.	Melbeck Vicarage
Taylor, Mr. R. E.	... Elloughton
Tenney. Mr. W. ...	Hazleton, Iowa, U.S.A.
Thompson, Joseph, Esq.,	Wauldby, Brough
Thornham, Mr. Chas.	South Cave
Tindale, Mr. Richard	Newbald
Tindill, Mr. Henry ...	Sancton
Tindle, Mr. Robt.	... Bromfleet
Todd, Mr. Frank P.	Rowley, Mass., U.S.A.
Todd, W. H. Esq.	... ... Hull
Tudor, Rev. W. L. ...	... Sheffield
Turner, J. Horsfall, Esq. ...	... Idel, Bradford
Turner, Mrs. ...	North Ferriby
Vause, Mr. Richard ...	Hull
Venus, Mr. Alfred	... Hull
Voase, Mrs. ...	... Anlaby House
Wade, J. E. Esq., J.P.	Brantingham-Thorpe
Walker, Mr. John	... ... Hull
Walker, Mr. J. E. ...	... ... ,,
Wallgate, Mr. Elgey	... ... South Cave
Warcup, Mr. Isaac ...	Oakville, Ontario, Canada
Wares, J. McIntosh, Esq.	... ... Elloughton Garth
Watkins, Mr. U. Gwynne	Pentwyn House, Llangwm, Mon.
Watson, Mr. R.	... ... Hotham Carrs
Watson, Mr. George	South Cave
Wauldby, Rev. F. ...	... ... Hull
Weddall, Mr. G. E. ...	Thornton House

Westmorland, Rev. Thomas	Brantingham Vicarage
Westoby, Mr. George ...	... Hull
West, T. H. Esq. ...	... ... Hull
West, L. H., Esq., LL.D.	Glenrock, Brough
Whitby, Mr. S. B.	... ... Hull
White, A. E., Esq.	... Borough Surveyor, Hull
Whitehead, Hy. Esq.	Bleak House, Wallingfen
Wiley, E. F., Esq.	Brough
Wilkinson, Mr. John	... Hull
Wilson, Arthur Esq., J.P.	Tranby Croft
Wilson, John, Esq. ...	South Cave
Wilson, Geo. T. Esq.	Cottingham
Wilson, Mr. Benjamin	Hotham
Wilson, Mr. E. B. ...	Brough
Wilson, Edwd. S. Esq., F.S.A.	... ... Melton
Wilson-Todd, W. H., Esq. ...	Halnaby Hall, Croft
Wimbush, Mrs.	... ... South Cave
Withill, Mr. G. ...	Rusk View, Ontario, Canada
Withill, Mr. Geo. Wm. ...	South Cave
Witty, Henry, Esq. ...	... ... Cottingham
Woodd, Basil T., Esq. ...	Conyngham Hall, Knaresborough
Woodhouse, Alderman, J. T.	... Elloughton
Woodhouse, Alderman Saml., F.R.H.S.	... ... Hull
Wrangham, W. F. Esq., J.P.	Hotham-House

CORRIGENDA.

Page, 23, line 11 : delete " In 1669 " and read " The Manor was afterwards," &c.

Page, 41, 4th line from bottom : delete comma after " proprietor "

„   123, line 18, for " wood," read " woad."

„   134, line 3, read : " The Living is in the gift of the Arch-bishop of York, and is now held by the Rev. H. T. Hutchinson."

Page 136 : heading, should read " Hotham " instead of " Sancton."

INDEX.

EDWIN OMBLER, PRINTER,
7, GEORGE STREET & 27, DOCK STREET, HULL.

www.ingramcontent.com/pod-product-compliance
Lightning Source LLC
Chambersburg PA
CBHW031359270326
41929CB00010BA/1254